The Stroessner Regime and Indigenous Resistance in Paraguay

UNIVERSITY PRESS OF FLORIDA

Florida A&M University, Tallahassee
Florida Atlantic University, Boca Raton
Florida Gulf Coast University, Ft. Myers
Florida International University, Miami
Florida State University, Tallahassee
New College of Florida, Sarasota
University of Central Florida, Orlando
University of Florida, Gainesville
University of North Florida, Jacksonville
University of South Florida, Tampa
University of West Florida, Pensacola

The Stroessner Regime and Indigenous Resistance in Paraguay

René D. Harder Horst

University Press of Florida
Gainesville/Tallahassee/Tampa/Boca Raton
Pensacola/Orlando/Miami/Jacksonville/Ft. Myers/Sarasota

Copyright 2007 by René D. Harder Horst
Printed in the United States of America on acid-free paper
All rights reserved

First cloth printing, 2007
First paperback printing, 2010

Library of Congress Cataloging-in-Publication Data
Horst, René Harder, 1967–
The Stroessner regime and indigenous resistance in Paraguay / René D. Harder Horst.
p. cm.
Includes bibliographical references and index.
ISBN-13: 978–0–8130–3056–2 (alk. paper); ISBN-13: 978-0-8130-3547-5 (pbk.)
1. Paraguay—History—1938–1989. 2. Indians of South America—Paraguay—
Government policy. 3. Indians of South America—Paraguay—Government relations.
4. Indians of South America—Missions—Paraguay. I. Title.
F2689.H67   2007
989.2079–dc22   2006030871

The University Press of Florida is the scholarly publishing agency for the State
University System of Florida, comprising Florida A&M University, Florida Atlantic
University, Florida Gulf Coast University, Florida International University, Florida
State University, New College of Florida, University of Central Florida, University of
Florida, University of North Florida, University of South Florida, and University of
West Florida.

University Press of Florida
15 Northwest 15th Street
Gainesville, FL 32611-2079
http://www.upf.com

To Marlene, my soul mate, for everything.

To Matías and Tali, for hope for the future and joy along the way.

Contents

Acknowledgments

The following organizations provided funds and assistance: the Institute of International Education Fulbright Grant, Indiana University, and Appalachian State University.

The following people in Paraguay were especially helpful to my research: Serafina de Álvarez, Jonathan Beachy, Ruth Beachy, Ed Bryce, Jerónimo Irala Burgos, Felipe Caballero, Francisco Cáceres, Oscar Centurión, Julio César Frutos, Edwin Fry, Modesto Gómez, Stephen Kidd, Cristóbal Ortiz, Reyes Pargas, Alcides Pintos, René Ramírez, Verena Regeher, Sinforiano Rodríguez, Enrique Romero, Miguel Chase Sardi, Mirna Vázquez, Oleg Vysokolán, Balbino Vargas Zárate.

I am indebted to my professors and colleagues. David Edmunds, Jeffrey Gould, Peter Guardino, and Muriel Nazzari at Indiana University offered advice at many points and wrote recommendations for me. Dennis Grafflin was a faithful colleague at Bates College. At Appalachian State University I am grateful to Ed Behrend-Martínez, Michael Krenn,Ralph Lentz, and many other members of our excellent history team.

My family is extremely supportive. My parents, Willis and Byrdalene Horst, helped track down details in Asunción, and my sisters, Carmen, Emily, and Cristina, inspired my work and read and proofed chapters along the way. I am indebted also to my grandparents, as well as to Tomasa Benítez, Albert Buckwalter, Lois Buckwalter, Leonida Garcia, Juan Mareco, Feliciano García, Betty Harder, Keith Kingsley, Gretchen Kingsley, Helen Lindhorst, Lon Sherer, Christine Weaver, Rosemary Wyse Reimer, Norma Wyse-Wenger, Sara Wyse, and Ned Wyse for their encouragement and prayers over the years.

I am grateful to Amy Hudnall, Amy Gorelick, and Jacqueline Kinghorn Brown, as well as anonymous readers for the University Press of Florida, all of whom helped shape this manuscript into a book. Christopher Knoll crafted the maps with extreme attention to detail. I alone am responsible for any problems in the manuscript. My thanks to all those I have not mentioned but who have contributed to my life and my research.

Abbreviations

AIAP—Inglesia Angelicana Paraguaya (Paraguayan Anglican Church), Asunción

AIM—American Indian Movement

AIP—Asociación Indigenista del Paraguay (Paraguayan Indigenist Association)

API—Asociación de Parcialidades Indígenas (Association of Indigenous Groups)

ASCIM—Asociación de Servicios de Cooperación Indígena-Mennonita (Indigenous-Mennonite Association for Cooperation Services)

CAIG—Comisión de Ayuda a los Indígenas Guayakí (Guayakí Indian Aid Commission

CEP—Conferencia Episcopal Paraguaya (Episcopal Conference of the Paraguayan Catholic Church)

DAI—Departamento de Asuntos Indígenas (Department of Indigenous Affairs)

ENM—Equipo Nacional de Misiones (National Catholic Missions Team)

IAII—Instituto Indigenista Interamericano (Inter-American Indigenist Institute)

IBR—Instituto de Bienestar Rural (Rural Welfare Institute)

INDI—Instituto Paraguayo del Indígena (Paraguayan Indigenous Institute; formerly called National Indigenous Institute)

IWGIA—International Work Group for Indian Affairs

NTM—New Tribes Mission

PCP—Partido Comunista Paraguayo (Paraguayan Communist Party)

PPÑ—Proyecto Guaraní-Ñandeva (Guaraní-Ñandeva Project)

PPT—Proyecto Païȳ Tavyterã (Project Païȳ Tavyterã)

SEPSAJ—Servicios Profesionales Antropológicos y Jurídicos (Professional Legal and Anthropological Services)

SPI—Serviço de Proteção aos Índios (Service for the Protection of Indians)

Introduction

Late in the afternoon of 17 May 1988, seven hundred indigenous people from Paraguay, Argentina, and Brazil welcomed Pope John Paul II to the Catholic Mission of Santa Teresita in the dry western Paraguayan Chaco. The people had chosen Enenlhit leader René Ramírez to present their collective statements to the pontiff. Ramírez was a chief from the Maskoy tribes, of which the Enenlhit are one tribe, which had only months before finally reclaimed their homeland territories at Riacho Mosquito after years of struggle against the Stroessner regime and the powerful Carlos Casado Ranching Company. Ramírez had traveled widely for a year to collect statements from indigenous peoples that he and advocates from the Catholic Church had compiled into a moving speech. Presenting this message to the highest Catholic leader, even though it forced him into seven months in hiding, culminated the chief's endeavors to reclaim his people's tribal territory. Accustomed, from his people's long struggle to recover their land, to addressing authorities, the Enenlhit leader proudly concluded: "Whites say we should become civilized. We invite the whites to be civilized and respect us as people, to respect our communities and our leaders, to respect our lands and our forests, and to return even a small part of what they have taken from us. Indigenous people wish to be friends with all Paraguayans. We wish for them to let us live in peace and without difficulties."[1]

Chief Ramírez thus summarized the difficulties that indigenous people in these nations faced in their daily struggle to secure food and work and to oppose heavy-handed state policies that encouraged them to disappear into the larger peasant population. The Enenlhit leader accused the regime's Instituto Paraguayo del Indígena (Paraguayan Indigenous Institute, INDI), the agency that was by law supposed to defend native rights, of working against the long indigenous struggles to reclaim land. Pope John Paul II concluded his response with a pointed criticism of the regime's treatment of Paraguay's indigenous population: "I know the great problems you face; in particular your need for land and property titles. For these I appeal to a sense of justice and humanity by all those responsible to favour the most deprived."[2]

The encounter with the pope was a symbolic victory for indigenous people throughout the Southern Cone, especially in the country that hosted his visit, Paraguay. Ramírez's testimony highlights how the Maskoy struggle for land had encouraged his people and Ramírez himself to strongly identify with their indigenous heritage. The pope's visit also shows that the preparation for the visit and the encounter with the pope reinforced indigenous identity, moving the people from the tribal allegiance expressed early in their struggle for land to a pan-indigenous unity that fortified Ramírez's presentation. The event presents evidence of strong support from the Catholic Church for native territorial claims. Perhaps even more important, it highlights the successful cooperation between the Catholic Church, other allies, and indigenous communities in successfully opposing the Stroessner regime.

When Stroessner bade the pope farewell the following day at the President Stroessner International Airport, he referred to his government's "special attention" to the native population. The dictator's ploy was an obvious attempt to repair the negative impression of his regime that Ramírez had provoked at Santa Teresita. John Paul II responded with a distinct gesture of surprise directed at the television cameras and thus lent further support to Stroessner's critics.[3]

As if to confirm its loss of papal approval, the regime immediately forced Chief Ramírez into hiding.[4] He later recalled the difficult seven months he spent secluded in the forest and living off the land near his tribal homeland of Riacho Mosquito, assisted by gifts of food and by information from his Maskoy community. Not until Stroessner's long rule came to an end, in January 1989, was the Maskoy leader finally able to return to his home. My interview with Ramírez, in May 2001, was the first time in over ten years that the chief had ventured back to the capital city of Asunción because of his very real fears of state retaliation, even though the regime had collapsed a decade before, and Paraguayans had a democratic government and a new constitution.

Ramírez's testimony and experience confirm that, rather than being isolated and marginal, indigenous people in Paraguay were savvy actors who were clearly integrated into the national political, economic, and social systems. His address to the pope and the international attention that indigenous people in Paraguay attracted as a result also highlight their astute attempts to make their difficult situation known to both domestic and foreign communities. As in other Latin American nations, by the late twentieth century, indigenous people in Paraguay were manipulating the media, capitalizing on contacts with individuals and nongovernmental organizations (NGOs) both at home and abroad, and publicly embarrassed the regime as often as possible by exposing its corruption. During the 1980s, throughout what became Stroessner's last decade in power, indigenous people created multiple alliances with opponents of the regime in an attempt to defend their natural resources and recover their tribal territories.

If it indeed presents a picture of an organized and politically active indigenous population, the natives' encounter with the pope also demonstrates their economic and political integration into the national community. Although indigenous people clearly resented the heavy-handed way the regime had tried to exclude them from the benefits of national development while stealing their land, timber, and resources, native groups were obviously in greater contact with and more dependent than ever before on non-Indian leaders, NGOs, and religious agencies. Throughout Stroessner's last decade in power, indigenous people organized widely to oppose the negative effects that his massive development projects were having on their communities. Yet, despite all their struggles to determine their own future and control their own resources, the very act of forming alliances with the dictator's opponents only drew indigenous communities into closer interaction and dependence on national structures and agencies loyal to the regime.

Were indigenous people in fact successfully integrated into national society? Elite supporters of the regime had created an elaborate policy—similar to policies elsewhere in the Americas—that promised to extend the benefits of civilization to the indigenous population. By "integration," the regime meant making indigenous people live as the Paraguayans did and abandon their distinctive indigenous identities and cultural practices. (I use "nationals," "Paraguayans," and the Spanish term *Paraguayos* throughout to designate nonindigenous people from Paraguay.) Integration meant farming and contributing to local economies and living in towns alongside the national population. At the same time, the integration program also tried to decrease prejudice and make nationals more welcoming toward native peoples, so the latter would stop regarding outsiders with suspicion. Stroessner wanted integration based on reciprocal contributions to create a more cohesive, unified state. Throughout his regime, this vague policy fluctuated in response to national and foreign pressures.

On a superficial level, the dictatorship promised to accomplish the successful integration of native communities into the majority population. In practice, though, the government had actually long attempted to exclude indigenous people from the benefits of national development. The state's policies had often failed to protect the very people they were supposed to defend. A closer look at Stroessner's agenda shows that policies portrayed as inclusive and designed to benefit indigenous people were not enforced or were even misused to permit the theft of indigenous resources and land.

A politically mobilized indigenous population, then, as evidenced distinctly when Chief Ramírez addressed the pope at Santa Teresita, actually represented the results of the regime's economic and political strategy gone awry. Stroessner had focused on national economic development as a way to secure popular support. As the corruption and graft—facilitated by his grandiose construction and elaborate rural development projects—declined during the mid-1980s, the elite who had built their fortunes on Stroessner's economic plans withdrew their support. His development programs had also damaged indigenous communities and their resources more seriously than ever before, and indigenous people throughout the country had joined forces to oppose the regime's plans to exclude them from the benefits of national growth.

Native struggles to keep and recover their territories in Paraguay exemplify the great themes of recent native mobilization. In *Contemporary Indigenous Movements in Latin America*, Erick Langer argues that, because most indigenous people live directly off the land, control over their territory has been critical to their continued survival.[5] It should come as no surprise, then, that, as Stroessner's development plans infringed on indigenous territory and tried to make the native population disappear, indigenous people throughout the country organized and joined forces to protect their resources and land.

This book examines the dialectical relationship between the indigenous population of modern Paraguay, the Stroessner dictatorship, and the religious missions. The historical importance of indigenous people within this borderland nation makes them more relevant than in other countries with smaller native populations and sheds light on the recent dynamics between indigenous peoples and states in Latin America.

My principal argument is that Stroessner's plans for the indigenous population were organic and evolved along with the regime in a somewhat haphazard manner. Sometimes the policy changes were directed from above and purposeful, while at other times they changed in reaction to outside events and pressures that the regime could not control. Initially, during the late 1950s, the dictatorship planned to integrate the indigenous population into society by way of a heavy-handed indigenist guardianship common throughout the continent. When this policy failed in the 1970s because of attention to human rights and as economic development came to motivate popular support for the regime, Stroessner began trying to exclude the indigenous population from national development policy and to make them "disappear" by whatever means possible. Although policy had shifted from inclusion to exclusion by the 1980s, increased international scrutiny caused the dictator to mask these goals within a policy of integration employed for similar reasons in much of Latin America.

The regime's actions shed light on Paraguay's political culture, its indigenist policies, its reaction to foreign influence, and the effects of its development programs on the nation's indigenous people. I will explore how the native population resisted, responded to, and adapted to the dictatorship's goals and plans. Indigenous agency provides examples of native responses to coercive national policies, religious proselytism, changing environments, and the loss of ancestral territories. Both indigenous people and the regime attempted to manipulate and alter one another, and each succeeded to a significant degree.

Still, the violent interaction in and of itself changed both sides in unexpected ways. Even as indigenous people joined forces and used their identities strategically to protect their resources, the dynamic exchange with the regime brought them into greater contact with national society than ever before. Stroessner's attempt to exclude them, even while framed within a policy of integration, in the end helped focus negative criticism on his regime. Thus, both the indigenous population and the regime achieved part of their goals while compromising central components of their political, social, and economic agendas.

A Racially Mixed Nation and
an Authoritarian Political Culture

Indigenous people have always accepted a forced alliance due to a lack of survival alternatives. In this case, the apparent acceptance of white suggestions, for the indigenous person . . . [is] to find in some sectors a defense for their group's interests.

Severo Flores, "Las comunidades"

Even more, at the very center of colonial domination a culture of alliance systematically developed that is no more than the pure and simple suppression of one of the components of the cultural duality . . . a harmony of the dominant classes.

Bartomeu Melià, *Una nación dos culturas*

The Indian within you has sprouted forth.

Paraguayan saying

Paraguay entered the twentieth century with unique patterns of interaction between its indigenous people and nationals. The first pattern was an exceptional case of *mestizaje*, or racial mixture. Second, following independence in 1811, the elite consistently tolerated dictatorial rule. In the 1860s, moreover, Paraguay fought a war with neighbors Argentina and Brazil that decimated its population and shaped labor, land, and political rule for decades. These patterns contributed to the fourth pattern: Paraguay is the only Latin American country with an official bilingual policy. Finally, these patterns contributed to unequal land distribution and created difficult living conditions for the lower classes, both peasants and native peoples.

Most scholars of Paraguay have attributed the extensive racial mixing during colonial Spanish rule to cooperation between Europeans and indigenous Guaraní near Asunción, where foreigners first settled in 1537. The exploitation of indigenous laborers and native women by the European settlers contributed to widespread miscegenation. By 1556, colonists had had at least six thousand children with indigenous women. Some Spaniards claimed to have as many as seventy indigenous wives. Local *encomienda* (entrusted) laws forced indigenous people to live close to Europeans and to work for them on a permanent basis. Women provided year-round household service to settlers, and daily contact led to cultural mixing and adoption of cultural traits by both sides. While they retained some indigenous practices, people of mixed race came to see themselves as superior and collectively developed pejorative attitudes toward their indigenous servants, even as they continued to practice Guaraní cooking and child-rearing customs.

Despite evidence of some accommodation, Paraguay's indigenous people rose up repeatedly to resist colonial Spanish rule. Between 1537 and 1609, the Guaraní revolted violently twenty-three times against the system of imposed labor.[1]

Also important during the colonial period were the thirty famous seventeenth-century mission towns, called the Paraguay Reductions (Reducciones Paraguayas), that the Jesuits created among the Guaraní people in what later became eastern Paraguay and across the Paraná River in neighboring Argentina and Brazil. Missionaries converted the Guaraní to Christianity and organized them into militias to counter the armed Brazilian *bandeirantes* (raiders) who led slaving raids deep into mission territory.

Although the European missionaries offered some protection against the slavers, the Guaraní continued to revolt. In 1753, when Spain gave the easternmost missions to Portugal following the 1750 Treaty of Madrid, the Guaraní rose up against the Portuguese crown. Several mission groups, under the direction of the great Guaraní orator Ñeengirú, assumed leadership of their communities in a small rebellion but were later crushed by a combined Spanish and Portuguese army.[2]

After King Charles III expelled the Jesuits from the Spanish territories in 1767, the Guaraní fled the missions. Barbara Ganson shows, in *The Guaraní under Spanish Rule in the Río de la Plata*, that, following the Jesuits' departure, measles and influenza decimated Guaraní communities. Mission reorganization under new administrators led to the imposition of the Spanish language, and the indigenous people showed their dissatisfaction with this turn of events by rustling cattle, stealing, taking their grievances to Spanish courts, and relocating to major cities in the Southern Cone. As the colonial period came to an end in the early nineteenth century, the plundering of missions contributed to the creation of a peasantry in Paraguay and the collapse of any significant Guaraní resistance. Nevertheless, as Ganson emphasizes: "The Guaraní still managed to retain distinctive elements of their indigenous culture, despite the efforts of Catholic missionaries, and in the

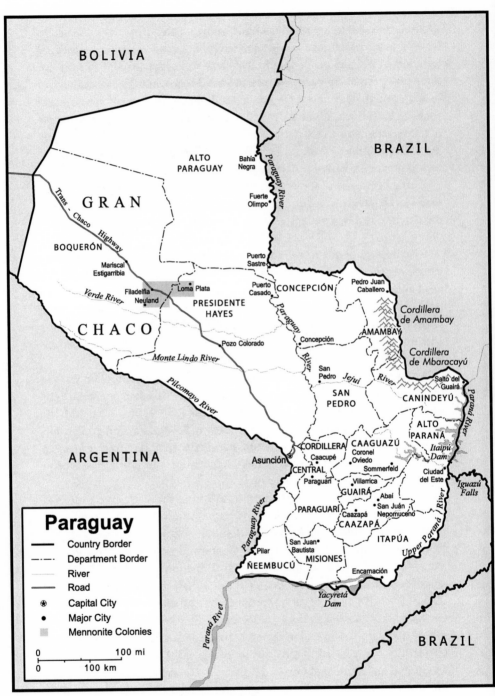

1.1. Paraguay. Cartography by Christopher Knoll.

face of the overwhelming political, economic, social, and cultural pressures from the Europeans they encountered."[3]

Also by the early nineteenth century, the encomienda system in Paraguay had integrated many indigenous people into colonial society and had produced a large racially mixed population whose most salient retention of native culture was the use of the Guaraní language. Only a few groups of Guaraní in eastern Paraguay and most of the western Chaco tribes remained free from national control. A few isolated communities of Païmbía Tavyterã, Avá Guaraní, Mbyá, and Ache still resided in wooded eastern locations, supporting themselves through horticulture or hunting and gathering. They fiercely maintained their independence. Still, the cultural markers that distinguished them from the Paraguayan majority were minimal: group identity; religious beliefs; and, especially, where they lived.

Perhaps it was because the differences between peasants and the indigenous population were seemingly so small that José Gaspar Rodríguez de Francia, the first leader to follow independence, took a conservative position toward his nation's remaining native population. Francia ruled as "dictator for life" between 1816 and 1840 with the title "El Supremo Dictador." While regimes elsewhere tried to dismantle or even eliminate native communities, as Argentine dictator Manuel de Rosas did during his Desert Campaign of 1833, Paraguay's dictator instead "strengthened the special status of the indigenous people."[4] To bolster his plans to diminish the power of the elite, Francia extended state recognition to the remaining indigenous communities even as he took territory from the church and landowners. He divided private land equally between indigenous people and peasants, which secured territory for select native groups and protected them from the elites who had exploited their resources.

Some indigenous groups responded positively to Francia's initiatives. By the end of the seventeenth century, a fierce tribe of traders that called itself the Evueví, known popularly as the Payaguá, dominated the northern Paraguay River. They attacked in canoe flotillas and terrorized European commerce on the river.[5] By the time Francia took control of the country, after decades of conflict, Evueví canoemen were serving the state as river police. The first dictatorship in Paraguay's national period thus strengthened indigenous landholdings and ties to the state, encouraged racial mixing, and largely isolated Paraguay from the rest of Latin America.

Gen. Carlos Antonio López assumed control of Paraguay following Francia's death in 1840 and began to change his isolated country into a modern nation-state. His economic policy led to momentous changes for the indigenous people in eastern Paraguay. To encourage natives to participate in wage labor and to gain access to their forest resources, the dictator "liberated" them. In 1842, López "undercut the communal structure of the pueblos" and set indigenous people against one another by limiting landownership to "capable Indians, those most deserving and well behaved."[6] This decree divided the indigenous population into those who could and those who could not own land and subjected the latter to legal discrimination.

Alleging long-standing abuse and humiliation of the native population, in 1848, López declared all people in the twenty-one native pueblos to be citizens of the republic. This much-lauded "emancipation" masked a hidden agenda. By "freeing" the native population, the dictator divested pueblos of their special status; seized all their cattle, goods, and properties; and subjected the native inhabitants to military service and taxes payable in yerba mate, the tea from Paraguay common by this time throughout the Southern Cone. This decree forced the six thousand Guaraní still living in the missions to move to villages and pushed as many as twenty-five thousand native workers into the wage-labor market.[7]

By this time, the remaining indigenous people east of the Paraguay River spoke some form of Guaraní and all belonged to the Tupí-Guaraní language family. In the northern Amambay region the Paï Tavyterã practiced subsistence horticulture and resided in large close-knit communities. The Avá Guaraní, culturally the closest to Paraguayans, lived in the eastern region. Both peoples had contact with peasants and some even worked as peons on ranches or sold yerba mate to outsiders. In the central-east lived the Mbyá Guaraní, who still avoided contact with national society by living in small wooded communities. The most isolated were the small groups of Ache, who used a form of the Guaraní language and hunted and gathered in small nomadic bands in the central-eastern regions. In pre-Columbian times, some Tupí-Guaraní had also migrated west of the Paraguay River. The western Guaraní—also called Chiriguanos—and the Guaraní-Ñandeva, both Guaraní speakers, lived in the dry territory that became the western border with Bolivia.

Many of the Guaraní people in eastern Paraguay participated in wider markets, some as wage laborers but primarily through the sale of yerba mate. Nearly all of the Jesuit missions had owned sizeable yerba plantations by 1762 and shipped the tea to Santa Fé and Buenos Aires, from where it was sold to Chile and Peru. The tea became the Jesuits' most lucrative product. Although production was strenuous, at times requiring trips of hundreds of miles into and out of the forests carrying heavy loads, as demand increased, more indigenous people joined the market as producers and harvesters of yerba.[8]

Historian Rafael Barrett has described the nineteenth-century yerba fields in eastern Paraguay. When they worked for nationals, conditions for the Guaraní were arduous. As many as 90 percent of the yerba mate harvesters commonly received only food as pay, and most suffered from alcoholism and tropical fevers. Owners used alcohol as an *enganche*, a means to secure and indebt indigenous workers for the backbreaking work. Often, workers sought relief in alcohol, Barrett argues, and drank to forget their dismal working conditions.[9]

In the northeastern Mbaracayú region, the Guaraní produced and sold yerba to outsiders but retained control over their land and avoided extensive relationships with outsiders by spending most of their time in secluded forest homes.[10] López's decree also authorized the seizure of the fertile agricultural lands that belonged to the twenty-one principal native Guaraní communities in eastern Paraguay. By breaking up these settlements, the state removed the most important marker that still differentiated indigenous people from Paraguayans: a distinct geographic location. Following this edict, census takers labeled the relocated natives as peasants, and the recognized native population dropped to less than one percent of the population.[11]

Francisco Solano López, who succeeded his father in 1862, expanded economic growth and pushed to occupy the Chaco, which led to greater contact with the indigenous people. By this time, the dry Chaco region west of the Paraguay River was populated by peasants and a variety of non-Guaraní indigenous people from four linguistic families. The Ayoreode and the Ïshïro were members of the Zamuco linguistic group who had traditionally inhabited the northern Chaco, the Ayoreode closer to Bolivia and the Ïshïro nearer the Paraguay River. Traditionally hunters and gatherers, the Ayoreode were the last native people in Paraguay to establish contact with outsiders, and the last known extended family left the forests in 2004 as ranchers deforested their remaining hunting grounds.

The Enlhit and closely related Enxet, farther east in the lower Chaco, were two groups of the same tribe whom Paraguayos pejoratively referred to as Lengua. Togeher with the Angaité, Sanapaná, Guan'a, and Enenlhit these tribes belonged to the Lengua-Maskoy linguistic group. These larger groups lived in the central and eastern areas of the Chaco, nearer the Paraguay River. The Yofuaxa, formerly called Choroti by nationals, the Nivaklé, and the Mak'a shared Mataco-Mataguayo linguistic ties and had in historical times lived in the central and southern areas of the Chaco.

Finally, the Toba-Qom, of Guaicurú linguistic ancestry, had tradition-

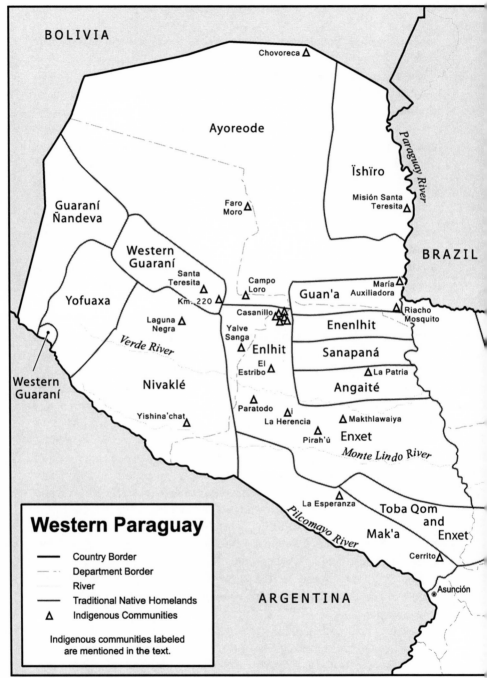

1.2. Selected western indigenous communities. Cartography by Christopher Knoll.

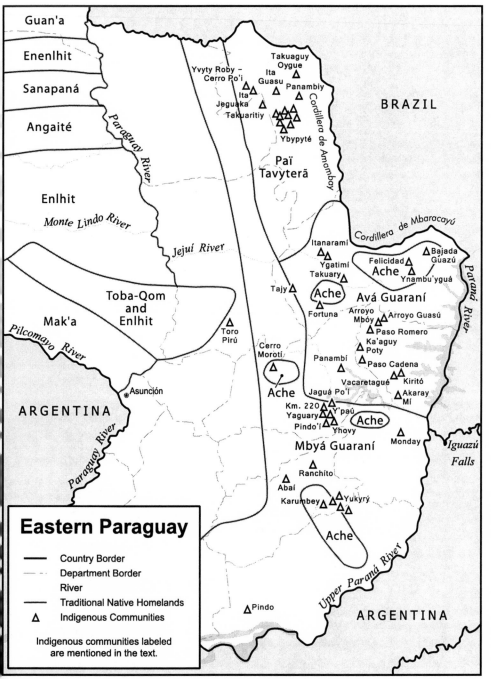

1.3. Selected eastern indigenous communities. Cartography by Christopher Knoll.

ally resided in the southeastern Chaco. Except for the two Guaraní peoples, tribes west of the Paraguay River shared linguistic ties with natives elsewhere in the Gran Chaco, an area covering parts of western Paraguay, northern Argentina, southeastern Bolivia, and southwestern Brazil.

To increase production, President López began to employ indigenous laborers. He forced the remaining Evueví to oversee state-owned lumber barges along the Paraguay River. As a result of increasing contact and disease, numbers diminished, and the tribe became extinct.[12]

The demise of the Evueví allowed the Maskoy people to move east and settle along the upper Paraguay River. The Maskoy of Paraguay's eastern Chaco are composed of five ethnic groups—the Guaná, the Sanapaná, the Enlhit, the Enenlhit, and the Angaité—who all speak regional dialects of the same general language. Traditionally farmers, on their new lands the Maskoy, especially the Guaná tribe, cultivated sweet potatoes, corn, manioc, and squash.[13] Branislava Susnik has argued that the Enenlhit were Toba-Takshik who migrated north from the Argentine province of Formosa to Paraguay in 1870 and settled among the Enlhit people near Puerto Sastre. Non-Indians in the nineteenth century confused these people with the Toba-Qom from the northern Argentine Chaco, who spoke a Guaicurúan language, and collectively called them the Toba-Maskoy.[14] The Enenlhit themselves claim that their tribe arrived from the west, from an area known today as Casanillo.[15] Though they claimed the new lands as tribal homelands, the Maskoy were relative newcomers to the eastern Chaco, where they joined the regional economy as harvesters of hardwoods and as ranch hands.

More important than his use of native labor was López's buildup of the military to assert hegemony over land that Paraguay claimed along its borders with Argentina and Brazil. This led the country into the War of the Triple Alliance with Brazil, Argentina, and Uruguay, a disastrous mistake for Paraguay. Even after drafting all males and forcing women into nonmilitary labor, Paraguay lost the war miserably. When the war finally ended in 1870, half of the country's population had been killed, and the male population had decreased from 220,000 to 28,000. The years that followed saw the increased use of Guaraní to resist the occupying Argentine forces.

Colonial patterns, the dictatorships, and the war all contributed to unequal land distribution in Paraguay. Strapped for cash after the War of the Triple Alliance and eager to attract foreign investment, as attested by the passage of the Civil Code of 1877, Paraguay sold 7,035 leagues of its western territory to seventy-nine persons or companies, mostly Argentine and European ranchers, for an average of less than three cents an acre.[16]

Bernardino Caballero, who seized power in 1880, sold the remaining state-owned land in western Paraguay to foreigners to replenish his bank-rupt treasury, and soon British businesses entered the Chaco. In 1886, for instance, Anglo-Argentine banker Carlos Casado del Alisal purchased 13,995,000 acres of land west of the Paraguay River. Although by law a single person could not own over 220 square leagues, through a variety of machi-nations Casado acquired 14 percent of Paraguay's territory. President Cabal-lero also founded the conservative Colorado Party, and many of his followers benefited from the Chaco sales. By 1900 seventy-nine people owned half the country's land and began to force peasant and native squatters to vacate their properties.[17] It was at this time that most indigenous land in the Chaco passed into private ownership.

In the last decade of the nineteenth century, when Casado began to ex-tract tannin, his company employed indigenous workers to build a railroad to its factories and increasingly relied on cheap native labor to extract lum-ber and tannin. The company's need for cheap labor and the indigenous population's growing desire for cash as a result of increasing loss of land, led the Maskoy people to harvest quebracho for the outsiders, who boiled down the hardwood trees for tannin to cure hides. Susnik has shown that labor at the tannin plants affected Maskoy workers negatively by changing tribal relationships. One traveler at the time argued that contact with non-Indians had made the Angaité "sweet with outsiders, angry with their own, selfish, demanding, beggars, drunks, deceitful, disloyal and thieves."[18]

Even more important, work in the cash economy fragmented Maskoy society. Work as *braceros* and *hacheros* in the extraction of quebracho broke up families and communities, even, for instance, among tribes such as the Sanapaná, who did not migrate to the Paraguay River. By the end of the nineteenth century, the Maskoy had joined the cash economy.

It was during this time that British missionaries first arrived in Paraguay. In 1889, when Anglicans began to proselytize in the Chaco with the govern-ment's encouragement, missionaries described their role as "influencing the Indians so that . . . by fair dealing and preparation of hearts and minds they may be led to welcome future settlers, and to share with them the advantages of civilization in return for their land surrendered to its service."[19] Anglicans enjoyed close ties to the British businesses that by the late nineteenth cen-tury dominated the Paraguayan economy and owned most of the Maskoy lands. The missionaries hoped to prepare native people for labor in the mar-ket economy, as missionary Barbrooke Grubb explained in 1909: "[Those] who have an interest in Chaco lands can surely not fail to see the benefit of a numerous, trained and willing population of workers, with whom to develop the lands in which they have placed their capital . . . we are practical enough to not neglect such training as will fit these people to take their proper place in the world."[20] Over the years, missionaries helped landowners survey, explore, and extend their control over the lower Chaco. Their efforts to help integrate the indigenous population seem to have been largely successful, since by 1950 the Maskoy people served as cheap laborers on the ranches, some as large as 300,000 hectares, that occupied their former territory.[21]

Although the sale of public lands and the arrival of Protestants encouraged foreign investment, they angered the Paraguayan public. The bitter outcry helped the Liberals return to power, though they advocated similar economic policies.

The Liberal Party dominated politics until 1936 and, although deeply divided, founded a constitutional state based, in theory, on free enterprise, elections, and trade. Liberal politicians also tried to disestablish the remaining native communities to force indigenous people into national settlements. The 1907 Ley de Reducciones de Tribus Indígenas, legislation that promoted the settlement of native tribes, promised native land to any religious organization that could successfully "reduce" the indigenous people, using the same term employed by former Jesuit missionaries to invite missions to settle native people close to nationals and place them under state guardianship.[22] Few missions, though, were interested in the state's offer, at least yet. More important, the Liberals encouraged large groups of foreign immigrants to settle in rural areas.

It was during these Liberal administrations that German Mennonite settlers purchased huge tracts of land in the western Chaco. The first group of 1,765 Mennonites arrived from Canada in 1926 to settle the Menno Colony, while a second group of 2,000 from the Soviet Union settled in the Chaco in 1930 at Fernheim Colony. Liberal politicians intended these settlements to secure the Chaco for Paraguay and promised that immigration would bolster economic growth. Politically, however, the Liberals proved to be just as authoritarian as former dictators and certainly did not abide by their own electoral promises. From 1904 to 1954, Paraguay had thirty-one presidents, only eight of whom finished out their full terms peacefully.

It was during these Liberal administrations that reports about abuses of indigenous people on the frontier began to reach the capital. In 1907, German immigrant Federico Maynzhusen described macabre hunts to kill and capture Ache in eastern Paraguay:

> The persecution of the Guayakí Indians . . . took on horrible characteristics, conducted with the authorization of military leaders. In one case in 1907, organized to avenge the death of a mare by indigenous ar-

rows, a group of *vecinos* (Paraguayan ranchers), with police initiative, attacked an Ache camp and killed many men, women, and children, except for five children they took alive. When the mothers called from the woods to the children, and the men were unable to quiet their crying, they choked them to death. And all this to avenge the death of a horse.[23]

In 1925, the German journal *Zeitschrift für Ethnologie* reported that Paraguayos sold Ache slaves for the price of a cow. Jean Vellard, a French scholar who traveled in Paraguay during the 1930s, saw ranchers purchase Ache children for two hundred to three hundred pesos.[24] Peasants bragged that they raped and killed Ache women to steal their children:

> The Axe [Ache] were hunted as if they were beasts; they were usually killed with one shot after being spotted; but sometimes they were [captured] alive to be used as labor. The captured children were sometimes treated kindly. Kidnapping seems to have been the most common reason for the surprise assaults. . . . The captive children usually died before reaching the age of fifteen, while adults usually escaped again to the woods . . . kidnapping children . . . was a common way to keep the little Indians as a kind of domesticated monkey.[25]

Growing stories about violence on Paraguay's internal frontiers make the widespread use of the Guaraní language all the more notable as the final uniquely Paraguayan trait produced by colonial and early national political choices. No other Latin American nation still has an official bilingual policy, and no other people use a native tongue so extensively in conjunction with Spanish as do Paraguayans. As Paraguay recovered from its devastating war losses, the use of Guaraní spread still further. The legacy of a native heritage and language had, by 1950, assumed such mythical proportions that it significantly colored the cultural, social, and political situation in Paraguay.

It was another war that finally ended Liberal rule and contributed to more extensive use of Guaraní. Bolivians took advantage of political upheavals in Asunción to move their forts steadily eastward into the Chaco. In December 1928, Paraguayan Major Rafael Franco destroyed a Bolivian fort in a surprise attack. The resulting series of confrontations and growing nationalist sentiment forced out the Liberal Party and thrust the country into war with Bolivia in July 1932.[26] Throughout the conflict, which continued until July 1935, Major Franco urged the use of Guaraní to unify his troops.

Back in Asunción, the Chaco War increased political turmoil and united opposition against the Liberals. Soldiers who had seen the miserable state of the army joined the protesters. Poor treatment of disabled war veterans, including by then General Franco, led disgruntled army units to end thirty-two years of Liberal rule.

The Chaco War also disrupted western indigenous people because it brought them into greater contact with Paraguayos and Bolivians. The confrontation gave many indigenous people in the Chaco their first contact with outsiders and greater exposure to Western diseases and militarism. A Nivaklé elder named Alto Tsach'imaj recounted the difficulties of those violent years: "When I was a child, the Nivaklé were warring with the Mataco; but when I became a young man, fights began with the Bolivians who penetrated along the Pilcomayo River. This came to be a very dangerous period for our people, since the invaders had firearms. Many Nivaklé perished in the battles. My older brother also fell in one of the confrontations. One day, when there had already been many deaths among our people, Tofai invited all his group to go to Fis'chat . . . they were told how many people had been killed."[27]

Tajingvoy, an elder of mixed Nivaklé and Enlhit ancestry, attributed a rise in disease among his people to the military conflict: "Following the war, an epidemic of mumps attacked our groups. It was a terrible time! There were settlements where most of the people perished. My wife also contracted the disease and died. In the terror of the situation I picked up my small son and fled to live alone."[28] Occupying forces terrorized the people they encountered, including this Nivaklé man: "When the combat between Bolivians and Paraguayans began, our groups escaped to the woods. . . . One day . . . suddenly we fell into an ambush set up by a contingent of Bolivian soldiers. . . . The soldiers, all armed with rifles, encircled us. In the middle was a table. There sat the leader. He was cleaning his pistol. He accused us of being Paraguayans. Finally he asked: 'How do you prefer to die, with a machete or with a pistol?'"[29]

Indigenous testimonies show that, while there were previous confrontations between native people in the Chaco, because non-Indians brought firearms and disease, the Chaco War proved a new and devastating experience for western indigenous people. Contact with outsiders introduced new diseases and disrupted native communities to a greater degree than ever before. Some indigenous people nevertheless began to work for the national forces. Gen. Juan Belaieff, a Russian soldier with whom Paraguay contracted to direct its war strategy, turned to indigenous people for assistance. The Mak'a were a nomadic hunting and fishing tribe that had traditionally lived along the Pilcomayo River and that knew the southern Chaco intimately.

They had also fought against Bolivians since the initial strife in 1928, so Belaieff used them in the war as trackers and guides.

Paraguay was ultimately able to push Bolivia out of the Chaco, but the economic chaos that followed brought down the Liberal government. In the 1936 February Revolt, General Franco led Conservatives back to power and promised a national revolution marked by a new era of social justice. Early in his rule, Franco expropriated 200,000 hectares of land for 10,000 peasant families. The new leader guaranteed workers the right to strike and created an eight-hour workday. He appealed to war-generated nationalism and, in his Mussolini-style speeches, declared Solano López a hero "without precedent" and interred his remains in the National Pantheon of Heroes.[30] For recently contacted Chaco indigenous people, Franco created the Patronato Militar de los Indígenas del Chaco (National Indigenous Patronage), which made them wards of the armed forces.[31]

President Franco, named president in February 1936, also encouraged the glorification of a racially mixed heritage. Wartime nationalism led to a resurgence of Guaraní, and Franco officially made it the second national language. To undergird his resolve, the president published official documents in both Spanish and Guaraní. Concurrently, however, the military Hispanicized conscripts' Guaraní surnames.

Such ambiguity was typical of indigenist policies elsewhere: being too indigenous was considered backward, but officials appropriated the native language and employed it to strengthen national identity.[32] Such nationalism encouraged patriotism and ensured the continued use of Guaraní.[33]

Paraguayan literature produced during Franco's rule mirrors the state's indigenismo and glorifies what writers saw as the indigenous heritage and foundation of national society. As had happened earlier in Mexico and Peru, Paraguayans exalted the indigenous past in the face of widespread racism and argued that indigenous people contributed to a glorious national society.[34] Moisés Bertoni, Narciso Colmán, and Natalicio González held that the mixture of European Spanish and indigenous Guaraní had forged a superior race in Paraguay.[35] These writers elevated the Guaraní to the status of noble savage but concurrently used positivist theory to argue that indigenous people were, in fact, inferior to the racially mixed society they had unwillingly helped produce.

The nationalist-indigenist writers encouraged the creation of a local indigenist movement. While they helped revalidate the use of Guaraní, their denigration of native people also left its mark. "In these writers," argues Wayne Robins, "we find some of the causes that have contributed to the creation and perpetuation of an attitude of depreciation toward the indigenous people of this country. Given this negative situation it has been difficult to validate indigenous people within Paraguay's sociocultural panorama and more difficult to create a space in which indigenous people could contribute their cultural richness to the nation."[36]

The indigenist writers influenced the first politicians who displayed an active interest in the indigenous population. The Ministry of Agriculture created an agency called the Patronato Nacional de Indígenas (National Indigenous Patronage Office) in 1936 to study and help indigenous people improve their lives. In April 1938, sponsored by the agency, seventy Mak'a dancers and musicians performed in the capital at what the indigenists advertised as an "Indian Fantasy." Later, well-meaning philanthropists even took native artists south to perform in Buenos Aires, Argentina.[37] Only ten years before, the elite in Cuzco, Peru, had similarly employed theatrical troupes and pageants of Incaic customs to glorify their city as the capital of the former Inca Empire, ratify indigenismo as the intellectual and political ideology of the elite *cuzqueños*, and represent the very "essence of their race."[38]

The theatrical presentations highlighted the exotic nature of indigenous people but furthered their depiction as inferior. By denigrating indigenous people, authors and the elite contributed to popular prejudice against them.[39] The new indigenist program in Paraguay was confusing in its emphasis on the use of Guaraní coupled with the literary glorification of an indigenous ancestry but accompanied by growing popular deprecation of indigenous people and cultures. Alan Knight has discovered similar pejorative foundations for postrevolutionary indigenismo in Mexico: "Indians are discriminated against for being Indian and at the same time admired for being the 'real soul' of Mexico, living proof of Mexico's noble pre-Hispanic heritage . . . where Indians remain, racism remains."[40] As in Mexico, racism continued to be a visible feature of Paraguayan indigenismo.

The years that followed the indigenist florescence saw renewed political chaos and authoritarianism. Mariscal Estigarribia, who ousted Franco in 1937, brought Liberals back into power and assumed dictatorial rule in February 1940. A mild reformer, Estigarribia's new Agrarian Statute, much as had the 1887 Dawes Allotment Act in the United States, encouraged indigenous people to farm individual plots and offered land to native groups that "demonstrated undeniable aptitude to become landowners."[41] Estigarribia also urged religious missions to settle indigenous people in permanent locations and gave land to churches in proportion to the number of natives they planned to manage. The president's attempted reforms were short-lived, however, for in 1941 Estigarribia perished in an airplane crash.

With support from the Liberal cabinet, minister of war Higinio Morínigo assumed the presidency in 1941. The new leader promptly banned Franco's Febrerista Party and the Liberal Party, his political opponents, and sharply curtailed free speech and individual liberties. Without popular backing, the shrewd new dictator survived by carefully manipulating a group of young military officers who held key positions. Morínigo led his pro-Axis regime throughout the Second World War with open support for European fascists. The chief of police at the time named his son Adolfo Hirohito, in fact. Morínigo's ties to Colorado hard-liners and their Guión Rojo paramilitary force finally led to a full-scale civil war in 1947. By 1950, there was a clear precedent in Paraguay for one-party rule, public order at the expense of political liberty, and acceptance of the army as a political actor.

Meanwhile, newspapers and travelers renewed attention to violent encounters on the eastern frontiers, where ranchers had, by the 1950s, started to clear forests. The reports focused on the native people who called themselves the Ache, spoke a dialect of Guaraní, and were only distantly related to the larger groups. These people had always been nomads who lived from hunting and gathering deep in the eastern forests. By the late 1950s, reports of the enslavement and murder of the Ache and of the sale of indigenous children were common.[42] In May 1957 *Patria* reported that indigenists had rescued a small Ache girl from Paraguayos who had kept her as a domestic slave.[43]

Luis Miraglia recorded in 1941 that ranchers collected Ache skulls as trophies, kept Ache women as concubines, and rewarded peons with cash for every Ache they killed. Landlords used the town of San Juan Nepomuceno, newspapers asserted, as a marketplace in which to sell Ache children as slaves.[44]

The startling accounts show that the violence against the Ache was in part due to national prejudice and racial differences. Peasants considered indigenous people less than fully human. As one reporter argued: "Campesinos saw Ache as animals and felt no remorse in killing them."[45] At the time, Paraguayos attributed their prejudice to the indigenous people's persistent refusal to be baptized into the Catholic Church.[46] The natives' rejection of Catholicism enraged non-Indians because it symbolized an aloofness that flew in the face of Paraguayan racism.

While Morínigo trod a careful path between the Axis and the Allies, a few members of the upper class took greater interest in the country's indigenous people. The years of war and dictatorship, with news of struggling people overseas and reports about the enslaved Ache, saw the development of a more active indigenist movement at the nongovernmental level. In October

1942, General Belaieff and a young ethnographer named León Cadogan created the Asociación Indigenist Paraguaya (Paraguayan Indigenist Association, AIP), a "philanthropic entity to protect indigenous people."[47] The new NGO secured 335 hectares across the Paraguay River from Asunción and settled the Mak'a tribe, displaced by the Chaco War and subsequent ranching, in order to quickly integrate them into national society. To gather support for a Spanish school for the Mak'a, the AIP pledged: "It is important to focus on the problems of those who, distanced from civilization, need to be incorporated into it by means of instruction."[48] Morínigo, at the time openly profascist and dictatorial, enacted for the first time a specific indigenist policy in Paraguay geared toward integrating indigenous peoples.

The Chaco War and nationalistic fervor during World War II led not only to greater contact with indigenous people, they also again encouraged widespread use of the Guaraní language. By 1950, the government had begun to promote the use and instruction of the language in Paraguay's schools. The Escuela Superior de Humanidades (College of Humanities), founded in 1944, was the first university-level institution to offer courses in Guaraní. The 1950 census shows that 92 percent of the country spoke the indigenous language, with 40 percent monolingual in Guaraní, and only 52 percent speaking some Spanish.[49] Political decisions, military conflicts, the indigenist movement, and increasing contact with indigenous peoples had, by the mid-twentieth century, created in Paraguay a bilingual society without precedence in Latin America.

Alfredo Stroessner: A Temporary Substitute?

Following the Allies' victory in 1945, Colorado factions in Paraguay struggled to win the presidency with assistance from paramilitary groups loyal to the party. It was the Democráticos, led by Federico Chávez, who finally took control of the economically devastated country. Chávez had claimed to favor free elections and a power-sharing agreement while running for the presidency, but he imposed a state of siege only three weeks after assuming power late in 1949.

Chávez inherited a difficult job. Two decades of political and social unrest had crippled the economy; national and per capita income had fallen, inflation was rampant, and corruption, widespread. When he ran for reelection in 1953, the seventy-three-year-old president frustrated political hopefuls and further divided the military. In May of 1954, Alfredo Stroessner, commander-in-chief of the armed forces, overthrew Chávez with support from members of the Colorado Party, who saw the young commander as only an interim and temporary substitute.[50] The young military officer soon proved the Colorados wrong. Despite the goals of some members of the upper classes, Stroessner retained his control of the presidency.

He was born in the town of Encarnación in 1912, the son of a Paraguayan woman and a German immigrant. After military school, Stroessner gained a reputation for bravery in the Chaco War, rose quickly through the ranks, and came to be known as a thorough and hard worker. In August 1954, when he became president, no one expected him to become Paraguay's longest-lasting dictator.

The new leader was unlike caudillos elsewhere in Latin America, who flaunted their charisma.[51] In fact, rivals underestimated Stroessner because he seemed so dull, plodding, and uninspiring. Nevertheless, the new president proved a successful dictator because he was a disciplined worker, an adept administrator, and careful manager of even the most minute details of his administration.[52] From his position as commander-in-chief and with widespread military loyalty, Stroessner united his Colorado Party and allied it with the armed forces. This three-part agreement between both military branches and the party became the foundation for Stroessner's political longevity.[53]

Even as the new president worked to establish the bases of his regime, additional violence on the frontier showed that conflicts between native people and settlers in the countryside were becoming increasingly common. In 1955, several Ayoreode attacked Mennonite immigrants in the Chaco and drew new attention to the northwestern frontier. Christian L. Graber describes the encounters:

> Very soon afterward, the Moros overtook Mr. Sawatsky and attacked him. The first spear was meant for his head, but missed slightly, making only a surface wound on the back of his neck. The second spear was aimed directly at his body, but it struck the hip bone and glanced off, cutting a slight gash in the abdomen. Next came a club blow to the head. Sawatsky's arm was broken as he protected his skull from the club. . . . Sawatsky pulled the spear from his abdomen, and together the men made some gestures of resistance toward the Indians. The Moros retreated and . . . quietly vanished into the impenetrable thorny bush, as only Moros could.
>
> The Moros also attacked Chulupí [Nivaklé] and Lengua [Enlhit] Indians and Paraguayans. Reliable rumors tell of three or four attacks which resulted in . . . death.
>
> Once they brought an Indian woman of the Chulupí tribe to our

hospital—she held part of her skull in her hand; the brain lay bare and was partially damaged, the scalp hung down in smashed flaps.[54]

The reports that portrayed Ayoreode as uncivilized and primitive high-lighted their supposedly savage nature. Graber even uses the highly pejora-tive term *moro*, a name that Paraguayos used to describe the dark Ayoreode phenotype. Such designations, rooted in the Spanish expulsion of the Mus-lims (Moors, or moros) from the Iberian Peninsula and adapted by explor-ers to Latin America, reflect the widespread racism in Paraguay at the time. The writers of these accounts ignored, however, the cause of such violence: growing intrusions by prospectors, trappers, and pioneers into indigenous territory. The revelation that there were hunter-and-gatherer people in the Chaco who resisted these incursions caused widespread interest in Para-guay.

Even as development increased in the Chaco, violence continued to grow on Paraguay's eastern frontiers. The colonization of eastern Paraguay, which began in earnest during the 1950s, increased peasant occupation of lands that indigenous people had traditionally used. Soon after Stroessner came to power he forced Industrial Paraguaya, the largest yerba mate extraction company, to sell its two million hectares in the east to new investors. The president's loyal military elite resold the land to Brazilian and U.S. ranchers and agroindustrialists, who began to clear the forests to plant soybeans and raise cattle.[55] Industrial Paraguaya had, since the 1890s, encouraged indig-enous people to remain on their land and harvest yerba from the forests, but the new ranchers resented indigenous "poaching" and evicted the na-tives. Pressure for land created difficulties for Mbyá, Avá Guaraní, and Païi Tavyterã groups, which had lived off of subsistence farming and gathering, but it especially threatened the Ache.

Ultimately, the difficulties indigenous people had in keeping their for-est reserves resulted from the inequitable distribution of land. By the mid-twentieth century, the land-tenure situation in Paraguay was one of the worst in Latin America, and land scarcity made living conditions difficult for peasants as well as for indigenous people. By 1956, 49 percent of all farmers were squatting on the land they were farming. Brazilian, U.S., and Argentine agribusinesses owned enormous tracts of land for ranching, cotton, and tim-ber extraction. The Stroessner years only exacerbated these trends. By as late as 1981, one percent of the nation's 273,000 farms still owned 79 percent of the farmland in use.[56]

To make matters worse for native peoples, as peasants' land tenure wors-ened, they organized and began to press the state for farmland. Between

1950 and 1960, the number of cooperative peasant organizations in rural areas grew from four to sixty. Japanese and European immigrants formed several of these cooperatives, but Paraguayans created the majority.[57]

Although indigenous people did not participate in the new cooperatives, they had started to interact to a greater degree with non-Indians. For a century, the three large Guaraní tribes had sold their yerba tea to Paraguayos, but the animosity between both groups was too severe to allow for joint cooperation. This was especially the case when both competed for the same land. Although some native peoples worked as peons for ranchers, they largely continued using land as a group and living in isolated communities. A distinct way of life was especially the case for the Ache, who, even more than other Guaraní, had preserved some independence within their forest homes. By 1950, there were four bands of Ache in eastern Paraguay. These groups remained hostile to outsiders because, as they recounted, they were "constantly harassed and attacked by Paraguayan colonists."[58] As peasants built roads and fences in traditional Ache hunting territory, the indigenous peoples increasingly looked to the outside world for food and sustenance.

At the same time, ranchers sometimes turned to indigenous workers, even the Ache, as a source of cheap labor. The scarcity of workers in northeastern Paraguay was a result of the War of the Triple Alliance, when Paraguay had lost so many people that the demand for field hands in the eastern region grew significantly.[59] Not only did ranchers import large numbers of campesinos from areas where land was scarce, they also sought indigenous workers and employed them through an often exploitative and even violent debt peonage system.[60] Even poorer peasants held Ache laborers through force and debt or captured their children to use as servants. The coercive nature of these relations led city folk, especially, to call the labor system outright slavery.

The widespread *criado* system in Paraguay helps explain the references to Ache slavery. It has been common in Paraguay for wealthy families to raise poor children as household servants, educating and feeding them in return for work. The fact that Ache skin pigment is lighter than that of other Guaraní natives and even than that of many peasants only complicated the Aches' situation. Paraguayos adopted Ache children as criados and kept them as their own children and thus lightened their progeny.[61] Sometimes, non-Indians took these youngsters during raids, but the Ache themselves also gave some children away voluntarily after their parents perished in epidemics that followed contact. Kim Hill argues that Paraguayos never believed they owned the Ache servants' person. Rather, they claimed to own the childhood services that non-Indians traded.[62]

Still, frontier news had little impact in the capital, where Stroessner began to use the Colorado Party to consolidate his personal control. The new president made the party serve his political purposes by creating a network of wards called *seccionales* throughout the country. These small cells functioned as a major system of patronage and surveillance of political dissent by organizing party affiliates and carefully monitoring opposition. Employment in the public sector, posts in state schools, and jobs in state hospitals and public services were all limited to party members. In addition, as early as 1955, the dictator began to require members of the armed forces to join his party and limited entrance into the elite officer corps to Colorado families.[63] With thorough control and oversight, Stroessner maintained the illusion of a large popular base of support. In return for his patronage, after 1954, the party always nominated him as its candidate for president.

The new president proved an able strategist who not only capitalized on current political and social trends but also did not hesitate to use brutal force to retain power. As the struggle between the United States and the Soviet Union intensified and permeated Latin America, Stroessner labeled opponents as Communists to imply that their goals were subversive or evil.[64] The dictator employed strong anti-Communist nationalism as a strategy for social control. To legitimate his rule, Stroessner employed the Doctrine of National Security and the perceived Communist threat to justify his tight control over the internal population, as well as to retain the United States' financial and military support. The small underground Partido Comunista Paraguayo (Paraguayan Communist Party, PCP) became a scapegoat the dictator used to intimidate and control those not firmly aligned with and loyal to his Colorado Party.

In his insightful analysis of Stroessner's rule, Carlos R. Miranda shows that he relied on several strategies to keep his authoritarian regime in power and uphold what came to be known as the *stronista* doctrine. While in the late 1950s the doctrine seemed to represent just one more neofascist regime and promised to guide the nation to a brighter future, Stroessner's tactics soon became evident. First, he allowed practices that kept the population in constant fear, so that Paraguayans even came to doubt their own thoughts, values, and speech. Second, the people came to see the state as an institution that worked pragmatically in pursuit of measurable goals, which minimized internal political controversy. Third, the regime emphasized the need to keep peace and order. Given the earlier political turmoil, a strong, stable government was highly popular in Paraguay.[65]

President Stroessner's principal goal and political strategy became the development of Paraguay's economic potential. He used a growing economy to reward his supporters in the upper class; this closed-minded group of political leaders benefited financially from Stroessner's retention of power. Unlike Juán Perón, the populist president of neighboring Argentina, Paraguay's president did not seek support from the lower and working classes. While "the professed motive for economic development was to raise the standard of living," as Miranda has argued, Stroessner's "unspoken motive was to win political acquiescence."[66] As the national economy responded under his rule, Stroessner's boom repaid the elite for the political price they paid by tolerating authoritarian rule.

Even though agricultural production dramatically increased, the regime achieved growth at a high cost to the lower classes. By 1956, Stroessner had instituted an International Monetary Fund economic austerity program that drove down real wages and led, two years later, to a general strike. Security forces arrested three hundred trade union leaders to quell the disturbance, but popular discontent prevailed. When Congress complained of police brutality, the president dissolved it and exiled all remaining dissidents from inside his party. Hundreds of people left Paraguay for neighboring countries.

After this initial purge of labor dissenters, the president "did not even bother with a facade of democracy," argues Cockroft.[67] On the contrary, Stroessner's treatment of indigenous people shows that he attempted year after year to maintain his popular legitimacy and an appearance of having a popular mandate. In 1967, he had congress approve a new constitution to provide a legal framework for his rule and thereafter held elections every six years.

Throughout the remainder of his long rule, the dictator used repression and any other means to ensure a stable political climate, a submissive population, and a subject labor force. These tactics attracted foreign investors, and steady economic growth followed throughout most of Stroessner's rule.

The Doctrine of National Security and toleration of corruption helped rally the elite at first, but the initial crackdown on labor leaders shows that heavy-handed political techniques did not ensure passive popular compliance for long, especially among the lower classes, which did not benefit from state corruption. Stroessner did not hesitate to use brutal measures to enforce a stable political climate. Security forces imprisoned, deported, tortured, and killed those who objected too strongly to Colorado rule. In larger towns and cities, the party created the Guardia Urbana (Urban Guard) to terrorize dissidents and discourage political meetings. Secret police called *pyragues* ("people with hairy feet") closely monitored the population.[68]

The constant search for legitimacy was perhaps most evident in the dictatorship's policies toward the indigenous population, because these measures attracted international attention as anthropological advocacy work increased in the 1970s. Although Stroessner himself had no interest in the indigenous population, because of their historical importance, the regime at first tried to use the country's indigenous legacy to bolster its hegemony. Only two years after becoming president, Stroessner instituted Guaraní as a high school subject in Asunción. To train instructors, in 1961, the Ministry of Education organized the Instituto Lingüistico Guaraní del Paraguay (Guaraní Linguistic Institute of Paraguay). The use of Guaraní also increased because of the rise in immigration that Stroessner encouraged from Brazil, Europe, and Asia. In the face of growing competition for jobs, Paraguayos used Guaraní to assert their national identity. Finally, to unite the population around the use of a native tongue, the regime initially encouraged the indigenist explanation that Paraguayan society was the glorious product of an alliance between Europeans and the Guaraní. The young president used many of what Benedict Anderson has termed the "imagined" components of modern nationality: horizontal comradeship; solidarity among whites; and, especially, a background based on a common heritage of race mixture.[69]

Nevertheless, because Stroessner focused so much attention on his party, development, and repression, it might seem to be a contradiction in terms to call the regime's treatment of the indigenous population an official "Indian policy." The dictator's development plans produced such adverse effects for the indigenous population that they showed a complete lack of concern for the indigenous people.[70] A reporter who claimed to be a personal friend of Stroessner's had a completely different opinion. Rafael Trinidad interviewed the dictator and argued that he was very interested in the indigenous population. When he learned of difficult conditions in a community, the reporter claimed, the president called his minister of defense and ordered him to quickly send provisions. "Stroessner loved to speak Guaraní," Trinidad recalled, and whenever possible would speak to native people in their own language. "It may be true," he admitted, "that some state functionaries treated *indígenas* badly. But Stroessner himself was 100 percent supportive of the indigenous people."[71] Trinidad was a state employee who had worked for the regime and was clearly interested in portraying the former president in a positive light. But his opinion should not be ignored, for it creates yet another controversial image of the dictatorship's relationship with the indigenous population.

Whether or not Stroessner was personally interested in the indigenous population, his development plans affected their rural communities directly. By the time he had consolidated his control, there were only sixty thousand

to seventy thousand indigenous people in Paraguay who considered themselves ethnically distinct from the Paraguayo majority. The seventeen different indigenous peoples belonged to five language families and were divided
geographically by the Paraguay River. The native groups had distinct histories of interaction with national society and with other native peoples, but
all shared the legacy of discrimination and inadequate access to legal protection. Some tribes actively avoided interaction with Paraguayans, but in the
eastern region especially, a few people shared close linguistic and cultural
traits with nationals. By 1954 every tribe had established contact with the
national population and had also lost much of its traditionally held land. In
addition, settlers and ranchers were extending farming, grazing cattle, and
cutting timber near most indigenous communities. The accelerating pace
of economic development promised to cause significant changes within indigenous communities as they maneuvered cultural, political, and religious
adaptation and changes.

Nevertheless, because Stroessner's attempts to develop the nation took
place in the late twentieth century, when economic development infringed on
indigenous rights, it attracted worldwide attention. Moreover, the expansion
of communication networks and anthropological advocacy in the last decades of the twentieth century fostered indigenous organization throughout
Latin America. Native demands forced nation-states to at least acknowledge
their indigenous populations. For these reasons, although the Stroessner regime paid little attention to indigenous people within Paraguay's borders,
by the time Paraguayans joined forces during the 1980s to overthrow the
Stronato (Stroessner's dictatorship), indigenous people had capitalized on
the political conditions to organize, form alliances with other opponents of
the regime, and lobby for the achievement of their tribal goals.

Conclusion

My interview with Enenlhit chief René Ramírez, in May 2001, demonstrates
that, ten years after the collapse of Stroessner's regime, indigenous people
in Paraguay had become savvy actors and were clearly integrated into the
national political, economic, and social systems. The Enenlhit leader elo-
quently recounted to me the great excitement he felt as he addressed the
Catholic pontiff, despite his real fear of retaliation from the regime.[72] His
trepidation was based on personal experience while working on the brutal
frontier created by the dictator's economic development plans. The dictator
soon made him pay for having focused renewed attention on the state's poor
treatment of indigenous people. The seven months that Ramírez spent hid-

ing out in the forest proves that the regime had no tolerance for a mobilized indigenous population. Nevertheless, the cooperation between the Catholic Church and the Maskoy people highlights the successful alliances that an organized indigenous population had forged with Stroessner's opponents in their efforts to defend their land and resources. Contrary to the state's efforts to exclude the native people from economic development, a host of causes had actually mobilized them enough to help discredit the dictator's social policies.

In this book I study the relationship between Paraguay's indigenous population, the Stroessner regime, and religious missions. My argument throughout is that Stroessner's haphazard plans for indigenous people evolved along with the regime, from an initial policy of integration common throughout Latin America in the early indigenist period to one of exclusion designed to make natives disappear by whatever means possible. Although the state's plans had shifted from inclusion to exclusion by the 1980s, because of increased foreign scrutiny, the dictator continued to mask this goal within a policy of integration employed for similar reasons in the surrounding nations. The indigenist agenda borrowed from abroad was vague enough to accommodate discrepancies and changing goals.

Paraguay presents a case of racial mixture unique in Latin America. No other country has created a bilingual policy and state based on such extensive interaction between settlers and indigenous people. While popular folklore in Paraguay portrays this process as the result of an alliance between natives and explorers, land and labor in colonial Paraguay forced indigenous people into daily and often exploitative contact with settlers. Native people served the Europeans and, with help from mission tutelage, by independence, Paraguay's population was racially mixed and largely bilingual.

Still, the use of an indigenous tongue during the colonial period does not explain why Guaraní persists until the twenty-first century and has become a national symbol. Instead, political choices ensured the perdurability of Guaraní. Paraguay's nineteenth-century dictators encouraged the idiom's use to strengthen their authority and forced the elite to mix with indigenous people. The Guaraní language became a symbol of nationalism and resistance, especially during the Argentine occupation after the War of the Triple Alliance. Dictators throughout the early twentieth century used the language and the indigenous heritage to unite their troops. Conditions that perpetuated an authoritarian culture also encouraged Paraguayans to use Guaraní and glorify a nearly mythical indigenous ancestry.

By the time Gen. Alfredo Stroessner assumed the presidency in 1954, the national population widely employed the Guaraní language but harbored deep-seated prejudice against indigenous people.

At first, Stroessner struggled to consolidate power and unite his party. It was a few years before he had to deal with the indigenous people in the rural areas. Soon, however, native people reminded ranchers of their enduring presence, and stories of growing violence as a result of competition for land began to reach the capital. Eventually, the new dictator had to add indigenous people to his domestic agenda and find interested followers to oversee his regime's policies toward the rural native population.

3

A State Policy of Integration, 1958–1966

Tekotevé ñande rovatavy ñañe mo-ngaraí uka haguá (One needs to be an imbecile to let oneself be baptized).

Remigio Benítez, from Cadogan, "Los mbyá-guaraní del Guairá"

Given the need to adopt measures tending to centralize the indigenous people scattered throughout . . . the Republic into organized colonies, [and] in order to avoid their extinction and adapt them to a sedentary way of life, the Department of Indigenous Affairs is hereby created.

Departamento de Asuntos Indígenas Charter

Your collaboration will make possible the *Christian* and *Patriotic* goals of the Superior National Government, of *assimilating aborigines into active national life.*

Juan Borgognón (emphasis added)

After fighting his way into power, Alfredo Stroessner faced another uphill battle to consolidate his position. This was especially the case in the countryside, where opposition parties still resisted the new regime. Stroessner also tried to unite peasants behind his plans to boost agricultural production. The indigenous population, scattered in isolated rural pockets, presented a unique dilemma. Their very presence challenged official social goals based on racist "whitening" ideals common in Latin America. The regime's perception of indigenous people as obstacles to economic progress seemed to undermine Stroessner's plan to bring Paraguay into the modern world. In the eyes of conservative politicians, communal landholding and production made native settlements potential sites for Communist infiltration. The regime sought to integrate indigenous populations into the wider society and to force natives into wage labor, and thus eliminate these minority communities.

As part of this goal, Stroessner endeavored to extend "civilization" to even the most remote areas. The state encouraged religious missions to settle nomadic indigenous bands and to teach natives to farm. Proselytizing was thought to be the key to integrating indigenous people. In less than a decade, in fact, these policies did lead to a transformation, although they rarely proceeded as planned. Instead, indigenous peoples shaped the interaction with outsiders and altered the regime's plans for social inclusion.

In November 1958, Stroessner created a state agency, the Departamento de Asuntos Indígenas (Department of Indigenous Affairs, DAI), to settle the remaining native population into colonies. Following indigenist policies common at the time in larger Latin American nations, the regime, paternalistically believing that indigenous people were unable to defend themselves, also promised to protect indigenous cultures from extinction. The DAI encouraged missionary proselytism as the fastest way to both defend and integrate natives and began to supply missions with clothing, food, and medicine. The DAI urged native groups to participate in the market economy but based its plans on misguided conceptions of native cultures. Nearly all its early projects failed.

Indigenous groups, however, took advantage of state assistance to secure necessary medicine and food as well as the tools needed for farming. During nearly a decade of concerted state action, native peoples increased their agricultural production and wage labor. When they had cash, they also purchased domestic goods. Despite obvious cultural changes, however, native groups showed that they intended to help shape the integration process.

But the regime did more than just supply indigenous communities with food and encourage them to grow crops. Although short of funds, personnel, and official support, the DAI tried to raise national awareness of the indigenous population. The agency tried to diminish prejudice through lectures and performances by indigenous people. It also suggested that, once natives abandoned communal land tenure and joined the capitalist marketplace, the "indigenous" components of their cultures would somehow wither away. Because Paraguayans lauded the role of the indigenous population in their national history, though, the DAI preserved indigenous artifacts in a museum so they would not entirely disappear. Thus began the integration of the indigenous population of Paraguay, which over the next two decades dramatically altered native communities.

Sources of Stroessner's Indigenist Policy

Faced with the dilemma of a small but visible indigenous population, the regime studied examples of policies directed at indigenous populations from surrounding nations. Chile and Argentina had both tried to physically eliminate their native populations by force during the nineteenth century. This was not a viable course of action for Paraguay because the World Wars had cast a negative shadow on state-sponsored extermination of minorities. By the time Brazil started to "civilize" its vast rural areas after World War I, for instance, the world no longer accepted genocide as a way to remove indigenous people from desirable land. Instead, Brazil chose to change native minorities by teaching them to become Brazilians. Since Brazilian law treated them as relatively incapable of taking care of themselves, Brazil had created a central agency to assimilate native groups, act on their behalf in encounters with Brazilians, and ensure that they did not impede development.[1] Brazilian integration became an example for Paraguay.

An even more pertinent model came from Mexico, which had enacted a set of paternalistic, welfare-oriented policies to integrate its large indigenous population and also to reap political dividends.[2] In 1940, Mexico created the Instituto Nacional Indígena (National Indigenous Institute) to extend health care, education, and equal legal rights to its native people. That same year, Mexico sponsored the Congreso Interamericano Indigenista (Inter-American Indigenist Congress) at Pátzcuaro, at which Latin American nations—including Paraguay—expressed respect for native cultures but agreed on guidelines for their incorporation.[3] The assembly founded the Inter-American Indian Institute (IAII)—part of the Organization of American States—and encouraged all nations to create national Indian institutes to oversee integration.[4]

The new IAII focused some attention on indigenous people but, ultimately, did little to improve their situation. Its creation was, in a sense, a desperate attempt by the Latin American nations to "shore up" their global image. Although governments discussed the indigenous situation, the IAII had no legislative authority; therefore, each nation was free to decide its own policies. The IAII focused on the collection of data that might interest tourists instead of on legal problems involving indigenous land and populations. As Vine Deloria has argued: "For nearly thirty years the nations met in conference, shared anecdotes, and adjourned to mourn the passing of the noble red race."[5] From the beginning, then, the institute did little to further the natives' own political or economic agendas.

In the 1940s and the 1950s, the integration of indigenous people throughout Latin America generally resulted in the loss of their ancestral lands and in cultural changes. Still, natives everywhere influenced the extent and speed of their individual incorporation into the state.[6] Given their importance as larger nations on a continent that already had centuries of documented interaction with native people, it should not be surprising that Mexico's and

Brazil's indigenist policies weighed heavily on smaller nations and that Stroessner followed their examples.

The need to settle all the indigenous population permanently was especially applicable to the Ache, who were coming into more and more conflict with national development policy. The growing accounts of Ache labor practices and their increasingly violent interaction with ranchers were confusing and contradictory and helped obscure the period in which Stroessner first shaped his policies toward indigenous peoples. Observers at the time used the term *slavery* to draw attention to the situation of indigenous peoples. In 1960, an ethnographer concerned about deteriorating conditions counted fifty-one Ache children working as slaves in Guairá Department.[7]

Roger Casement's 1913 statement to Britain's Parliament provides an example of a confusing report about indigenous labor. Casement's report shows in graphic detail the tactics of "torture, starvation, and terror" used by the Peruvian Rubber Company to produce four thousand tons of rubber at the expense of thirty thousand Indian lives.[8] Reporting obviously horrific events, Casement manipulated sources to make his argument even stronger. He used the term *slavery* to describe debt peonage, for instance, which only complicated the picture.[9] Because of accounts such as Casement's, condemnation of abuses against the Ache created problems of interpretation and motivation.

Growing accounts of violence and Ache slavery aroused public curiosity about the situation in eastern Paraguay. Newspaper accounts of torture, abuse, and murder created a highly charged situation that quickly put the regime in a defensive position and fueled Stroessner's eagerness to once and for all settle these nomadic bands. The presence of nomadic indigenous people especially heightened the regime's sensitivity about being branded as less civilized than neighboring Argentina and Brazil.

The perceived need to bring Paraguay up to the level of its neighbors became clear as the dictator's plans for the rural areas and populations developed. The Guaraní language had given Paraguay the reputation of being a nation of *indios*, a designation that Paraguayans deeply resented. As Richard Reed has argued: "Brazilians and Argentines refer disparagingly to this 'uncivilized' country, painting the picture of naked savages, living in huts in the deep forest. (The intended slight is even more onerous in that Paraguayan mestizos share their neighbors' antipathy toward indigenous populations.)"[10] Media coverage made Stroessner eager to, once and for all, solve what his regime by now referred to as the "Indian problem."

First, the regime tried to quiet reports about violence on the frontier.

In June 1957, the Ministry of the Interior decreed: "Under no pretext shall Guayakí of any age or sex be killed, abused, or kidnapped, under penalty that those who proceed to do so will be punished to the full extent of the law." The regime prohibited the trade, purchase, and coercion of Ache labor. To condemn the widespread racism that contributed to unequal labor practices, in September, the Supreme Court also ruled that "the Indians are as human as the other inhabitants of this native soil."[11] For the first time, Paraguay legally acknowledged the humanity of its indigenous population.

Growing discontent about Stroessner's heavy-handed rule helps explain why the regime began to employ anything at its disposal, even indigenous affairs, to portray its social legislation as positive. By 1958, the dictator's popularity had fallen to a low point because of police brutality and a continued state of siege. In August, the Confederación Paraguaya de Obreros (Paraguayan Workers Confederation) called a general strike to demand a 30 percent wage increase. In response, the regime occupied the union's headquarters and arrested over two hundred militants.[12] When protests against repression increased, in April 1959, Stroessner lifted the twelve-year state of siege and welcomed back several exiled opposition parties.

The demonstrating workers in Asunción were almost certainly not interested in the fate of indigenous people, so the enactment of legislation to protect native people might seem surprising. Nevertheless, the decrees show how the dictator began strategically to use indigenous rights to position himself—both at home and abroad—as a beneficent ruler, precisely because this image allowed him some flexibility in ignoring the urban populace and its rising demands.

By the late 1950s, in fact, even Colorado Party members began to encourage the president to improve the conditions of the indigenous population as a way to solidify popular support. León Cadogan, former chief of police in the eastern town of Villarrica, sent adamant messages to this effect. The son of Australian immigrants, Cadogan had first developed an interest in the Mbyá in the 1920s while managing his father-in-law's yerba mate plantation.[13] Later, he recorded Mbyá legends, and by 1946 had published his first articles about the Guaraní tribes.[14]

As he rose through the Colorado Party ranks, Cadogan drew attention to native rights. In December 1949, Guairá Department created a small agency to protect indigenous people from the ranchers. Governor Arza appointed Cadogan director of the new Curaduría de los Indígenas del Guairá (Protectorate for the Indigenous People of Guairá) because of his knowledge of the Mbyá and Ache, and ordered him to "seek the worthy means necessary to incorporate the indigenous population into civilized life."[15] The governor's use of the term *curar*, from the same root as the word *curator*, indicates his paternalistic goal of looking after, curing, and civilizing the allegedly inferior, deviant, and unhealthy people who still self-identified as indigenous. With financial assistance from the Ministry of Education and well-versed in Mexican indigenismo, Cadogan began to provide food to the Mbyá and draw attention to the growing threats to their land.[16]

Cadogan's articles about the Guaraní in the IAII journal *América Indígena* attracted the attention of foreign scholars. In 1954, Brazilian anthropologist Egon Schaden visited Villarrica and encouraged Cadogan.[17] In his growing contacts with authorities, the tall, thin ethnographer argued that the inclusion of native people in the wider society would occur only after the regime encouraged further Catholic proselytism to "acculturate" and eliminate "negative" indigenous practices. Missions would improve conditions among the indigenous population and encourage them to adopt capitalist values, Cadogan held, and ultimately save Paraguay considerable expense.

Cadogan was the first to describe how Paraguayos praised their Guaraní ancestors but concurrently "deprecated, exploited, and pursued" native people in the countryside.[18] In fact, he saw national racism as the greatest stumbling block for "assimilating" indigenous people. When he asked Remigio Benítez, a Mbyá chief in Caaguazú, why he refused baptism into the Catholic Church, Benítez answered: "Yes, let myself be baptized so that when they see me pass they point at me and say: Look at that imbecile Avá who puts on civilized airs!" [19]

Fueled by such indigenous statements, the relentless Cadogan finally grew extremely frustrated at the lack of state action on behalf of his charges and in 1958 traveled to Asunción and personally reminded minister of defense Marcial Samaniego that Paraguay urgently needed an indigenist agency.[20]

Although he directed the dictator's repressive forces, Samaniego took Cadogan's advice seriously because of his own interest in the native population. Gen. Marcial Samaniego created the regime's program for the indigenous population almost by himself while serving Stroessner as minister of defense between 1956 and 1983 (except for a hiatus between 1962 and 1975, when he directed the Ministry of Public Works). His concerted action highlights two important points about the dictatorship: first, Stroessner did not manage all facets of his regime alone, as Paul Lewis has argued; second, social policies, including native issues, were less important to the state than was economic development.[21] A methodical planner and ruthlessly loyal to the dictator, Samaniego developed a fascination with Guaraní religious beliefs while building roads in eastern Paraguay as a military engineer. There he befriended Paï Tavyterã leaders and recorded many ritual songs while living in a native community. These personal contacts raised the general's concern that conditions might deteriorate to the point that all indigenous people could become extinct. As a sign of his concern, by 1956, he had convinced the regime to give the title to thirteen thousand hectares of tribal land to Paï Tavyterã at Yvypyté.[22]

Samaniego's vision of integrating native people back into the society he believed they had helped create was romantic at best, but the general ultimately intended to serve his president. He hoped that, once nationals fully respected them, native people would contribute crops to the local economy.[23]

With Cadogan's encouragement, General Samaniego convinced Stroessner to create an agency that could aid in improving native conditions. In November 1958, the regime established guardianship over indigenous people as wards of the Ministry of Defense and created the DAI. According to the charter:

> Given the need to adopt measures to nucleate the indigenous people scattered throughout the eastern and western regions of the Republic into organized colonies, in order to avoid their extinction and adapt them to a sedentary way of life, and considering that Paraguay has assumed commitments to this effect in its role as a member state of the Inter-American Indigenist Institute; that investigations conducted by the Ministry of National Defense . . . prove the existence of an important autochthonous population in a defenseless and helpless state; it is impossible to postpone the need to adopt measures to direct their reinstatement into national civilized life, we create the Department of Indigenous Affairs . . . with the purpose of centralizing the indigenist activities in the national territory.[24]

The charter shows that Stroessner's generals believed native people led an unorganized, uncivilized, and miserable existence because they did not live in permanent locations. In reality, however, only the Ache and the Ayoreode were seminomadic. Because frontier violence had recently attracted media attention, the regime hoped to quickly and quietly settle these "helpless minors" in "organized" colonies. The charter for the new agency clearly tied Stroessner's policy to other Latin American programs for integration. The curious order calling for "reinstatement into national civilized life" emphasizes the belief that at one point indigenous people were more active participants in Paraguayan society but had, shamefully, "left the fold." Now the new regime would gloriously restore them to their rightful place in the nation.

The tribute to the importance of Guaraní and the concurrent juxtaposition of deep-seated racism mirror indigenist policies elsewhere.

The reference to centralizing indigenist activities shows that integration was initially attractive because it might increase control over sparsely populated rural areas. Splinter groups of Paraguayan guerrillas from the Febrerista and Liberal parties, exiled in Argentina, returned to Paraguay in 1958 to combat the new regime, attacking military outposts that bordered Argentina's Misiones Province. Fearing that peasants might join the insurgency, the dictator took several years to extend his rule over the countryside by torturing and executing dissidents at isolated camps. Guerrilla violence and police counterterror raised tensions in the countryside to a new high.[25]

Still, officials continued to be largely unaware of events in secluded native communities that, with different religious beliefs and communal farming, had remained outside of state control. Not surprisingly, then, the regime did not want these mysterious native communities infiltrated by its opponents. The desperate struggle for hegemony helps explain the state's initial eagerness for integration of the indigenous population.

Communist Party activities in rural areas only heightened the dictator's paranoia. Virulently anti-Communist, he feared that the rural population might join the leftists. Communists had in fact been active in Paraguay since 1928, when they founded the PCP. The PCP controlled labor through the 1930s, but the civil war of 1947 forced it into exile. The Communists held their last party conference in 1949 and throughout the Stronato, as Stroessner became stronger, never attracted more than four thousand members.[26] Stroessner outlawed the party in his 1955 Ley para la Defensa de Democracia (Law for the Defense of Democracy) and then monitored Communist activities through Colorado Party neighborhood committees, which kept the PCP from influencing rural peasants.[27]

Still, whenever peasants challenged the existing land-tenure system, Stroessner, to legitimize repression, publicized a "Communist threat." Given such paranoia, it should not be surprising that his generals feared that isolated native settlements' communal lands were actually hotbeds for potential Communist infiltration.

Because of difficulties in controlling rural areas, Stroessner put the Ministry of Defense in charge of indigenous integration from the start.[28] As in other nations, soldiers were often the only authorities posted near native communities; Samaniego's experience shows that military doctors were the only health professionals available to native people and that soldiers built the roads.[29] The military was also the government branch with the most resources.

Military direction had drawbacks for both the DAI and the indigenous population. The DAI relied totally on the defense minister's personal commitment to the indigenist cause. As Paul Lewis has argued, moreover, Stroessner often allocated posts in state-run monopolies to military personnel to provide opportunities for smuggling and to ensure support. The DAI was no different, and the dictator appointed its staff purely for political purposes rather than on the basis of experience. As a result, the DAI received castoffs with no interest in the natives' situation, so its success was compromised from its inception.[30]

Strategies to Integrate the Indigenous Population

Integrating the indigenous population was a difficult assignment. During its first four years, the DAI worked without an official budget and depended on the Ministry of Defense for intermittent appropriations. Often, the DAI could not perform even its most basic tasks—such as food distribution and medical relief—nor did the regime provide clear direction about how to accomplish integration.

Because integration proved daunting, the DAI focused on three basic tasks. The first was settling the seminomadic tribes and teaching them to farm. The second involved documenting the existence of communities and providing food, clothing, and medical assistance to improve conditions, make the indigenous population into consumers, and include them in the legal framework. Finally, the DAI tried to diminish widespread prejudice in hopes that natives would more readily join national society if they felt welcomed.

General Samaniego appointed a minor officer named Juan Alfonso Borgognón to direct the DAI's ambiguous program. Borgognón was kind and energetic, and employees remember him as well-suited for running the new agency. Native people respected him and called him "*taita*," a Guaraní word for "father."[31] The director set out to discover how many indigenous people there were and in what conditions they lived, so his employees began to gather information from missions and military outposts.[32]

The fortuitous appearance of an Ache group in eastern Paraguay, though, provided Borgognón with a timely opportunity to settle a nomadic indigenous band. In 1958, a southern Ache named Pikygi led part of his Ypety band to a ranch near Abaí, in Guairá Department, where he had previously worked. Because of increasing peasant attacks, the twenty Ache approached a rancher named Manuel de Jesús Pereira and requested protection. These people belonged to one of three southern Ache groups, of between 30 to 60 people each, who lived east of Villarrica in the Yvyturuzú hills. The related northern Ache numbered nearly 550 before extensive contact and lived between the headwaters of the Jejuí and the Paraná rivers.[33] Pereira had been a well-known hunter and seller of Ache laborers and had worked for Pichín López, the most notorious Ache trader in the area.[34] López had fled abroad after the regime prohibited the sale of Ache, but Pereira had returned to ranching. The law passed in 1957 against killing the Ache made Pereira afraid to sell Pikygi's family; instead, he allowed them to work for food.

Given Pereira's notoriety as an Ache trader, it is puzzling that Pikygi's group asked him for protection. The Ache explained that Pereira had treated Pikygi well. Mark Münzel argues that natives sought protection from Pereira "mainly because he [was] unable to have children, which meant more tranquillity for their wives and daughters than with other slave owners."[35] Pereira was clearly pleased at the prospect of cheap labor, for he tried to attract more Ache to his land.

Once Pereira had collected two dozen Ache, he realized that despite their labor it would prove a financial burden to provide them with food. So in 1959 the rancher visited León Cadogan at the *curaduría* and promised to protect the Ache from other ranchers if the state would cover the cost of feeding them. Authorities gave Pereira a line of credit at a bank to "create a permanent assistance post for the Guayakí Indians, with the intent of later colonization."[36]

Cadogan knew that Pereira had a reputation as a drunkard and an abuser of indigenous women, but he was also aware of the regime's eagerness to settle and remove the Ache from the path of ranching and commercial agriculture. Cadogan first counseled Borgognón to appoint someone else as overseer, but the latter feared that, in anger, Pereira might sell the Ache. Borgognón also hoped to facilitate the study of Ache culture, for he wrote to a friend: "Recently a group of Guayakí appeared that had remained in a primitive state, systematically reacting to any intent at assimilation. This unexpected event makes it possible to carry out scientific studies that are of interest to the DAI."[37] The regime agreed to provide Pereira with resources to settle and teach the Ache to farm, so the DAI sent him food and medicine from a Catholic relief agency and designated his ranch the Puesto de Asistencia y Nacionalización No. 1 de los Indios Guayakíes "Gral. Marcial Samaniego" ("Guayakí Indian Assistance and Nationalization Post No. 1 General Marcial Samaniego").[38] Not only did the rancher's request present the regime with an excellent opportunity for settling people who had been hunting on private land, rustling cattle, and raiding peasant gardens, but it allowed the army to borrow Ache from Pereira's farm to track guerrilla forces in the area.[39]

In August 1959, still uncertain about how to proceed with other native groups, Borgognón invited missionaries, scholars, and indigenists to brainstorm about integration at the Ministry of Defense. At the Primer Congreso Indigenista (First Indigenist Congress), participants discussed indigenous people's legal and health situations, as well as plans to settle and educate them. They recommended that the state rely heavily on missions to hasten native inclusion.[40] Missionaries and the DAI alike promised to cooperate closely. The state asked church organizations to "exert their religious influence in order to attract the indigenous people and win their confidence." Missions promised to enroll native people in the official registry of persons and to inform the DAI about conditions in rural settlements. Church workers also agreed to provide health care but requested supplies and workers from the state. Participants requested "that missions continue to situate indigenous persons according to race in permanent settlements, which would facilitate their education and social, economic, and educational development."[41]

Frequent references to sedentary farming and permanent, stable communities show that both the authorities and the missionaries viewed nomadism as the most "backward" element of native culture. This was an inaccurate stereotype, since by 1959, only the Ache and the Ayoreode still migrated seasonally in search of game. Other people moved occasionally in search of work, food, or even to visit relatives but were in no way truly nomadic.

Authorities were clearly most eager to change the image of natives as shiftless, lazy vagrants—people too irresponsible to raise crops—views they themselves projected onto indigenous people. When missionaries agreed to teach indigenous people to live as "civilized" Paraguayans, the regime in return granted religious organizations permission to increase proselytism among the native population.[42]

Following the congress, the DAI began to work closely with the religious agencies. During the winter of 1959, the Paraguay River flooded the low settlement across from Asunción where Belaieff had settled the Mak'a tribe. The Catholic relief agency Cáritas Paraguaya promptly contributed food and clothing for the Mak'a.[43] From then on, Cáritas frequently donated food for native settlements and even appointed Borgognón to its board of directors.

The missions, for their part, began to request all types of favors from the DAI, from legal protection to medicine.[44] In January of 1960, a Salesian missionary in Bahía Negra requested two thousand hectares to build a school and church for Ïshïro in the area.[45] The following year, Father José Seelwische, director of the western mission of Santa Teresita, asked the DAI to build a health center for the two thousand Nivaklé under his care.[46] The cooperation clearly benefited both parties. The DAI, severely limited in financial resources, depended on missions to influence and provide for indigenous communities. The religious agencies relied on the DAI to procure support from the regime.

During its first years, as the DAI contacted indigenous communities, it also tried to decrease national prejudice. In 1959, Borgognón created two soccer teams and a dance troupe of Mak'a youth to introduce Paraguayans to native people. The Mak'a often sold artifacts in Asunción and were therefore the indigenous group most accessible to the DAI. Soccer games between Cerro and Olimpia Mak'a, which added the names of the most popular national soccer teams to their own teams, became a popular way for schools and clubs to entertain guests at their fund-raisers. In 1959 alone, the soccer teams and a troupe of dancers performed at over two dozen events around the country.[47] In September 1960, Borgognón even sent the Mak'a teams and dance troupe to Buenos Aires.[48] The Mak'a performers traveled until 1966 and served as a source of revenue for both the DAI and the Mak'a community.[49] School directors, entertainers, and private club owners seem to have used the Mak'a shows for fund-raising and praised the state for increasing cultural sensitivity.[50] Those who hosted Mak'a performances frequently expressed the belief that the shows helped break down historical barriers between natives and the larger society.[51] While the Mak'a displays brought people from both groups into closer proximity, it is doubtful that these brief and gaudy performances actually increased Paraguayan understanding of indigenous people.

Indigenous Responses to the State's Indigenismo

Borgognón began to inform Paraguayans that there was a new agency charged with improving the lot of the indigenous population, and the natives also spread the news. Indigenous leaders began to visit the capital to ask the DAI for clothing, food, and medical assistance. In 1961, Borgognón received sixty-seven indigenous leaders in Asunción, and the requests grew rapidly over the next years. When they could not afford to travel, leaders made their needs known through missionaries or military commanders, who described the difficult conditions in agonizing detail. In July 1959, one missionary conveyed the following: "I write to inform you that Vicente Gauto, chief of a small group of catechized indios living at Paijhá, fears being evicted from their land."[52] Two months later, Cadogan complained about the Guaraní near Monday, numbering ten thousand, who were "literally rotting from sores for lack of [medicine]. I have not received anything for them because the DAI lacks resources."[53] Military officers and missionaries in rural areas likewise stressed the horrible conditions.

The urgent requests from the interior showed that indigenous peoples intended to make sure that the new DAI was aware of their situation. Appeals for assistance centered on the growing need for food, medicine, and especially land on which to hunt and grow subsistence crops. The letters provide evidence of significant changes taking place as ranchers expanded herds onto indigenous land and settlers chopped down forests to plant crops for export. Indigenous people either turned to outsiders for assistance or took desperate measures. In October 1960, eighty native people attacked the Campos y Quebrachales ranch, west of Puerto Sastre, and killed eight Paraguayans with spears and arrows. Conflicts such as this one impressed upon the DAI the need to settle the indigenous population permanently.[54]

Desperate reports from the interior coupled with the pleas for assistance encouraged Borgognón to explore ways that indigenous communities might earn a living and participate more fully in the broader economy after leaving their tribal way of life. The director's first plan was to teach native people to harvest fish.[55] Over the next few years, DAI employees built experimental fish tanks and explored how to preserve fish for later use.[56]

Native people, though, responded negatively to the DAI proposal. Ironically, they had extensive experience fishing in natural ponds or rivers, but the concept of raising fish for food was completely foreign to them, an outside imposition that they did not accept.

The following year, Borgognón suggested that indigenous people might sell *caraguatá* cactus fibers to businesses that made shoes. Though native communities in the Chaco had traditionally employed caraguatá to weave bags, belts, and nets, the director suggested that the sale of these plants might boost shoe production and also turn a handsome profit for needy native communities. Under missionary supervision, he argued, indigenous people could easily produce up to thirty thousand kilograms of the fiber annually.[57]

Borgognón's most ambitious plan was to increase the sale of yerba mate. Eastern Guaraní had, for two centuries, harvested the herb from their forests and sold it to national producers.[58] Now the DAI encouraged indigenous people to increase their output and market the yerba "more intelligently." The director asked missionaries to monitor production carefully and to teach indigenous people how to handle the business of sales.[59]

Obviously, Borgognón hoped that development projects would turn in-digenous people into more active consumers and producers in wider mar-kets. Yet, his projects never bore fruit. While the director's plans were re-lated to native subsistence economies, they required indigenous people to approach natural resources with a market economy in mind. What is more, ignoring the reality that they had already interacted economically for cen-turies with outsiders, Borgognón saw indigenous people as too naïve and inexperienced to successfully engage in the capitalist system and thus sought non-Indians to oversee their work. Indigenous people must have found such oversight patronizing and demeaning, anthropologists have argued, because they rejected the projects. National prejudice and especially a misunder-standing of native cultures hampered the success of the DAI's integration efforts from the start.[60]

In fact, it was often the Paraguayan overseers who caused difficulties for the DAI. Manuel Pereira quickly proved to be a dishonest manager of the new Ache settlement. To help settle the Ache, the DAI sent more cloth-ing, food, and basic provisions to Pereira's than to any other reservation.[61] Nevertheless, the administrator still frequently complained that he was un-able to adequately feed or clothe his charges and that they became ill as a result.[62]

The problem was that Pereira regularly embezzled the DAI supplies. He resold provisions to other farmers and pocketed the profits instead of feed-ing the Ache.[63] Most food or clothing never reached the Ache and forced them to hunt for food while they worked in Pereira's fields. Pierre Clastres, a French ethnologist who visited the reservation in 1962, describes the over-seer's theft:

The days passed peacefully, especially when the Paraguayan chief [Pereira] disappeared. His absences sometimes extended for weeks on end, which he devoted to endless bouts of drunkenness in the villages of the area. When he returned, almost unable to keep himself on the saddle, he would explode in a fury impossible to understand, pulling out his gun and firing it in all directions, and shouting vague threats in Guaraní. From his new power he drew direct advantages, not the least of which was access to the young girls of the tribe. . . . If the sal-ary he received was modest, the quantity of food—flour, grease, sugar, and powdered milk—sent for the Indians from Asunción, was, on the other hand, rather important. The Ache certainly received part of it, but the rest was diverted by the white chief, who sold it, for his exclu-sive profit, to the farmers of the region.[64]

Borgognón was aware that conditions at the Ache reservation were poor, and he certainly knew of Pereira's dishonesty, because León Cadogan denounced the overseer's theft and abuse regularly in great detail. The DAI was so eager to settle the Ache, however, that it overlooked the theft. Borgognón also took advantage of Pereira's dishonesty to supply young Ache women to military friends.[65] The DAI saw the criado labor system, with its inherent potential for sexual abuse, as helping to change and integrate the Ache.[66] Thus, the DAI tolerated Pereira's poor treatment of the Ache in hopes that he would finally help change and settle them permanently.

Borgognón was so keen to ensure that the Ache remain with Pereira that he ignored Cadogan's warnings and periodically increased shipments of clothing and food. In fact, when, in 1961, Pereira insisted that his facilities were too crowded to support fifty Ache, the DAI purchased adjacent land and increased the reservation to two thousand hectares. Borgognón renamed Pereira's farm the Colonia Nacional Guayakí "Beato Roque González de Santa Cruz" (National Guayakí Colony Pious Roque González of the Holy Cross) to procure financial assistance from the bishop in Villarrica.[67]

While he gathered supplies for the Ache and other communities, Borgognón contacted foreign indigenists, and it is notable that he invited scholars from Mexico rather than neighboring Brazil to visit his country. In 1961, Mexican anthropologist Leonardo Manrique Castañeda arrived to organize the Anthropology Ministry at the National University in Asunción. Castañeda visited native communities, helped organize the DAI's files, and encouraged the fledgling organization.[68] In October, noted Mexican anthropologist Miguel León-Portilla visited in his role as director of the IAII. To show off the regime's commitment to the indigenist cause and the integration program, General Samaniego laid out the "red carpet" for the visiting scholars.[69]

It is curious that the regime first approached Mexican anthropologists rather than scholars from neighboring Brazil for advice on shaping its indigenist program. Indeed, Brazil had created the Serviço de Proteção ao Índio (Indian Protection Service, SPI) in 1910, to increase knowledge about native people, to protect them from massacre and exploitation, to defend their land, and to provide them with the education they would need to enter national society successfully. Still, although Mexico had more recently created an agency to integrate indigenous people, its history of race mixing made it much closer to the Paraguayan case than Brazil was, where small groups in the vast and unexplored interior still evaded contact. Following the Mexican scholars' visits, Borgognón, basing the changes on the original goals of the state, increased the educational component of the integration program significantly.[70]

To make other Paraguayans more receptive to indigenous people, Borgognón presented lectures about the DAI and native cultures. In 1962, employees of the DAI gave eleven talks about its integration program and hosted seven fund-raising events. Borgognón used a weekly radio broadcast to explain why the "assimilation" program was a "superior military conquest" and even had the postal service issue stamps to commemorate the DAI.[71] Visiting indigenists also encouraged the DAI to display its growing collection of indigenous pottery, instruments, and weapons. The director believed these specimens would inform future generations about native people, because integration was sure to quickly do away with their old way of life.

Borgognón's efforts show just how urgently his superiors wanted to alter the "backward" and "archaic" indigenous cultures. In October 1962, the DAI exhibited its artifacts at the Centro Cultural Paraguayo Americano (Paraguayan-American Cultural Center).[72] The culmination of this public-awareness campaign was the erection of a monument to Guaraní Indians in Concepción, a growing port city two hundred kilometers north of Asunción on the Paraguay River.[73] The location of the statue, far from Asunción, shows that, although Borgognón had gotten his message across, the DAI and the indigenous population were still a low priority for the regime.

While Stroessner had been able to ignore the indigenous population during the first years of his presidency, the Mexican indigenists and the flurry of activity their visit caused impressed both Borgognón and his superiors. Shortly after León-Portilla's departure, Borgognón pressed General Samaniego for more funds and precise instructions. In August 1962, the minister of defense moved the DAI to a new building, wrote new bylaws, and finally gave the agency a formal budget.[74]

Far more than in 1958, the new guidelines focused on altering indigenous cultures to bring native ways of life as close to Paraguayo practices as possible. The regime strongly contrasted "civilized" non-Indian culture with indigenous practices and promised that complete integration would eliminate such differences. The proposed changes in how the native population was to earn a living continued to center around a sedentary lifestyle, religious affiliation, and agriculture. A significant departure was the new admonition to protect indigenous communities, especially their people but also their land. The DAI would still preserve examples of indigenous cultures as relics with historical value, but now the agency was also strongly to protect the people from perishing in the process of integration. Samaniego also intended the missions to play a more active role in helping to both alter and defend native people. The new goals showed the contradiction inherent in the indigenist policy: while the DAI was supposed to convince indigenous people to live as Paraguayos, it was also to value and preserve examples of their original native cultures.

A notable development was the way the regime tried to improve ties to religious organizations via the DAI. New bylaws emphasized, even more strongly, that the DAI should closely cooperate with the missions. This should not come as a surprise, considering that by 1960 the Catholic Church had started to organize peasants in rural areas as part of its religious outreach. The DAI was to regard missions as their strongest allies and assistants in permanently settling indigenous groups and making them producers and consumers. The regime still considered Christian education, regardless of denominational emphasis, the fastest and, in fact, the only way to completely civilize and integrate native people. In the years that followed the institution of the new bylaws, the DAI and the missions joined forces even more closely in their attempts to change the indigenous population.

Mission Cooperation with the Regime

For years, religious agencies in Paraguay had tried to influence indigenous cultures, so the regime's integration program coincided closely with their goals. Both Anglicans and Mennonites had long tried to make indigenous people in western Paraguay good workers and participants in the market economy. Even before Stroessner assumed power, the Paraguayan state had largely ignored the colonization of rural areas, leaving the task, instead, to foreign ranching companies. After the dictator began to extend state control over the countryside and urged the DAI to encourage mission work, religious organizations began to work closely with the regime.

The Mennonite settlers belonged to a Protestant denomination whose work coincided closely with the regime's plans for integration. For nearly three decades, these immigrants had lived in the Chaco and by 1960 were directing the largest evangelistic effort in Paraguay. The third wave of Mennonite settlers, twenty-five hundred people, had arrived from the Soviet Union in 1947. The immigrants were conservative and continued to speak German and remain separate from Paraguayan society. Indigenous people had helped settlers clear land and plant crops in the dry territory soon after their arrival. With overseas contributions and help from native laborers, by the 1960s, the settlers had built a prosperous but isolated enclave.

When they first arrived, Mennonites found only several hundred native people on the 510,936 hectares they bought from the state. The immigrants needed field hands and actively sought indigenous workers. Enlhit workers from the eastern Chaco with experience on ranches and in tannin factories along the Paraguay River arrived quickly in search of work. Mennonite laypeople began preaching to the indigenous workers as early as 1932, and after the Chaco War continued serious preaching of fundamental Christian principles among the Enlhit under the aegis of an agency called Light to the Indians.[75] By 1935, Enlhit converts had permission to settle among the Mennonites on small lots on their colony's property.[76]

In addition to providing religious instruction, Mennonites promised to "civilize" the indigenous population to "bind these nomads to a stable place with the goal of educating them to be good and useful citizens of the Paraguayan state." By 1946, the immigrants had settled one thousand Enlhit at Yalve Sanga and by 1962 had organized the Enlhit into twelve villages.[77]

The native people provided cheap labor for Mennonite ranchers but also found the arrangement advantageous. One indigenous person favorably compared the new landlords to Paraguayans: "Mennonites pay more, make us work less, and do not beat us."[78]

Although Mennonites actively settled and converted the Enlhit, they refused to provide land to the Nivaklé people who arrived from the southwestern Chaco in search of work. To the foreigners, the Nivaklé practice of gathering instead of farming had not "culturally prepared" them to raise crops. People in this indigenous group had also developed an extremely negative self-image as a result of dire poverty and widespread discrimination. "One wants to become a person," Nivaklé commonly responded in the early 1960s when asked their deepest desire.[79] Working for the Mennonites taught the Nivaklé that the acquisition of property and agriculture led to economic success. "This drive to obtain first class status via agriculture was intense beyond expectation," observed anthropologist Jacob Loewen in the early 1960s.[80]

The Nivaklé asked colony administrators for land to improve their economic position, but Mennonites denied these requests. The Nivaklé grew resentful. One leader expressed his frustration: "We have worked for the settlers for over 30 years. Now it is time that they help us to also get something. When they came here 30 years ago they had nothing, and we have worked for them ever since. We have helped them get land, houses, cattle, horses, much equipment, and we ourselves are still living in the same shelters that we used to have."[81]

The Nivaklé requests show how native people changed their economic practices to adapt to new conditions. Because natives depended on ranchers so extensively for wages, labor, and food, their demands for land were also an attempt to regain some degree of economic independence.

In response to the Nivaklé pressure, the three Mennonite colonies and missionaries finally agreed in 1961 to increase the number of indigenous settlements.[82] But these concessions came too late to satisfy indigenous workers, especially when the worst drought in thirty-three years hit western Paraguay in 1962 and destroyed crops. Mennonite farmers laid off their laborers, and conditions deteriorated until the native population grew desperate. This was especially true for the Nivaklé, who had no land on which to eke out a subsistence living. The drought brought to a climax their frustration at having been consistently denied colony land. In September 1962, close to seven hundred desperate Nivaklé under the leadership of Chief Manuel rose up in arms against the Mennonite settlers, marched to colony headquarters, and demanded equipment and land. Native women, who bore the brunt of protecting their families during the crisis in the matriarchal Nivaklé society, encouraged the uprising. The rebel leader promised his people that the government in Asunción would send trucks to transport them to their own land and provide them all that they needed. He reminded the women that once they left the colonies they would regain their authority. Mennonite leaders calmed the Nivaklé but gave them no land, so they "stomped out of the colonies in anger."[83]

Scholars have focused on this uprising as a sign of severe cultural stress for the Nivaklé people and the subsequent tension between them and the Mennonite administrators. Loewen used the events to highlight a "drastic sign of growing demand by the Indians for land," and he was the first to describe the event as an "uprising."[84] Peter Klassen, writing from a pro-Mennonite perspective, argues that native testimony shows only an indigenous desire for independent management. "The Indians said: 'We don't want to stop working for the Mennonites. All we want is to try to become independent people.'" What is more, Klassen claims that the conflict did not lead Mennonites to begin planning for a large settlement project, which, he believes, had commenced as early as 1961.[85]

Following the uprising, Mennonites began to work more closely with the Stroessner regime to integrate indigenous people. Settlers blamed the revolt on "outside influence [that] aggravated the situation," but Mennonite administrators offered no tangible proof of Communist infiltration, and the creation of a scapegoat was clearly an attempt to secure drought relief from the conservative regime. The following year, in fact, as if to confirm both positions, Samaniego told Mennonite administrators that "building up backward people in [the] country is the best defense against communism."[86]

For their part, the immigrants promised to settle the indigenous population and "to convert them into productive farmers and artisans and into better Paraguayan citizens." As mission administrators later wrote: "The national government desires that the country's cultural minorities be integrated into national society by means of schools. Mennonite leaders are inclined to advise indigenous people to draw nearer to national society."[87]

The Nivaklé who had left the Mennonite colonies turned to Catholic missionaries at Mariscal Estigarribia for relief. With assistance from the DAI, the Catholic Church promptly resettled the five hundred Nivaklé near Mariscal Estigarribia's Santa Teresita mission. Cáritas Paraguayas donated fifteen thousand kilograms of food and the DAI distributed powdered milk, oil, and beans to drought victims.[88]

Unlike the Mennonites, Catholic priests and the DAI encouraged the Nivaklé to farm despite the dry conditions. The new managers, however, left no decisions to the Nivaklé and tried to oversee the settlement process completely. Borgognón experimented with artificial irrigation to sustain the people during the drought, but when this project failed, the DAI dug two new wells.[89] The Nivaklé resettlement plan showed that the regime intended to carefully direct integration and leave nothing to the indigenous people's initiative. Even more important, the regime would assist the Catholic Church in keeping native groups free of Protestant influence.

Once they were through the worst of the drought, the Mennonites created new native settlements, this time even including some Nivaklé. By 1963, immigrants had organized four agricultural communities composed of thirty-six indigenous villages. Mennonite goals now closely resembled those of the DAI. Mennonite administrators offered work programs and extended credit to encourage native farmers. Every community received its own health center and school, tying religious instruction to further cultural changes within the native communities.

Meanwhile, the settlers continued mission work among the indigenous people. Most active in this sense were the Mennonites from Fernheim Colony, who had proselytized in Russia and Prussia as early as 1854 and shared a long-established "idea of missions to heathens."[90] Mennonite evangelism resulted in the creation of one dozen indigenous churches by the early 1960s, and close proximity to the European colonists began to alter indigenous ways of life significantly. The immigrants were highly patriarchal and emphasized male dominance. Women, in contrast, had traditionally been the leaders among the Nivaklé. These patterns began to change; women became dependent on men to buy provisions and lost the power to make economic decisions.[91] In effect, as government officials had hoped, life near the Mennonites was integrating indigenous people into wider markets and the labor pool and introducing them to non-Indian ways of life.

Besides assisting the church in relocating the Nivaklé, in 1962, the regime helped Catholic Salesian missionaries settle Ayoreode people in the north-western Chaco.[92] Ranchers and soldiers were overrunning Ayoreode land in growing numbers, and violent encounters with non-Indians had increased. The demand for furs was especially high, and by the mid-1960s, seven hundred Brazilian, Bolivian, and Argentine trappers passed through Ayoreode territory every year to collect pelts.[93] The Ayoreode, much like the Ache, contacted outsiders for assistance when the decline of animals for hunting and non-Indian intrusions made their life too difficult. The DAI located a band of Ayoreode in August and, after their first peaceful encounter with outsiders, made plans with the Catholic Church to settle them at the new Mission of María Auxiliadora along the upper Paraguay River.[94]

Salesians at the mission requested assistance from the DAI and promised to "take to these beings the benefits that the orientation of our Catholic doctrine offers. Offering in this way the ideal form of Assimilation of Aborigines into Active National Life."[95] The Salesians of Don Bosco, organized late in the nineteenth century, focused on teaching trades to young people so they might find jobs and become "contributing members of society."[96]

Once the group was settled at the new mission, missionaries took eight newly contacted Ayoreode to Asunción and showed them the major tourist sights.[97] Borgognón met with the Ayoreode, whom he continued to call "moros," and proclaimed the entire expedition a great success for the regime and especially for his department.

Even as he settled Nivaklé and Ayoreode in the Chaco, Borgognón expanded the Ache settlement in Abaí. With the regime's blessing, by 1963, Pereira had used Ache hunters to convince all of the two southern groups, the Ypety and the Yvytyruzú, to move to and work at his ranch.[98] The DAI continued to send Pereira large shipments of clothing and food, even as he continued embezzling supplies. Cadogan blamed the terrible conditions at the camp directly on the rancher: "The government waste[s] large sums of money . . . to support the Guayakí, yet today the camp is a filthy pigsty and an insult to national image." When he discovered that the DAI had invited scholars from European universities to study the Ache, Cadogan advised against such visits. "The Ache camp lacks even the most elemental comforts," he wrote, "and I believe it would be in the government's interest to remedy this deficiency."[99] In response, Borgognón finally took his concerns about Pereira directly to Marcial Samaniego. Rather than bringing the overseer to justice, though, the minister simply sent additional supplies for his indigenous charges.[100]

In reality, the mismanaged settlement project was deadly for the Ache. Donated corn, manioc, and fat, when they were available, were poor substitutes for the diet high in fiber and protein that the Ache had enjoyed in the woods. A terrible diet only worsened conditions already made bad from exposure to Western diseases. Between 1963 and 1968, over fifty people, half of the southern Ache, died at the reservation from respiratory infections against which they had no immunity or medication.[101]

The regime could have prevented these deaths easily by replacing the corrupt manager, so why did the DAI instead tolerate and even encourage Pereira's theft by sending him an ever-larger supply of food and medicine? The botched attempt to settle the Ache, even at this early stage, could be viewed as a deliberate attempt to kill them. Had Borgognón received financial benefits from Pereira's dishonest behavior, the settlement would have been only one more fraudulent scandal that Stroessner's officials used to enrich themselves. Still, Borgognón continued to collect supplies for the Ache and apparently believed that at least some of the provisions reached them and helped toward their integration.

Land Tenure and Peasant Mobilization

We can explain the urgency to settle indigenous people only within the context of the regime's wider agrarian policy and the growing mobilization of the peasantry. By the late 1950s, Stroessner had begun to develop the rural areas and to expand agricultural production. His first plans for agrarian reform, presented in July 1958, produced few visible changes in the latifundio system of unequal land distribution. At the time, critics charged that "the rural problem in Paraguay is one of the most scandalous in Latin America . . . in terms of the concentration of land in the hands of the few."[102] The opposition Christian Democratic Party, formed in 1960, insisted on "the need to incorporate the large rural masses into national development by means of true agrarian reform that should be radical, and at the same time integrated them into a general plan to restructure rural life."[103]

Opposition calls for more equitable land distribution were certainly well founded, as rural organization over the next years made clear. Squatters and peasants joined forces and together began to defend the land they had traditionally used, even when they did not hold legal title. In 1960, 300 peasants marched to San Juan Bautista, capital of Misiones Department, and successfully prevented a rancher from fencing off the land where 420 families grazed their cattle.[104] The Catholic Church actively helped organize peasant movements, and by 1965, the Catholic Worker Youth, the Third Franciscan Order, the National Federation of Christian Agrarian Leagues, and the Christian Campesino Federation had formed forty Christian agrarian leagues to defend peasant rights.[105] Campesinos began to make their demands for land reform known.

As Christian Democrats and recently organized peasants increased their protests, in 1963, the regime revised the agrarian legal framework. Stroessner had a new agrarian law enacted and created the Instituto de Bienestar Rural (Rural Welfare Institute, IBR) to enforce the policy and thus increase Paraguay's agricultural capacity and production. To improve access to land, in 1964, the IBR resettled hundreds of campesinos from the heavily populated central region to state-owned lands in the north and east. By 1962, this area still had a population density of only 1.8 persons per square kilometer.[106]

The IBR also offered cheap land to foreigners, especially Brazilians. Over the next twenty years, it transferred title to millions of hectares of land to peasants and created hundreds of settlements where one quarter of the national population came to reside.[107] The Agrarian Statute limited the size of a single property to ten thousand hectares and promised to break up large landholdings, but in reality the IBR rarely enforced the law, and it led to little actual reform.[108]

The new statute nevertheless had far-reaching effects for the indigenous population because it made integration part of the plan to settle and develop the countryside. To keep native people from hunting, poaching, and migrating in search of work, the new statute promised to settle them in colonies, of course, solely for their own benefit:

Concerning the Beneficiaries of the Agrarian Statute

Art. 16. The surviving nuclei of indigenous groups that still exist in the country will be assisted by the Rural Welfare Institute to organize in colonies. This goal will affect the land needed for settlement and may require collaboration with state organisms and pertinent entities to promote the steady incorporation of said groups into the economic and social development of the country.[109]

The statute highlighted integration but emphasized that a stable residence would contribute more fully to the national economy, so it provided for the expropriation of private land to create "colonias indígenas nacionales" (national indigenous colonies). Finally, the statute again stressed that missions would help speed up integration and pressured the DAI to increase cooperation with religious agencies.

The Agrarian Statute of 1963 ultimately ensured that many indigenous communities lost much of their remaining land. In his analysis of the statute, Wayne Robins argues that indigenous people did not yet pose a threat, because the state still viewed them as a source of labor for yerba mate production and timber extraction; hence, in 1963, the state still intended to integrate indigenous people into national society.[110] Robins's analysis confirms that the policy shift from inclusion to exclusion occurred later, during the 1970s, when indigenous people became a liability to Stroessner's international reputation.

To uphold the spirit of the new law and to increase the rate of native settlement, in September 1963, minister of defense Leodegar Cabello replaced DAI director Borgognón with Col. Anancio Zárate. The new director met immediately with Ministry heads to "coordinate the efforts of the different organisms interested in indigenous problems, to *hasten the work of assimilation* of the Paraguayan Indian into national society" (emphasis added). Increasing the rate of integration, Zárate told his colleagues, "demands the joint action of all state organisms."[111]

With reassurance that the whole regime backed his indigenist program, Zárate also encouraged the missions to redouble their efforts. During the new director's administration, the regime worked even more closely with the religious agencies to settle and integrate native communities.

Religious Missions and Indigenous Integration

To deepen religious influence, Zárate encouraged missions to undertake new outreach efforts where the DAI had had no influence. This was the case when, in 1964, the new director asked Salesians to provide religious and literacy instruction to the Paï Tavyterã village of Ybypyté.[112] The DAI hoped that missionaries would also protect the Paï from the peasants who, with increasing frequency, planted crops on and stole lumber from Paï land.[113] Later that year, Mennonites and the DAI settled more indigenous people on one thousand hectares within the Mennonite colonies. Closer proximity to Mennonite farms, argued the director, would turn natives into good farmers and stop their seasonal migration in search of work.[114]

To include indigenous people more fully in the wider economy, Zárate created small offices near the communities to distribute food, clothes, and tools. In 1963, the DAI used these assistance posts to distribute shovels, machetes, wheelbarrows, and axes to the twenty-four Avá Guaraní families recently settled at Santa Cecilia and to reward Mbyá at Plácido with donations when they farmed instead of hunted.[115] When the DAI sent the military at Fort Ingavi provisions to distribute among the Ayoreode, the director explained that "the work of assimilation is long, trying, and requires many economic resources." Zárate promised the fort's officers that such gifts would make natives dependent on the government and encourage them to move "toward a new socioeconomic standard."[116]

Because the DAI focused so intently on managing changes in native communities, it ignored the indigenous peoples' own efforts to improve their living conditions. At the community of Plácido, the Mbyá raised corn in a communal field and used the proceeds to purchase Cáritas supplies. The Avá Guaraní at Paso Cadena sold lumber from forest reserves to build new homes, an airfield, and a sawmill and to purchase farm implements. Though the indigenous people were making obvious changes on their own initiative, in 1963, the DAI still encouraged the Norwegian Pentecostal mission, NORMA, to begin proselytizing at Paso Cadena. This religious effort, an outreach of the Norwegian Pentecostal movement, emphasized a charismatic renewal experience focused on speaking in tongues. Most important for the DAI, the mission was generously funded from Europe. Soon, NORMA missionaries provided literacy, health-care, and religious instruction to the Avá Guaraní.[117]

When Chief Juan Vera visited Asunción in March 1963, he described the changes in his community and impressed Zárate, who cited Paso Cadena as an example of successful integration in progress. In a very similar way, because settlers wanted Indian land, U.S. officials had overlooked efforts by the five civilized southern tribes to adopt white practices in the early nineteenth century. In Paraguay the regime ignored Avá community efforts to alter their living conditions and economic situation when such initiatives lay outside of state management.[118]

To impress his superiors with examples of DAI success, in 1964, Zárate brought a group of the Ache from Pereira's reservation to Asunción. The regime showed them the tourist sites, and the Ache met with the infantry commander who had earlier used them to track guerrillas. The director privately admitted that his job was going to be difficult because of the Ache's "shy and introspective demeanor." He made a promise, however: "But once we incorporate those who still live in the jungles . . . place more in Paraguayan homes, we can expect acculturation to proceed more rapidly."[119] Despite private reservations, the DAI continued to present a positive face to the regime.

Despite the successful Ache tour, the DAI's work remained difficult. As it spread meager resources to still more communities, the quality and quantity of services declined. The shortage of funds made Zárate's goals for integration a distant illusion. When the DAI increased allocations after receiving a budget, natives flooded it with requests for assistance. By 1964, despite more help from the missions, demand had so overextended the department's resources that it became notoriously ineffective. The director begged for assistance from almost any NGO willing to contribute financial aid, especially religious missions.

Instead of prompt assistance from the regime, the DAI's difficulties attracted the attention of Stroessner's critics, who began to blame the department for deteriorating conditions in indigenous communities. Early in 1965, amateur ethnographer Miguel Chase Sardi accused DAI officials of incompetence. In a scathing article, he blamed the regime for twenty-four deaths at Pereira's reserve and poor conditions elsewhere.[120]

Chase Sardi clearly shared the DAI's sense of urgency to integrate native people, or at least to improve their living conditions. He agreed that, since national society was Catholic, such integration required more work from the religious missions. He lauded the famous seventeenth-century Jesuit missions and claimed that similar work could again improve the natives' situation. His attack attracted attention to the ineffectiveness of the DAI.

Growing criticism, and especially the rise in indigenous requests for assistance, frustrated the DAI's director. Zárate soon admitted to his superiors that he had not dealt with the "indigenous problem" as efficiently as they had directed. The DAI agreed that most native people, especially in the Chaco, continued to live in "extreme indigence" and in a "primitive state," Zárate's terms for destitution. In other words, the DAI recognized that the indigenous population had not conformed to the majority's way of life or the market economy as quickly as the regime had hoped. If the regime intended the DAI to succeed, Zárate begged, it would have to increase his budget and number of employees.[121]

President Stroessner, however, was in no position to increase funding for, or even pay attention to, the DAI. By 1965, the regime was undergoing a "liberalization," a difficult period in which Stroessner negotiated with opponents to strengthen his position. Years of exile and fruitless violent struggle had finally brought opposition parties to their knees; they sued for peace and asked to participate in the electoral process. The Movimiento Renovador (Renewal Movement), a faction of the Liberal Party, returned from exile to become the officially tolerated opposition. The new Christian Democratic Party, closely allied with the Catholic Church, renounced violence and sought access to politics as an avenue for change. As opponents agreed to a dialogue, the president crushed his remaining enemies. First Stroessner finished off the remains of the small Communist Party. Then he dismissed minister of the interior Edgar Ynsfrán, who had brutally crushed opposition but had pretensions to the presidency.[122] By 1966, Stroessner was once again firmly in control of the government and made plans to be reelected and to amend the Constitution. The DAI and the indigenous population were, not surprisingly, the least of the dictator's worries.

When Anancio Zárate received no more financial assistance, he turned once again to the religious missions. In 1965, the DAI asked the Vatican to send a mission "to take charge of the catechization of the 40,000 remaining indígenas that live in our country without shepherds and professing their native religion." Because of financial problems, the director added: "We hope the mission will be, at the same time, provided with funding . . . channeled to at the same time assure the socioeconomic base of indigenous families."[123] Clearly in need of the means to carry out integration, Zárate argued that missionaries would protect natives from the pace of national development and also strengthen the DAI.

The missions did not disappoint the Ministry. In 1965, all the Christian missions fully agreed again to cooperate in the integration project. But while Protestant missions successfully increased their number of native adherents, the Catholic Church reported frustration in its efforts to proselytize. Catholic missionaries therefore worked even more closely with the DAI. In March 1965, the Conferencia Episcopal Paraguaya (Episcopal Conference of the Paraguayan Catholic Church, CEP), asked the pope to send missionaries to catechize the twenty-five thousand native people in the eastern dioceses of Villarrica and Encarnación.[124] Bishops requested that missionaries especially encourage indigenous groups to adopt "an agricultural way of life."[125] While it clearly intended to assist the DAI in boosting native agricultural production, without an anthropological perspective in mind, the CEP completely ignored the fact that the three principal Guaraní tribes were already subsistence farmers.

One reason that the Catholic Church urgently desired new missions was the growing success of Protestant missions and their increasing influence among native people in Paraguay. Protestant denominations generally had greater success than Catholics among indigenous people throughout Latin America, likely because the collective native memory linked Catholic proselytism to the conquest and loss of land. An analogous case of indigenous adherence to Protestantism occurred in Chimborazo, Ecuador, and shows that natives found in the Protestant faith "a new presentation of self, pride in their own language," and tools to strengthen kinship and family ties. Evangelical organizations enabled the Quichua to create boundaries between themselves and the largely Catholic mestizo society. The indigenous population employed Protestant beliefs to forge a new identity that opposed the state's ideology of inclusion and mestizaje and countered the "bourgeois system of domination" and Catholic mestizos.[126] Joanne Rappaport notes that, even though the Guambiano and Páez in the highlands of southern Colombia rejected the right-wing political agenda brought by conservative Protestant missionaries, they employed their doctrines to fortify a growing ethnic pride and consciousness.[127] The success that Protestant missions were enjoying by the mid-1960s in Paraguay shows that a similar process was under way among indigenous people there.[128]

The Anglican Church reported widespread indigenous adherence. Between 1964 and 1970, with 890 baptisms and confirmations, most of the Enxet joined the Anglican Church in a "wholesale conversion."[129] The Anglicans, alongside their traditional Protestant religious instruction, taught the indigenous people industrial arts and to function as peasant laborers within national society. This wave of baptisms was the latest in three periods of conversions. From 1899 to 1910, 149 Enxet accepted baptism and settled at the central mission of Makthlawaiya. Over 120 western Enxet joined from 1926 to 1936 and moved to a new mission station. Unlike Catholic efforts, conversion of natives to Anglicanism continued to grow, and by 1985, several thousand indígenas formed 90 percent of the Paraguayan Anglican Church.[130]

Despite its ties to the Catholic Church, the DAI was very pleased with the conversion of hundreds of Enxet to the Anglican Church, since from its beginning that mission promised to help integrate indigenous people. When even more Enxet joined the Anglican Church in the mid-1960s, the DAI began to take credit for positive movement toward the regime's integration goal.

One explanation for the eagerness with which the Enxet welcomed Anglican proselytism was their worsening economic condition. From their early contact with missionaries, the Enxet viewed the Anglicans as a source of provisions; this perception grew stronger as their economic situation deteriorated. Missionaries encouraged this view and provided for all needs during religious training at mission compounds. Anglicans built cattle ranches and small industries, such as carpentry and leather shops, where they employed as many as one thousand native people.[131]

Events between 1953 and 1959 support the economic basis for conversion.

During this time, the New Tribes Mission (NTM), a conservative and fundamentalist interdenominational Protestant group based in Florida, which had begun to proselytize in Paraguay in 1949 among the Ïshïro, briefly managed the central compound at Makthlawaiya. Nearly the entire population of the mission was rebaptized as NTM followers. Later, the NTM extended its work to six additional tribes and completed the translation of the New Testament into Enlhit in 1973.

The Enxet conversions to the New Tribes Mission were a pragmatic response, as Enxet recounted that they had joined NTM because North American missionaries traveled in two airplanes while their British predecessors had traveled only by horse and oxcart. The day after the Anglicans took ownership of the mission again in 1963, the Enxet requested the reintroduction of the Anglican communion service and realigned themselves with the new source of provisions.[132]

The enthusiastic Enxet response to Protestantism, then, was partly economically motivated. But wholesale conversion can be fully understood only by recognizing the extent to which native people continued to distinguish indigenous religious beliefs from their relationship with Anglican missionaries. To secure economic benefits, the Enxet deliberately hid their traditional spirituality from the missionaries. The *yohoxma*, or religious healers, learned to sing quietly and continued to perform healing ceremonies even at mission stations without the missionaries' knowing. Whenever the Enxet wished to drink or dance, they left the mission for a time. Thus, the indigenous population "created a façade of orthodox Anglicanism behind which they were able to develop an independent syncretistic religious system of which the missionaries remained blissfully unaware. In doing this they have manifested both an excellent understanding and parallel rejection of many aspects of the missionary message. Their success has been predicated on following a dual strategy of hiding their traditional culture and mastering an acceptable Anglican discourse."[133]

The creative way in which the Enxet adopted the Anglican message allowed them to secure financial assistance from the mission but continue traditional beliefs and rituals in secret. The persistence of indigenous religious practices sustained the natives' self-perception as distinct ethnic minorities within a surrounding non-Indian society and allowed them to adapt successfully to vast changes in their way of life.[134]

In 1966, the Anglican Church renewed its efforts to integrate indigenous people and equip the Enxet to survive as part of the rural peasant society. This time, the mission employed linguistic education to encourage cultural change. Anglicans created agricultural and cattle-raising projects that attracted more Enxet to Makthlawaiya. Administrator John Battman then discouraged the natives from using their own language. Missionaries introduced education in Guaraní and refused to speak Enxet in any context. Bishop Bill Flagg explained that the use of Guaraní "would help promote integration of the Indian people into national life."[135] The move was partly successful, since the Enxet adopted a negative attitude toward their tribal culture during the late 1960s.[136] Such obvious progress toward integration greatly pleased the DAI.

Mennonite missionaries farther west reported similar surges in conversions and cultural change. Starting in the late 1960s, almost all the indigenous settlements within the Mennonite colonies experienced messianic movements and increased participation in the Mennonite Church, again, in part an endeavor to improve their economic conditions.[137]

Another reason for widespread participation was the indigenous population's attempt to restore harmony and well-being in a rapidly changing way of life. The Toba and Pilagá tribes in the Argentine Chaco used Pentecostal revivals, at this same time, to reduce the tension that resulted from contact with non-Indians. Through the Pentecostal emphasis on healing and communication with the Holy Spirit, the Toba restored cultural harmony and balance to their rapidly changing society. Indigenous people in northern Argentina created their own native church during the 1960s, which eventually spread to hundreds of communities and four ethnic groups.[138]

In much the same way, native people in the Mennonite colonies used massive religious revivals to invoke the spiritual forces they thought had made Europeans successful farmers. Indigenous people understood their relationship with the Mennonites within the context of the rituals they had previously employed to assure control over their world. Natives traditionally attributed a spiritual dimension to hunting and gathering and correctly performed a series of rituals to ensure successful results. The move from scrub forests and ranches to a sedentary life among the Mennonites led them to transfer their traditional worldview to the relationship with their new overseers and providers.[139]

Native people rapidly came to believe that correct performance of the new religious rites would bring them economic success; baptism into the Mennonite Church, then, had not necessarily altered their traditional religious cosmology. The Enlhit and Nivaklé continued to embrace tribal spirituality even while performing Protestant rituals. Indigenous people in the Chaco thus greatly increased their participation in the Anglican and Mennonite churches by 1965. The regime was delighted with this turn of events, for, as a result, indigenous people often settled permanently and started to farm.

Director Zárate's reliance on the missions seemed to be paying off, so he again turned his attention to the reservation that still had no religious managers, Pereira's settlement for the Ache. The regime's plans to integrate indigenous people in eastern Paraguay seemed also to be progressing well. Because his income was directly proportional to the number of Ache that lived under his control, Pereira tried to attract still more people to his ranch.[140] In its eagerness to settle and "pacify" the Ache, the regime continued to tolerate Pereira's dishonesty. In 1966, forest-dwelling Ache wounded several peasants. Pereira and Borgognón, the latter of whom still worked for the DAI, set out with Ache trackers to contact the jungle group.[141] Pereira used reservation Ache to attract their recently contacted relatives with gifts of food.[142] His motives were greedy, but if conditions at the reservation were difficult, why did Ache themselves encourage their relatives to move to the settlement?

Ultimately, the Ache participated in Pereira's scheme because their tribal power structure had changed significantly after settling among Paraguayans. Young Ache men who had spent more time among non-Indians stole wives from the new arrivals. While this had been a common practice in the forests, younger men now usurped political power from elders who had previously led the tribe and used their new leverage to secure more wives and children than would previously have been possible. In addition, the Ache claimed to feel safer at the reservation because there ranchers could not kill them.[143]

The DAI was very pleased that by 1966 practically all the southern Ache, over one hundred people, were gathered at Pereira's settlement. Zárate believed that the Ache had adapted well, since they now grew crops instead of hunting and worked for neighboring farmers. In his zeal to alter Ache culture, the director even asked the government to build a school at Pereira's camp. Soon, Zárate promised, the Ache would be completely self-sufficient and well on their way toward complete integration.[144] Changes clearly had taken place in Ache society. What Zárate neglected to recognize, though, was how the Ache themselves had altered their lives to adjust to their new environment.

An important explanation of the regime's urgency to settle the Ache was its growing interest in developing eastern Paraguay. In 1965, the regime completed an asphalt road between Asunción and the Brazilian border. Brazil built a bridge across the Paraná River to the Paraguayan town of President

Stroessner and provided Paraguay with "free zone" custom privileges for exports and a direct link to ports on the Atlantic Ocean.[145] Thus, Paraguay sought to both decrease its historical dependence on Argentina and boost economic development along its eastern frontier. Opening the region to greater commerce, though, meant serious shifts in lifestyle and economic conditions for the area's indigenous Guaraní.

Other indigenous communities besides the Ache were also changing. Another sign of so-called economic progress was the placement of Avá youth from Paso Cadena in schools in surrounding Paraguayan towns.[146] Enlhit Sanapaná, at La Esperanza in the Chaco, by this time were marketing their own peanuts, kafir, wheat, and cotton in national markets. Other indigenous people in the Mennonite colonies labored as mechanics, chauffeurs, and field hands.[147] Zárate was pleased that the NTM had recently settled two hundred Ayoreode at Campo Loro Mission near Fort Lagarenza in the central Chaco.[148] Now both Protestants and Catholics were working with the DAI to change Ayoreode culture. Zárate could finally proclaim that his DAI, with close cooperation from the religious missions, had started to alter indigenous life. Only a few years before, the regime had been frustrated with the rate of integration, but by the end of 1966, growing mission cooperation suggested that the successful inclusion of native people in the wider society might be just around the corner.

In that same year, in fact, Stroessner made significant progress toward economic growth, which ultimately motivated the integration program. In exchange for the withdrawal of Brazilian troops from Salto del Guairá (Guairá Falls), on 22 June, Stroessner and Brazil's military president, Humberto de Alencar Castelo Branco, signed the Act of Iguazú. The pact resolved an old border dispute in favor of Brazil and removed restrictions on Brazilian colonization of Paraguay's eastern border region. Soon after, the IBR, hoping settlers would boost production of export crops, started selling large tracts of state-owned land to Brazilian land companies. Within a few years, Brazilian immigrants would pour into eastern Paraguay and seriously threaten the indigenous communities in the area.

Conclusion

By 1966, after nearly eight years of intense activity, the DAI seemed to be well on its way toward integrating the indigenous population. Stroessner had extended his control over all areas of the country and had tried to raise Paraguay to the economic level of the surrounding countries by improving living conditions and developing the nation's agricultural base. Rural indigenous communities—especially nomadic bands that still hunted in the few remaining forests—were obstacles to both economic progress and the nation's image. To modernize Paraguay, the regime hoped to alter native ways of life. Stroessner's plan to include indigenous people in national culture and markets would at the very least significantly change many communities.

Using indigenist examples from Mexico, Stroessner's generals embarked on a plan to integrate the indigenous population into Paraguayan society. First they created the DAI to settle native groups on reservations. The dictatorship promised to protect indigenous people from physical extinction but insisted that they change their way of life.

The small DAI tried to improve the economic situation of the natives, and while these programs largely failed, it did change communities. The DAI sent food, medicine, and clothing to indigenous villages to make the people more dependent on Western products and to improve their health. The regime also started to settle the nomadic Ache and Ayoreode tribes.

Sure that integration would change indigenous culture beyond recognition, the DAI collected native artifacts to preserve exotic examples of their earlier lifestyles. Finally, it used sporting and artistic events to decrease prejudice and raise national awareness of the native people.

The DAI cooperated extensively with religious organizations to change and influence the indigenous communities. The Catholic, Anglican, and Mennonite churches were sponsoring the largest missions in Paraguay by the 1960s. From the outset, missionary goals for the indigenous population coincided closely with those of the dictatorship. Religious agencies not only assisted the DAI, they also depended on the regime for permission to operate. In return, missions worked hard to acculturate the tribal groups. Both Catholics and Protestants encouraged native people to produce agricultural products for a wider market and to associate more fully with national society. Native people's widespread response to the Protestant missions, especially, showed that missions had significantly influenced and changed their lives.

Indigenous people responded cautiously to the regime's integration plan. Largely isolated and losing their land, they rejected the state's development projects, but many accepted food, medicine, and tools from the government. Numerous indigenous communities joined Protestant denominations in part to access the economic resources these religious organizations provided. While native groups had in the past largely rejected Catholic proselytism due to its associations with the Paraguayan majority, natives nonetheless gratefully welcomed drought relief, medication, and food from Catholic relief agencies.

During the first eight years of the Stroessner regime's indigenist policy, indigenous people cautiously increased their participation in non-Indian markets and religious organizations. Thus began the integration of Paraguay's native population, which over the next decades dramatically altered indigenous communities and their relationship with national society.

Integration Turns to Exclusion, 1967–1976

The Guajakí dead we are . . . now our Great Father . . . owner of the corn.
He rules over all of us now.

Kanexirigi

In 1972 the Paraguayan authorities showed the obvious intention of get-
ting rid of all the Aché, and even of extending this policy to other Indian
groups in Paraguay.

Mark Münzel, *The Aché*

The indigenous cultures are perhaps in danger, at least if they do not
receive our help. We need to become conscious of the indigenous situation.

Juan Usher, "Proyecto 'Marandú'"

After eight years of work, the DAI seemed well on its way to changing indigenous life and increasing the natives' participation in national society.
The department had started to settle both seminomadic tribes—the Ache
and the Ayoreode—and to provide food and medicine to other communities. Indigenous people accepted the donations but relayed their increasing
need for land to the DAI. While they largely rejected development projects
and attempts to control their economic activities, indigenous communities
augmented their participation in national markets and the labor force on
their own initiative. This was certainly the case for communities that joined
missions, especially Protestant ones.

Churches continued to cooperate with these attempts to alter indigenous
people. Missionaries, not only to secure religious allegiance but also to assist
with integration, urged the people to farm and to speak Guaraní. The DAI
seemed to be moving steadily toward full incorporation of indigenous communities into national society.

The dictatorship, however, viewed the so-called indigenous problem otherwise and urged the DAI to increase the speed of integration. In so doing, the regime took advantage of political changes in 1967 to redirect its plans for native people. Earlier, Stroessner had weathered his most serious political crisis and, with some basic changes in framework, overcame opposition from those who resented his heavy-handed rule. Most important, Stroessner caused a new Constitution to be enacted that gave him two more terms and bolstered his Colorado Party. Next, the president gave loyal army comrades prominent party positions. General Samaniego left the Ministry of Defense to manage party finances and from there to direct patronage. A generation of new and younger politicians rose to prominence, so that by 1967, everyone in government posts, including in the DAI, owed their position to Stroessner.

Leaders of the DAI were especially beholden to Stroessner simply because the agency was unable to force indigenous integration as quickly as the government asked. To speed up the process, Stroessner reshuffled the DAI's leadership. To undermine indigenous self-sufficiency, the new director severely cut assistance to native communities and evicted indigenous groups from ranches when they poached cattle or obstructed the extension of cash-crop farming. Rather than improving the conditions of the natives, the DAI focused on settling the remaining independent Ache and Ayoreode.

While trying to force cultural changes, though, the DAI attracted the attention of outside NGOs, which highlighted the poor conditions of the natives to criticize the regime. The rise of anthropological advocacy changed the indigenous population's position because it increased their leverage in conflicts over land and resources. At the most obvious level, criticism by human rights organizations forced the regime to alter the discourse of its indigenous policy. In 1972, Mark Münzel, from Germany, focused attention on the regime's indigenous settlement programs, and critics chastised the dictator for human rights abuses. International scrutiny and declining aid forced the Stroessner regime to promise to protect indigenous cultures. Scholars joined forces with the Catholic Church and created ambitious projects to defend native rights and to secure land for the indigenous communities. These efforts improved the indigenous people's position and made it possible for them to organize broadly for the first time. Stroessner terminated the DAI in 1975 because of the abuses that marked integration, a rise in NGO advocacy, and pan-indigenous organization. These developments altered indigenous communities, helped undermine the regime's legitimacy, and changed the outcome of the state's plans to integrate indigenous people.

The Demise of the Department of Indigenous Affairs

In 1967, Stroessner made political changes to legally assure himself two more terms in office. Thus, secure enough to grant public petitioners some concessions, in February, he allowed the Liberal Party to become the official minority opposition in the Paraguayan Legislature.[1] In May, he had the fifth constitution since independence ratified. Billed as a defense of human rights, the new document only thinly veiled Stroessner's ambitious plans to retain control. The 1967 Constitution left intact the broad powers of the executive branch and gave citizens the liberty to form political parties that did not "advocate the destruction of the republic." Chapter Six of the document promised agrarian reform and equitable land distribution as well as state-sponsored colonization of rural areas.[2] Most important, the new law guaranteed Stroessner two more five-year terms. The legal revisions bought the dictator temporary compliance from the outlawed parties, which decreased their support for rural insurgents. Perhaps their goal was to give the new legislation a chance to work. In any case, Paraguay entered a brief period of political peace.

In the first year, Stroessner employed the new legal code to legitimate his rule. Some scholars have held that he maintained his position only through brutal force, which he referred to as "preventive repression," and that after 1959 he "did not even bother with the facade of democracy."[3] On the contrary, Stroessner found it important to maintain an appearance of legality. After he used the Constitution of 1967 to consolidate his power, he employed all available legal artifices, even indigenist legislation, to create a façade of legitimacy.

Stroessner's new executive powers allowed him to position loyal officers at all levels of the government. The DAI's leadership changed several times. The virtual shutdown of the agency shows what a small value the regime actually placed on indigenous people within its broader national development goals. The DAI changed teachers at the school for indigenous children at Fortuna and asked a rancher at Cerro Ipir to keep his cattle out of indigenous fields. The director ordered police to investigate a claim that a Mbyá had filed against a Mennonite rancher at Sommerfeld, an eastern settlement where foreign ranchers began to harass indigenous people to evict them from the colony's land.[4] Aside from such minor actions, the DAI virtually ignored the indigenous population.

Complaints from ranchers about indigenous squatters did finally lead to changes at the DAI. Increasingly frustrated landowners urged the regime to destroy native communities within their ranch boundaries and to once and for all settle native groups out of harm's way. In March 1967, nineteen land-owners from Cerro Sarambí sent a petition to Samaniego, who still oversaw work at the DAI, asking him to evict native people, who had "the damaging custom of trespassing on others' property and doing work belonging to wicked and unsavory crooks."[5] Ranchers were clearly frustrated with indigenous people within their property boundaries who at times rustled cattle. Only by contributing to the national economy, in their view, would these people become productive citizens, even real human beings, and cease to be a nuisance.

Pressure from the ranchers precisely when the regime began trying to augment rural production again encouraged high-ranking officials to try to speed up the integration process. The dictator named a new director for the DAI in May 1968: Col. Tristán Infanzon. Infanzon was a loyal member of the ruling Colorado Party. Visiting journalist Norman Lewis described him as a "man of mild aspect and outstanding courteous demeanor" but "one of the dictator's right hand men."[6] The new director was a good compromise, for he would not prove squeamish when implementing the coercive side of integration.

President Stroessner's skillful manipulation of his power base, especially after 1967, proves that Infanzon's appointment was not a coincidence. Not only did Stroessner personally choose each and every one of his staff members, down to junior military officers, but he relied on *personalismo*, a practice in which the elite attached their loyalty to a strong political leader.[7] Infanzon was a serious officer who would oversee the settlement of the Ache, for instance, but, since he owed his job to the regime, he would also favor the interests of the ranchers, the base of Stroessner's power, over native concerns. In this way, Stroessner planned to appease both integration goals and the ranchers bent on removing native people from their properties.

The degree to which Stroessner honored landowners in his plans for integration shows their growing prominence in the Colorado Party. As in neighboring nations, the elite in Paraguay still owned most of the land. As one lawyer explained: "Since the last century, in our country, politicians were those who owned ranches. To have status, a person had to be a rancher; he had the economic resources and that also gave him political status."[8] Most of Stroessner's cabinet members, ministers, and top military officers were landowners, and thus ranchers exerted a disproportionate amount of influence.

Ranchers depended on peasants for labor, but in the Chaco, especially, they also employed native people for work in the fields. Indigenous self-sufficiency based on hunting as an alternate form of sustenance, though, diminished their effectiveness as dependent laborers, especially when they had access to land. Beginning in the 1960s, therefore, ranchers evicted indigenous squatters to free land for ranching and to create a more dependent working class.

Growing demands from ranchers and the ambiguous orders for integration soon frustrated the new director of the DAI. Within only a few months—in July 1968—Infanzon made public his frustration with the state's attempts to change native communities. The director accused the government of not having a viable strategy to induce integration and charged that past efforts had been paternalistic and archaic.[9]

Infanzon's charge was not only personally risky, it also showed that his frustration was, at its base, economic; the DAI simply did not have enough funds to fulfill its charge. Since indigenous people did not pay taxes, the director held, any funds to improve their situation had to come from other sources. Infanzon argued that the dictatorship needed to define its indigenist goals and provide him with funds to execute its plans. "Once they formulate a true program of action for relating to Paraguay's indigenous population," Infanzon wrote, "then the DAI will have a mission on which it can act."[10] The director's complaint shows the futility that minor officials must have felt when working at the bottom of the regime structure. The deeper significance of his remarks, however, is their reflection of the regime's shifting priorities: economic growth had surpassed social concerns as Stroessner began to reward elite supporters.

In October 1968, former director Borgognón published the results of his ten-year investigation of the indigenous population, the first such examination conducted by a government official. After reportedly covering 67,000 kilometers in over 230 trips, DAI staff members reported that 50,000 indigenous people from 17 tribes lived in over 300 communities throughout country. This number, while seemingly low, actually inflated the number of indigenous people, most likely, to legitimate DAI requests for funds. Only three years later, in what was probably a more accurate count, Chase Sardi calculated the indigenous population at only 37,169.[11] Borgognón admitted that, regardless of their actual number, most indigenous people still lived in small, isolated communities, "conserved many of their autochthonous cultural markers," and showed no visible desire to join the larger society.[12]

The report from the DAI reflected the state's disappointment at the slow pace of integration. Borgognón acknowledged that indigenous people still lived very differently from the national norm and that ten years of indigenist action had done little to improve their situation. What is more, the DAI had been unable to convince indigenous people to leave their communities and settle among nationals. Strapped for cash, however, over the next few years the dictatorship provided the DAI with neither funding nor new guidelines. As a result, after 1968, the department's usefulness to both natives and the regime deteriorated as indigenous people moved low on the list of the regime's concerns.

Changes in the Catholic Church and Anthropology

Despite the intense frustration of its superiors, the DAI continued to work closely with the missions. Borgognón, who continued to help out at the department as needed, acknowledged that Paraguay owed them a great debt: "The foundations on which to base TRUE INDIGENIST WORK IN OUR COUNTRY have been built by [the] PRESENT MISSIONARIES OF PARA-GUAY. Let us agree that, if we still have jungle aborigines, we must accept that it is because our missions still exist."[13]

Even after ten years of official integration, employees of the state still regarded indigenous people as racially inferior and certainly different from nationals.[14] But religious proselytism could redeem these "backward" people, Borgognón claimed, and in fact had made their very survival possible.

Regardless of the regime's hopes to the contrary, the largest religious organization no longer intended to cooperate closely with the government to integrate the native population. While Protestants continued to support the state's indigenist plans, Catholic leaders had begun to oppose the dictatorship. The profound change was initially a result of the Second Vatican Council (1962–1965), in which Pope John XXIII called on his congregation to defend human rights as a new way to evangelize the modern world.[15] When bishops met at Medellín in 1968 to consider the pope's directives, they agreed to join politics and work for social justice to increase their influence in the lower classes and possibly to discourage Communist uprisings.[16] Some priests who began to call for social justice, however, adopted a Marxist critique of capitalist abuses. The church's move to the political Left thus elicited a severe response from conservative regimes such as the one that Stroessner directed.

The shifts in the wider church quickly arrived in Paraguay, where the Catholic approach to proselytism changed. Before Medellín, bishops still encouraged missions to change indigenous cultures and integrate the natives quickly into national society. In March 1965, the CEP urged the Vatican to send missionaries to catechize and encourage twenty-five thousand indigenous people in eastern Paraguay to adopt "an agricultural way of life."[17] Following Medellín, bishops canceled these plans and instead began to stress the importance of economic assistance. "It is necessary to do socioeconomic development, not evangelization; and even less to use the reduction system. Action with the indigenous people cannot be primarily evangelism but, rather, promotion and acculturation."[18]

The Catholic missions' new strategy reflected a sense of their past failure and was an attempt to exert more influence within the lower classes. Missionary José Seelwische argued that Catholics had failed to influence indigenous people: "The Catholic attempt to convert the pagan indigenous population, civilizing and educating them toward a Christian way of life [had] not succeed[ed] in any way, and many missionaries felt their work was impossible." The priest believed that Catholic missionaries had failed to "convince the indigenous population to abandon their superstitions, pagan rituals, and primitive customs." After Vatican II, Seelwische insisted, missionaries learned to respect indigenous cultures and tolerate religious freedom and had started to preach universal salvation.[19]

Changes in the Catholic Church profoundly influenced the DAI, which had relied on it to help integrate indigenous communities. While the CEP still promised to support indigenous people and peasants, it adopted a critical position toward the regime. During the late 1960s, the decline in Catholic contributions forced the DAI to curtail its assistance to indigenous communities.[20] With less funding from Cáritas and growing criticism from the CEP, Infanzon sharply cut provisions of food and medicine to native people and virtually ended DAI visits to the countryside.

Infanzon focused on what must have seemed his only manageable task, settling the northern Ache. By 1968, all the southern Ache had moved to Pereira's farm, where half of the group, sixty-nine individuals, had died from contact-related respiratory infections.[21] In August, Pereira asked for permission to move the Ache north to a property that was large enough to "be able to nucleate more . . . aboriginal people of the same group, but from the jungle and in a wild state."[22] So many Ache had perished that Pereira needed more people if he was to continue to embezzle supplies.

Another reason Pereira hoped to move was pressure from nearby peasants. Settlers were jealous that the regime allowed indigenous people, whom they despised, to use good farmland. The DAI reported that in 1967 alone the Ache had raised 20,000 kilos of maize, 120,000 kilos of manioc, 880 kilos of rice, and 500 kilos of potatoes and beans.[23] Angry peasants pressured the local Colorado Party Sectional to remove the Ache. In July, Pereira visited Stroessner and told him that he needed more land and additional financial assistance to settle the remaining Ache.[24]

Minister Samaniego sent inspectors, who confirmed that the Ache lived in poor sanitary conditions without medical or educational assistance.[25] To make matters worse for the DAI, in July 1968, León Cadogan again accused the agency of trying to exterminate the Ache by allowing conditions at the camp to deteriorate severely.[26] Inspectors observed that Pereira obviously mismanaged the Ache settlement but recommended that the government give the overseer more land farther north for "collecting others of the same Guayakí groups dispersed through that zone."[27] Tolerance of Pereira's duplicity can be explained only by the regime's urgent desire to clear the remaining Ache—the northern bands—from the path of development in Caaguazú. The IBR assigned twenty-five hectares of state-owned property to Pereira at Cerro Morotí (White Hill), and in September the army transported reservation Ache to their new home.[28]

The DAI renamed Pereira's new settlement the Colonia Nacional Guayakí (National Guayakí Colony) and reported that the Ache quickly planted six hectares of watermelon, corn, manioc, sugarcane, and soy beans.[29] Actual conditions, however, were far from optimal. Pereira still complained that he was unable to feed the Ache despite regular food shipments. The native people complained that their nomadic relatives still had food while "among the whites we don't eat anymore." When they threatened to return to the woods, Pereira warned the government that he would abandon his post if he did not receive still more provisions.[30]

At the heart of the issue was not only Pereira's continued embezzlement but also the regime's complicity. In 1968, it completed a highway between Coronel Oviedo and Saltos de Guairá. The new road divided the traditional northern Ache territory and increased violent encounters between indigenous people and nationals.[31] Peasants and ranchers alike pressured the state to settle the northern Ache and this, along with plans for integration, makes the DAI's tolerance of Pereira's theft and abuse more understandable.

Just as important as plans for development were Cadogan's complaints about abuses caused by integration. The ethnographer was aware of growing trends in the field of anthropology. During the 1960s, cultural ecologists led by Julian Steward, Eric Wolf, Sydney Mintz, and Marshall Sahlins studied the material base of society and economic relations within colonial contexts. In opposition to the Boasian school, which tended to ignore the material conditions of subjects, these scholars used an historical approach to study economic exploitation and the cultural adaptations to colonialism.[32] Within the context of the rise of racial consciousness in the United States, especially the new Red Power movement, these scholars charged that ignorance of the consequences of colonialism had benefited white society and U.S. expansion. They drew attention to the living conditions of the indigenous population and called on their colleagues to combat racism and make society more equitable for their subjects.[33]

Religious organizations paid attention to the new focus on exploitation, and several began to support the changes in anthropology. In 1969, the World Council of Churches declared that "churches must be actively concerned for the economic and political well-being of exploited groups" and help "victims of racism regain a sense of their own worth and determine their own future."[34] At the University of Bern, the council created the Program to Combat Racism to defuse potential racial conflict. In response, religious groups began to call attention to racism and indigenous conditions.

For the moment, foreign religious groups were far from Stroessner's highest concern. More pressing were changes in Paraguay's Catholic Church. In January 1969, the Conference of Bishops asked Stroessner to improve the treatment of political prisoners, and Monsignor Bogarín adopted a clear stance in favor of human rights: "The church cannot show itself to be indifferent or insensitive to the fate of the Paraguayan man . . . when this man finds himself oppressed or diminished by unjust socioeconomic structures or by excesses of power that hurt human rights, the church's mission also assumes the form of a prophetic denouncement and acts as a moral force to pressure for liberation and the respect of human rights."[35] The archbishop strongly criticized the dictator and demanded economic justice and an end to excessive force.

The church's growing radicalization brought a swift response from the security forces. Soon after Bogarín's pronouncement, soldiers closed a Catholic seminary, expelled Jesuit priests from the country, canceled Cáritas's reception of food and clothing from the United States, and violently repressed protesting students. On December 8, when the president traditionally led thousands of the faithful on a thirty-five-kilometer trek to the shrine of the Virgin of Caacupé, the church instead staged a dramatic protest and replaced the pilgrimage with a vigil of penitence to protest repression. During the vigil, security forces beat up a priest and squelched the peaceful demonstrations.[36]

Even as the church-state confrontation was deepening by 1969, native communities were seeking additional protection for their land.[37] Indigenous requests for land titles grew desperate by 1969, as settlers occupied native territories and ranchers evicted more indigenous squatters. Confronted with land invasions, the indigenous communities first requested assistance from Infanzon. Since the DAI had no authority to issue land titles, though, the director only passed petitions on to the IBR.[38]

The IBR, however, faced a serious conflict of interests. As part of the regime's plans to populate the frontier regions, the institute's president, Juan Manuel Frutos, wanted to resettle peasants from the overpopulated central region to the vast rural areas of the eastern border area. When indigenous people farmed the properties allotted to peasants, however, serious conflicts arose. While the IBR could have protected indigenous properties, more often than not, Frutos sided with the peasants he was also supposed to defend.[39]

Heavy-handed Integration

Conflicts between ranchers and indigenous people had a similar result. Even though Infanzon at times lobbied on behalf of indigenous communities, more often, he employed a heavy-handed approach and sided with the ranchers. In April 1969, La Gauloise, a company that owned several large cattle ranches in the eastern Chaco, asked the DAI to remove a group of Toba-Qom from its property at Paratodo. The state had granted the Toba ownership of their tribal territory in 1935, after they had helped fight Bolivians in the Chaco War. Shortly after, La Gauloise bought the Toba lands, located one hundred kilometers west of Asunción, as part of a larger sale of state-owned property. After growing conflicts, La Gauloise complained that the Toba were ruining its ranching business and called on the DAI to evict them.[40] The ranchers had grown tired of trying to prevent the Toba from ignoring fences, changing the location of their settlements, and poaching. La Gauloise offered trucks to help remove the Toba as well as six cows to supply milk during the resettlement. The company pledged all of this, of course, only if the DAI forced the Toba to promise never to return.

On 6 September 1969, Infanzon traveled to Paratodo with soldiers to evict the Toba. Firing rounds into the air, the soldiers approached the indigenous settlement, where the people hid in their houses. Once the shooting stopped, the Toba emerged and at first resisted the soldiers. Infanzon told their leaders that they must abandon their land. The Toba leader at the time of this writing, Francisco Cáceres, was only a child at the time, but he vividly recalled the strength of their chief, who responded: "I cannot go. We have always had these lands. [We] will not leave."[41] In response, Infanzon himself torched the Toba's homes. The people left their possessions and animals to the soldiers and fled to a nearby grove of trees. To reach cover they crossed a creek, where the only casualty occurred; an elderly grandmother fell from her horse and died when the horse stumbled in the muddy water.

Not surprisingly, the event left such an impression that in an interview twenty-five years later Cáceres still vividly recalled both the day of the eviction and Infanzon with distaste and anger: "Infanzon was very mean, his character was very unpleasant. He does nothing in the best interest of those who love indigenous people. He was mean. He solved the ranchers' problems, not ours. In favor of the ranchers, not for us. Then we thought that he sold out, that the ranchers had bought him. There was no one hurt that day, only the chief's grandmother fell from the horse . . . and died. The people stayed in the woods for three days, eating from the woods. But the people were very fearful, were afraid."[42] The chief's testimony reflects the general indigenous mistrust of non-Indians and ranchers and their great fear of the regime's officials. The Toba clearly understood what the official records show: bribes facilitated the changing nature of DAI support as other ranchers requested the removal of the indigenous people.[43]

Despite help from the ranchers, total integration still eluded the DAI. The director's excuses ranged from what he called the natives' backward and millennial culture to the national society's unwillingness to accept indigenous people into their midst.[44] Infanzon's rationalizations failed to impress his superiors, however, and by the end of 1969, he had terminated all visits to native communities as the DAI's activities ground to a halt.

The one exception still remained the Ache, whose settlement probably appealed to Infanzon because, unlike the rest of the ambiguous integration program, it appeared to be a task with concrete goals. In Pereira, moreover, the director had an ally who shared his heavy-handed approach to changing indigenous lifestyles. After moving the Ache to the San Joaquín hills in the Caaguazú Department, Pereira began to search for the northern Ache. It was not until November 1970, however, that he actually began to remove the people from their forested habitat. First, trackers captured a woman from the northern group, who led Pereira's Ache back to her people and convinced all but one family, thirty-six individuals, to visit Cerro Morotí.[45]

Why did the Ache abandon their forest homes in favor of life at the reservation? The indigenous people attributed their decision to family ties with the reservation Ache. Older people in both groups had known each other as adolescents. What is more, deadly illnesses were sweeping through the forest Ache, and their contacts with campesinos were becoming increasingly violent. A man named Kuchingi recalled that at this time relatives frequently told each other: "If we stay in the forests we will all be killed."[46] What happened to the Ache resembles virgin-soil epidemics that ravaged indigenous communities during the sixteenth- and seventeenth-century demographic collapse throughout the Americas.

Northern Ache claimed that, although southern relatives pressured them to move to Pereira's settlement, the decision was their own. Pereira had en-

couraged the move, yet the Ache recalled that at no point was any violent
or physical coercion employed to force them onto the reserve. In fact, the
Ache "emphatically den[ied] previous reports that individuals were forcibly
captured and brought to the reservation."[47] They recounted, moreover, that,
once the overseer realized how quickly the new arrivals succumbed to illness, he discouraged his charges from contacting their northern relatives.
"Kanegi took us to the white people's house. There the Ache all died. Pereira
was really angry. 'Why are you in such a hurry to bring all the Ache for no
reason?' 'Don't hurry, take your time,' he used to say. Pereira was really angry" that the Ache went back to make more contacts.[48] The testimony shows
that Pereira was aware that a slower settlement process might yield better
results, presumably because his flow of supplies would end if the Ache all
perished. By 1971, he was allowing his reservation charges to convince the
northern Ache to walk to the nearest road, where he met them and took
them back to the settlement. The Ache later recounted that almost as many
of them remained in the forest, where they presumably all died.[49]

Authorities actively encouraged Pereira to settle the northern Ache. In
November of 1970, when reservation Ache first established contact, AIP
president Luis Albospino and Infanzon both visited the reservation, urged
Pereira to attract more Ache, and left US$5,000 in supplies for new arriv-
als.[50] In turn, Pereira redoubled his efforts to settle all the forest Ache.

So concerned were entrepreneurs in the capital that the Ache not obstruct
rural development that, soon after the northern Ache arrived at the reservation, businessmen formed a small NGO to fund and assure positive publicity about the settlement. In January 1971, Milan Zeman—manager of the
German company Hoechst del Paraguay—created the Comisión de Ayuda
al Indigena Guayakí (Guayakí Indian Aid Commission, CAIG) along with
Thomas Holt—the managing director of the Bank of America in Paraguay—
Infanzon, and General Bejarano of the AIP. The CAIG convinced businesses
of the need to settle the Ache and in 1971 contributed US$14,000 to the DAI.
The following year, businesses and oil refineries donated US$22,500 so the
DAI could purchase more supplies to send to Pereira's reserve.[51]

These donations should have improved conditions, yet, because Pereira
was still reselling the donations, the supplies never reached the Ache. Infanzon clearly knew of Pereira's theft, for throughout 1971 he sent rations
intended for the army in addition to the DAI supplies he was sending to keep
the indigenous people from starving. Besides reselling supplies, Pereira even
forced the Ache to raise marijuana and hired them out to farmers in the area
who paid him for their labor.[52]

Even more serious than Pereira's dishonesty were the effects of initial contact for the arriving forty-seven northern Ache, who all contracted minor respiratory illnesses soon after moving to the reservation. Twenty died almost immediately.[53] The children who survived grew weak from malnutrition, and many died from pneumonia. Illness also killed those people who remained in the woods; the Ache recounted that they sometimes were forced to bury elderly stragglers alive to prevent vultures from eating them.[54] Whether or not they moved to the reservation, increased contact devastated the northern Ache.

Infanzon also focused his attention on settling the Ache because the church had begun to oppose the regime. As mentioned above, instead of assisting with the integration program, Catholic leaders were now focused on organizing peasant agrarian leagues and base communities. In 1971, the agrarian leagues' stated purposes still included fairly radical goals, such as socialized landownership and production.[55]

Because the regime, despite disclaimers, associated peasant cooperatives with communism, security forces attacked the co-ops. After one particularly severe period of repression in 1970, Catholic archbishop Bogarín himself asked Stroessner to respect church organizations and stop "persecuting" Christian peasant leaders.[56]

Despite the church's plea for greater tolerance, however, the conflict grew more severe. The CEP began to accuse the regime of human rights abuses, ignoring land reform, and allowing peasants' living conditions to deteriorate. In 1971, church leaders went as far as to excommunicate one of Stroessner's ministers and the chief of police. Security forces, in return, murdered priests found with the peasant leagues, evicted others, and clashed with students and layworkers.[57]

Even as the Catholic hierarchy severely curtailed cooperation with the DAI, Protestant agencies increased their support. The DAI responded positively because Protestants funded their own mission projects. The department waived customs duties for missions on imported medicine and tools and exempted personnel from registration costs in the civil registry.[58] Infanzon also authorized Protestants to initiate proselytism in indigenous settlements.[59] At this time, the NTM commenced work among the Yofuaxa tribe of southwestern Paraguay.[60] In 1971, the DAI director praised the "close bonds" with Protestant missions and concluded that such cooperation "improved and facilitated the DAI's work to acculturate our indigenous people."[61]

The expansion of Protestant missions coincided with a rise in the world's attention to indigenous affairs. The military government of Brazil had sparked an indigenous movement in the late sixties, when the international press had accused it of committing genocide.[62] Another catalyst was the American Indian Movement (AIM) in the United States, which used the National Council of Churches as a mediator during its 1973 occupation of Wounded Knee on the Pine Ridge Lakota reservation.

Deteriorating conditions and resulting demonstrations drew attention to the way nation-states treated native peoples. Religious agencies and academics, especially, with their traditional interest in minorities, began to encourage states to honor treaties and to improve indigenous people's conditions. In 1969, the World Council of Churches declared that "churches must be actively concerned for the economic and political well-being of exploited groups" and must encourage "victims of racism to regain a sense of their own worth and determine their own future."[63]

In response to growing indigenous outrage, the World Council of Churches invited anthropologists from South America to discuss the situation of their native forest-dwelling peoples.[64] In January 1971, scholars gathered in Barbados for the Symposium on Inter-ethnic Conflict in South America and compared the effects of industrialization on native people. Scholars criticized governments for imposing political and economic models on indigenous people with the "purpose of exterminating" and integrating them. It was vital to change what was viewed as an "oppressive" relationship, anthropologists agreed, and to encourage indigenous people to manage and determine their own economic future.[65]

Two scholars from Paraguay participated in the symposium: Georg Grünberg, an Austrian anthropologist who worked among the Paï Tavyterã; and Miguel Chase Sardi, who in his presentation suggested that natives in his country were in danger of imminent extinction because they were "affected by the vices and ills of national society." Chase Sardi cited the Avá Guaraní as the "most acculturated group in eastern Paraguay, already almost indistinguishable from mestizo peasants. No one in fact, judging by his clothes, behavior in the presence of strangers, way of speaking Guaraní, or facial features in the majority of cases, would say that a Chiripá [Avá Guaraní] was an Indian."[66] In his country, Chase Sardi argued, indigenous people were on the verge of disappearing.

Anthropologists depicted state integration programs as genocidal and called for an immediate halt to missionary proselytism. In their "Barbados Declaration," the scholars promised to apply their studies to improving conditions for native peoples.[67] The widely publicized Barbados agreement influenced native organizations, NGOs, and anthropologists throughout Latin America.

Paraguay responded quickly to the new international focus on indigenous affairs. Stroessner urged his ministers to once and for all integrate the native people. Late in 1971, the minister of agriculture accused indigenous people of destroying the nation's natural resources and of costing the nation over US$1 million every year because they killed game and gathered instead of farming.[68] The official admonition was not lost on the DAI, which stepped up efforts to settle the remaining Ache and clear more indigenous people from the path of further economic development.

During this same period, Mennonite ranchers evicted another group of indigenous people. This action, like the treatment of the Toba-Qom by La Gauloise, would return to haunt the DAI. Mennonites by this time housed their indigenous laborers in twelve major work camps, which a visitor described in 1980: "Not all the Indians have been able to become part of the settlement program. Over half of the Indians had been forced to remain in labor camps. . . . There are twelve major labor camps in the Mennonite colonies, and several less stable ones as well. These labor camps are very impoverished and conditions are rather primitive. There are no sewage disposal systems or water supplies. There are many problems involved, and the Mennonites cannot be blamed too harshly for the situation."[69] A group of Enenlhit at a large labor camp in Loma Plata, within the western Chaco Fernheim Colony, had a serious dispute in 1971 over wages, deteriorating conditions, and access to land. After the argument, Mennonites expelled forty of the protestors and, with armed soldiers, took them in trucks to Filadelfia, capital of Fernheim, and forced them to sign a statement agreeing not to protest their eviction. Within only a few years, though, because they had no land, the Enenlhit denounced their expulsion to Mennonite authorities and the DAI.

By the end of 1971, ranchers were evicting indigenous communities with increasing frequency. Native people not at missions had nowhere to turn for legal assistance, since the DAI was ineffective. The Catholic Church had also sharply cut its contributions to the indigenist effort. Moreover, the DAI director took only limited advantage of Protestant donations because he was more concerned with dismembering indigenous communities and settling the Ache still in the forests. In fact, the resettlement plans are what ultimately changed the dictatorship's goals for the indigenous population.

Münzel's Charges of Genocide

In the winter of 1971, a German anthropologist named Mark Münzel and his wife, Cristine, arrived at Cerro Morotí to study the Ache. They lived for the better part of a year at the reservation and witnessed the malnutrition, abuse, and death of the camp's newly arrived northern Ache. When Münzel spoke out on their behalf, the regime expelled him from the country. As a result of unpleasant experiences at the reservation, the anthropologist accused the regime of trying to exterminate the Ache. These charges ultimately altered the state's plans for integration and improved the indigenous population's position vis-à-vis the regime.

Münzel initially studied Ache culture, but he could not help noticing their poor living conditions and the ill effects of initial contact on the new arrivals. He saw Pereira and his armed indigenous assistants bring northern Ache by truck and keep them as prisoners, guarding them with machetes. The rancher denied them medicine and threatened to kill the northern Ache if they spoke with the Germans, whom he also prevented from assisting the new arrivals.[70]

On 29 February 1972, Pereira and his Ache assistants brought another group of northern Ache to the reservation. Over the next months, "about 171 'wild' Achés were captured and deported to the Ache reservation," where they explained their arrival to the anthropologist in detail:

> The hunters first surrounded them in silence, and then suddenly appeared and frightened them with a lot of noise. . . . The hunters first raped the young women, and then brought the entire band to Silvacué. . . . A military truck transported both hunters and hunted back to the Reservation. The Aché descended from the truck and marched into the Reservation, a spectacle which we filmed. The captured Aché's marched in the middle, surrounded by the Achés of the Reservation with machetes, and by Mr. Jesús Pereira and his Paraguayan fellows . . . thus we learned that the prisoners were angry about being in the reservation.[71]

Münzel suggested that there was a coercive and concealed plan to remove indigenous people from their traditional habitat. Once at the reservation, moreover, Pereira tried to keep the Ache from hunting, changed their names, prevented them from performing their ceremonies, forbade the use of their dialect, forced them to change their hairstyles, and made the men remove their *betá*, or lip ornaments. "The Ache are being convinced that it is a shame to be an Ache," recounted Münzel, and "are told that the only way to escape from this shame is to become a hunter of Indians like Jesús Pereira."[72]

The anthropologist also documented Pereira's abuse of Ache women, men, and children: "In January 1972, he raped a 10–year-old girl and then threatened her father with death if he dared to denounce the crime. . . . Of the five girls between around 6 and 12 years of age, four live in the household of that somewhat sexually abnormal Jesús Pereira. . . . As of February 1972, three adult girls also live in Pereira's house. All these women are accessible not only to Jesús Pereira, but also to friends of his who visit the Reservation; as such visitors the Indians cite . . . Infanzon and Arévalo Paris, president of the AIP."[73] Münzel charged that officials took full advantage of the settlement process for their own sexual diversions.

Given the new emphasis in anthropology, it should not be surprising that Münzel spoke out about Ache conditions. In November 1971, he informed Milan Zeman, president of the CAIG, that Pereira was embezzling their contributions. In January 1972, he told the German ambassador that Pereira was attempting to capture more indigenous people. After the northern Ache arrived, Münzel told the CAIG that they lacked medicine and food and that urgent care was necessary to prevent an epidemic. In March he informed Bejarano, of the AIP, about hunts to secure more Ache and conditions at the camp.[74] Neither the AIP nor the CAIG took steps to stop Pereira's expeditions or the abuse.

During the fall of 1972, an epidemic of influenza claimed the lives of at least fifty Ache, most of them recent arrivals. Although the CAIG had recently donated US$12,000 for medicine, Pereira failed to protect the Ache even from simple respiratory disease.[75] At the same time, a Peace Corps volunteer named Dave Griggs, who conducted forest surveys for the United Nations' Forestry Resources Inventory Program, happened on the reservation quite by accident. Griggs was overwhelmed by the sight of the Ache, starving and dying in their shelters with no heat to sustain them. Later, he returned with food and clothing and made their condition known to Bill Berry, Peace Corps director in Asunción. Berry visited and found the Ache in terrible conditions. One volunteer who took part in this visit, Steve Herrick, recounted: "The people were at the worst of decimation, people dying from hunger. They were just like in a concentration camp, the smell was just overwhelming."[76] In March Münzel again pressured Pereira to improve health conditions, but Pereira responded by personally shoving Münzel, his wife, and their luggage off the reservation and threatened to harm them if he ever saw them again.[77]

People in Asunción now began to pay attention to news about the Ache reserve. Münzel, whose research was cut short by the eviction, publicly denounced Pereira in the capital. He found ample support among Paraguayan ethnologists and especially from the Catholic Church. The church promptly sponsored a conference to debate the Barbados Declaration. The Consulta Indígena (Indigenous Consultation) of Asunción, with Chase Sardi, Bar-

tomeu Melià—director of the Equipo Nacional de Misiones (National Catholic Missions Team, ENM), and Grünberg present, created the "Documento
de Asunción," which called on missionaries and scholars to respect native
cultures and guarantee indigenous people the full benefits of state development.[78]

Conference participants paid close attention to Münzel's version of abuses
at the Ache reservation, and Peace Corps volunteers reported their experiences to the businesses that had raised funds for the Ache reserve. Bank
of America, a large contributor to the new settlement, became concerned
that the Ache experiment might draw negative press. The bank requested a
Peace Corps placement, and Bill Berry risked his job to assist the Ache. Steve
Herrick was assigned to the reservation and charged with producing food
so the people would not starve. "But at the same time I was to keep an eye
on what was happening at the reservation," Herrick recalled, "as far as how
much meat from the animals was being bought and how much was being
slaughtered. I was to document that the old man Pereira was basically stealing the money."[79]

Two months later, the Catholic University hosted yet another conference
to address the natives' situation. At this conference Münzel called on Paraguayans to help improve the deteriorating condition of the Ache.[80] In response, scholars and Catholic activists began to use the example of the Ache
to criticize the regime's integration policy. As director of the Anthropology
Department at the Catholic University, Chase Sardi was highly critical of
settlement efforts and suggested that integration of the native population
was genocidal.[81]

Cristine Münzel and Melià denounced the state's efforts as "ethnocidal."[82]
Both Melià and Chase Sardi riskily positioned themselves firmly behind
Mark Münzel's criticism of the state's indigenist policy. They argued that
settlement policies would physically exterminate the indigenous people. The
Catholic University published both articles late in 1972, thereby extending
church support to the Ache campaign.

Melià's position as the director of the ENM helps explain why the church
adopted indigenous rights as a weapon in its struggle with the dictatorship.
A Jesuit, Melià earned a PhD in anthropology at Strasbourg and in 1969
conducted fieldwork among the Avá and Mbyá Guaraní. His encounter with
them completely changed his view of proselytism, for he discovered that
indigenous people led profoundly spiritual lives without professing Christianity. Prayer, justice, contemplation, and mysticism, Melià found, were the
foundations of Guaraní historical consciousness and ethnic identity. Indigenous society was permeated, the Jesuit wrote, with so-called Christian prin-

ciples such as mutual respect and relative economic and political equality.[83] He argued that, because the Guaraní already led such a profoundly religious life, it was not necessary to catechize them; rather, we should learn from them with respect and humility.

In his position, Melià tried to bring Catholic proselytism in line with Vatican II and Medellín.[84] He instructed missionaries to foment indigenous religious expression, so they encouraged indigenous people to once again practice tribal rituals. After Catholic workers of the Divine Word Order applied Melià's instructions at the Mission of Akaray Mí, the Avá Guaraní recommenced the visible practice of their *jeroky ñemboʼé*, or prayer dances. Changes at Akaray Mí encouraged a wave of tribal ethnic identification that eventually spread to other Avá Guaraní communities.[85] Catholic missionaries thus began to support indigenous cultural distinctiveness, which contributed to a rise in ethnic Guaraní identification and pride in eastern Paraguay.

In Asunción, Melià, Chase Sardi, and journalist Luigi Miraglia spoke out with increasing frequency about what they by now all referred to as "the genocide."[86] Melià declared: "The Ache reservation is an Ache graveyard." Chase Sardi added: "The Ache of the reservation are real prisoners in a concentration camp."[87]

This denunciation was especially threatening because Chase Sardi had worked in the United States from 1971 to 1972 on a prestigious Guggenheim fellowship.[88] It was only his international recognition, in fact, that kept the regime from silencing him at this point. The ethnographer spoke out frequently against Ache settlement.[89] The Catholic Church notified the Holy See of recent Ache deaths, and opposition deputies presented the Ache abuses to Congress.[90]

The regime responded quickly to growing criticism of its integration policy. After the DAI denied the charges, Bejarano at the AIP and then Infanzon asked Melià to discontinue the "bad campaign against the reservation because contributions for the Ache had diminished."[91] Ties between the CAIG and German businesses led even the German embassy to pressure Melià and Cadogan to drop charges of genocide.

When initial efforts to quiet growing criticism did not work, the regime took its revenge on Münzel. Not only did Samaniego forbid the anthropologist from continuing his work, but the DAI ordered an end to his studies.[92] Finally, the dictator evicted Münzel from Paraguay on fabricated charges that he had become sexually involved with the people he studied.[93] From the AIP, Bejarano charged that Münzel had "become a disturbing element, having departed from his role as a scientist to become involved [in] administrative affairs and the government of the colony, for which we believe it fitting that he not return to it."[94] At the heart of the issue, then, was the regime's growing embarrassment over abuses and the resulting negative press.

If Münzel had indeed annoyed the regime, though, Pereira also suffered as a result of the state's frustration. After Münzel left, Infanzon finally fired Pereira. In September 1972, the regime pressed charges against the rancher for causing too many Ache to abandon the reserve. Police jailed him for embezzling state funds, and he served a brief sentence but was soon back at his ranch.[95]

The DAI moved quickly to change management of the Ache, and Infanzon invited the NTM to take charge. Missionaries arrived in June 1972, and immediately built new houses for the indigenous population.[96] This time the DAI was taking no chances with mismanagement or bad press. Instead of approaching the Catholic Church, Infanzon went directly to a Protestant agency whose stated goal was to assist indigenous people in becoming economically independent.[97] Since Catholic criticism had focused on the Ache settlement, the regime was not about to beg for church assistance. The United States placed Peace Corps volunteers, who started "teaching the Ache how to raise crops, cook food, and organize their households." With new but honest overseers, the DAI finished a health-care center and started building a school.[98] The regime had not changed its plans to alter the Ache's way of life, but the DAI realized it would have to maintain a positive public image throughout the integration process.

The Ache themselves, however, were not satisfied with the administrative changes. The missionaries may have improved living conditions, but the indigenous population seems to have been displeased with their conservative religious instruction. Hundreds of Ache left the reservation and wandered through eastern Paraguay. Some natives returned to the forest and some took on odd jobs for nationals. The regime took no steps to protect them, and "almost every individual was victimized in some way" by peasants and ranchers.[99] While the dictatorship was eager to oversee integration initially, it was far less concerned with how contact might actually affect the indigenous population.

Anthropological Advocacy Raises the Stakes

Scholars and missionaries with closer contact to native communities, though, were very worried about how the loss of land would affect living conditions. Beginning in 1972, scholars created projects to help indigenous people protect their land and natural resources. By strengthening indigenous communities, these projects stymied the regime's hope of easily integrating native people into the larger society.

Geörg Grünberg designed the first of such projects to improve the conditions of the natives in Amambay Department. The Paï Tavyterã had once shared communal houses in large agricultural villages there, but by 1972, these had fragmented into over one hundred small settlements where they worked as day laborers. Disease had destroyed Paï communities, and nearly 60 percent of the Paï Tavyterã suffered from tuberculosis.[100] Within two years, Grünberg and Melià's new Proyecto Paï Tavyterã (Paï Tavyterã Project, PPT) had assisted the people in securing land for ten original communities while extending health care and credit in the form of tools and seeds.[101]

Grünberg and his team worked among the Paï Tavyterã, yet the atmosphere in Asunción was still tense from the Münzel affair. Chase Sardi and Melià launched a new program named Marandú, which in Guaraní means "information," to assist indigenous leaders in defending their people's rights and in planning and developing their own future.[102] Chase Sardi presented the project at the UN's 1972 Conference on Human Environments in Stockholm and won the endorsement of the International Work Group for Indian Affairs (IWGIA).[103]

Meanwhile, Münzel had denounced the Paraguayan Ache settlement policy to the European public. This led Amnesty International, the Anti-Slavery Society for the Protection of Human Rights, and the International Commission of Jurists to protest the Ache deaths. Next, Münzel secured the support of French ethnologists Pierre Clastres and Claude Lévi-Strauss, and the Norwegian, Swedish, and Danish parliaments presented the Ache case at the United Nations. Münzel offered his own conclusions in February 1973, at an IWGIA conference in Copenhagen.

In Paraguay, Münzel had focused on the poor conditions at the reservation. After his expulsion, he concluded that the dictator was hiding a sinister plot to exterminate the Ache.[104] He exposed to the world outside of Paraguay abuses that the Paraguayan press had been reporting for over a decade. His report, though, lacked Ache testimonies and ignored the indigenous experience and motivation. Münzel focused his attention on the DAI's integration process and blamed the deaths principally on Pereira, whom he portrayed as a crook and a violent abuser of the indigenous population.

After the Münzels' expulsion, as noted, Mark Münzel also began to accuse the regime of intending to eliminate all of the nation's indigenous people.[105] His only hard evidence was a CAIG memo of which he claimed to have a copy and a newspaper article, which he did not cite. What is more, he used loaded terms such as "manhunt," "wild," "tame," "free," "captives," and "slaves" to generate suspicion of the regime. The combined effect was a damning portrayal of Stroessner's government as a brutal regime that planned to exterminate all of Paraguay's indigenous peoples. Münzel's goal appears to have been to focus enough international attention on the Ache that Stroessner would have to alter or improve his plans for integration.

After Münzel spoke at the IWGIA, letters about the Ache poured into Asunción. Members of the Ethnology Department at the University of Bern wrote in June 1973: "We stand appalled at the inhumanity of the methods with which the 'solution' of the 'Indian question' in Paraguay is being affected, and which are hardly conducive to the reputation of Paraguay as a civilized member of the world community. Above all, we demand the immediate cessation of the heinous manhunts."[106] These letters merely repeated Münzel's charges and added superlatives without further research. Terms such as "heinous manhunts" and phrases like "wipe them from the face of the earth" attracted the press, and British, German, and Swiss newspapers all published letters. In the wake of the postwar Nuremberg trials and UN proclamations condemning genocide, European states were eager to denounce the premeditated murder of groups of people.

In the United States, the AIM protests at Pine Ridge caused the Nixon administration to respond cautiously to charges of genocide in Paraguay. The United States had long supported Stroessner, so the State Department argued that the living conditions of the Ache were an internal Paraguayan matter.[107] Still, on 12 October 1973, Charles Rangel, Democrat from New York, denounced Ache deaths in the House of Representatives. Later that month, James Abourezk, a democratic senator from South Dakota who had grown up on the Rosebud Lakota Reservation and mediated the Wounded Knee standoff, demanded that the United States terminate aid to Paraguay and investigate the settlement of the Ache.[108] The Stroessner regime, worried about its international image, denied the charges and claimed that Ache deaths were only an unfortunate result of the settlement. Foreign diplomats argued that the Ache perished because they had not adapted well to the "very huge reserve" where the state had placed them for their own protection.[109] Repeating its charges of Münzel's sexual impropriety, the regime warned journalists to counter any foreign charges.

Accusations from abroad had the potential to affect international financing of the dictator's grandiose development plans. Early in 1973, Paraguay and Brazil had signed a treaty to construct Itaipú, a hydroelectric facility along the Paraná River with a capacity of twelve thousand megawatts, the world's largest. Later that year, the Stroessner regime and Argentina agreed to construct yet another dam farther down the river at Yacyretá. Work on Itaipú began in 1974, and it is no surprise that the regime tried to overcome obstacles to foreign investment.

Portraying the integration program as beneficial, however, did not dissuade critics. Instead, allusions to the coercive nature of the state's plans only fueled more attacks. The DAI soon realized that the rise of interest in indigenous affairs made it necessary to describe integration in a new way, by promising to do so without changing native culture.

Not surprisingly, then, Infanzon turned again to the Catholic Church, which had stopped emphasizing proselytism of indigenous groups and also had proclaimed 1974 to be the Year of Ecclesial Reflection to improve relations with the dictatorship. The shift in the church's position, ultimately part of a conservative backlash in the Vatican, reflected the difficulty of sustaining a long-term antiregime stance. Growing radical activism had caused serious breaches within the Catholic hierarchy, and state-sponsored repression had thinned the numbers of Paraguayan clergy. In their shift to the right, Catholic bishops even distanced themselves from the Agrarian Leagues. In 1974, Archbishop Rolón shook hands with President Stroessner for the first time in years, signaling an end to the standoff and prompting the DAI to request further church missionary activity.[110]

The DAI also encouraged Protestant efforts. Infanzon hoped that the NTM focus on the Ayoreode, for instance, would encourage and teach them to adopt agriculture. For their part, NTM administrators at El Faro Moro relied on the DAI to keep peasants from settling on their property.[111] Late in 1973, when indigenous people began leaving the mission to beg for work and food in the nearby Mennonite colonies, Infanzon used Mennonite and military guards to confine the Ayoreode once more within their mission.[112] In another case, an Anglican supervisor reassured the DAI that his denomination was still working to integrate the indigenous population.[113] Such promises of support nearly always accompanied a request for legal assistance and highlight how cooperation benefited both religious agencies and the state.

With international human rights agencies focused on regime abuses, however, by 1974, the DAI had changed the way it presented its cooperation with religious missions and begun to stress that missions actually respected indigenous cultures.[114] The DAI still clearly intended for proselytism to alter indigenous lifestyles. Nevertheless, because of the Münzel affair, the DAI now promised to respect native cultures, even within mission work. Within only a few years, the rise of anthropological interest had altered the way the regime portrayed its plans for Paraguay's indigenous population. As NGO advocacy grew, indigenous people gained some leverage in their struggle with the dictatorship.

Nongovernmental Organizations Alter the Regime's Plans

In the years that followed Münzel's initial charges, NGOs expanded their efforts to defend native rights and land. Human rights organizations and religious agencies pressed the dictatorship to alter and improve its integration policy. Even after the Catholic Church became less critical, the ENM encouraged native autonomy. The Catholic University sponsored the most important project to help the indigenous population, the Marandú Project, and while Stroessner repressed the initiative, indigenous people used the project's framework to launch a pan-indigenous organization. NGO projects thus provided a forum in which indigenous leaders could, for the first time, communicate with the government. Pan-indigenous organization, attempts by NGOs to secure indigenous territory, and the ongoing Münzel accusations finally forced the regime to alter the presentation of its integration policy and, later, the policy itself. These changes led to more native resistance.

While indigenists organized projects, concerned individuals overseas refused to lay the Ache controversy to rest. In March 1974, Senator Abourezk denounced Stroessner and accused the United States of playing a "typical ostrich-like role of sticking its head in the sand for fear of seeing something they do not want to admit is happening" and, despite accusations of genocide, of pouring "massive amounts of foreign aid into Paraguay" to support Stroessner's "ruthless regime."[115]

Shortly afterward, the United States recalled its ambassador to Paraguay, and relations between the two countries cooled considerably due to ongoing accusations of human rights abuses and the absence of political reform.[116] The State Department tried to forestall any congressional action considered "adverse to positive relations with the Stroessner government."[117] Gerald Ford had pardoned Nixon following the Watergate scandal, and in revenge, Democrats tried for months to restrict foreign aid to punish Republican administrators. Officials in Paraguay were fully aware that foreign states and human rights organizations were debating the accusations of genocide. Paraguayan diplomats in Europe and the United States received numerous inquiries about the Ache and briefed the regime as the case developed overseas. In April 1974, the president of the Organization of American States' Inter-American Commission on Human Rights, Justino Aréchaga, asked Paraguay to clarify Münzel's allegations of "serious human rights abuses against the Ache Guayakí." "Please send us any valid document," the commissioner wrote, "that in your judgment might indicate whether or not measures have been adopted to address this issue."[118]

As the investigation escalated overseas, the regime turned to what in Guaraní is known as *mbareté*, or direct force. In April and May 1974, Gen. Marcial Samaniego summoned state ministries, religious agencies, educational institutions, and even a U.S. diplomat to a series of meetings at the Ministry of Defense. He distributed copies of UN Resolution 96, which condemns genocide, and a heated debate took place over the exact definition of the crime. The United Nations had ruled, argued Samaniego, that premeditated intent was a critical component of genocide. Since the regime never purposely tried to eliminate any native tribe, the minister contended there was no genocide.[119] He explained that Münzel was incorrect and forced participants to deny that genocide had taken place.

Initially, those invited to the meetings refused to cooperate, but pressure to agree weighed heavily. "There was great manipulation," recalled Meliá about how Samaniego used threats to force their compliance. When Meliá refused to cooperate, Samaniego asked him at least not to publish anything else about the Ache.[120] Near midnight and after five hours of discussion, the entire group, except for Meliá and Franciscan missionary Amadeo Benz, finally signed the following statement:

> Given the United Nations documents of 11 December 1946, and 9 December 1948, both declarations against the crime of genocide, and taking into consideration the conditions of Indians within Paraguay, and since our government condemns genocide, the undersigned declare:
>
> 1. In Paraguay the crime of genocide does not exist in any of its forms.
>
> 2. We reject the accusations made by the international and local news media.
>
> 3. We agree to publish this declaration widely.[121]

The denial was a tenuous fabrication, based only on the regime's defense of its own actions. As Samaniego explained: "Although there are victims and victimizers, there is not the third element necessary to establish the crime of genocide—this is 'intent.' Therefore, since there is no intent, one cannot speak of 'genocide.'"[122]

Almost immediately, Catholic workers declared that they had signed this disavowal against their will, and bishops immediately demanded an "exhaustive investigation of this matter with particular regard to the situation of several Indian groups in Paraguay, whose survival is seriously imperiled."[123] Missionaries clearly intended to continue using native affairs to criticize the regime.

The Catholic Church's response was not surprising, given the Catholic University's sponsorship of the Marandú Project, finally launched in April 1974. Regime officials extended support to the initiative only after its directors promised it would help integrate native people into national society.[124] On July 16, Marandú offered its first course at Cerrito, the Toba settlement one hour west of Asunción at Benjamín Aceval. At the initial encounter, the Toba, the very people that Infanzon had expelled for La Gauloise in 1969, voiced their dire need for land. Toba leaders responded eagerly to the presentations of videos, puppets, and filmed interviews.[125] Soon afterward, Project Marandú leaders formed a council and organized a cooperative to help them market their crops.[126] Within only a year, Toba leaders began to pressure authorities in Asunción to return their ancestral lands.

While the Marandú team in Asunción prepared to host a conference for indigenous leaders, in Europe Mark Münzel continued to accuse the regime of genocide. In August 1974, the IWGIA published Münzel's second pamphlet, *The Aché: Genocide Continues in Paraguay*, in which he broadened his original charges. He claimed that missionaries continued to conduct "manhunts from the reservation" to bring related Ache to the reserve by force.[127] In the pamphlet he describes how missionaries encouraged the Ache to seek out their relatives in the forests. Finally, Münzel argues that the Ministry of Defense's recent denial, in effect, extended "the discussion about genocide now clearly not only to the Ache, but to other indigenous groups as well."[128] This pamphlet includes information that is, at best, secondhand evidence.

The Ache later recounted that they had initiated contacts with their northern relatives themselves but argued that missionaries had strongly urged them to do so.[129] Indigenous testimonies show that, while missionaries encouraged more Ache to come to the reservation, Münzel exaggerated his accusations about deliberate genocide, especially in reference to the other indigenous tribes.

In retrospect, it is clear that Pereira, backed by supporters in the DAI and the CAIG, permitted conditions at the reservation to deteriorate until many Ache perished. Many of these deaths were the result of exposure to diseases against which they had no immunity. Certainly, some foresight might have prevented such calamitous results. Individuals contributed to the mismanaged settlement attempt. The New Tribes missionary who followed Pereira, Jim Stoltz, had a "John Wayne mentality" and was very eager to attract more people to the reservation, but, ultimately, the Ache themselves made the initial contacts.[130] Still, even if authorities allowed such neglect because they were eager to remove Ache from the forests, there is no evidence that the Ache people were purposely killed as a result of settlement.

What becomes most clear is that Paraguayans employed Münzel's accusations to criticize the regime and assist indigenous peoples. Chase Sardi, in fact, admitted that Münzel had exaggerated his accusations: "It is true that Münzel was a liar. Münzel lied and exaggerated some things. But that exaggeration made international pressure so intense that General Samaniego called us and told us: 'What can we do to change Paraguay's image?' I recognize that Münzel lied, but I believe that in that lie he helped the indígenas."[131] When pressed, Chase Sardi admitted that he and his colleagues had readily added their voices to Münzel's in the belief that a concerted effort, with international support, might actually improve the regime's treatment of the indigenous population.

As Münzel intensified his campaign, in October 1974, Marandú hosted thirty indigenous leaders from Argentina, Bolivia, Brazil, Venezuela, and Paraguay at the Parlamento Indio Americano del Cono Sur (Southern Cone American Indian Parliament). Inspired by Canada's National Indian Brotherhood's recent attempts to organize indigenous tribes of the Americas, for three days native leaders discussed their socioeconomic situation and finally issued a strong call for greater attention from national governments:[132] "WE PROCLAIM THE VALIDITY OF OUR CULTURES before the men of all the earth . . . strangers to indigenous communities need to realize that we are united, and that in the future it will be more difficult to continue the extermination of our brothers."[133] Indigenous leaders employed a distinct ethnic discourse to highlight their economic difficulties and used the construction of a pre-Columbian cultural legacy to present a unified front to national governments. Participants accused missionaries and governments of perpetrating five centuries of abuse and demanded health care and legal protection at the minimum.[134]

The indigenous gathering had important effects for native organizations in Paraguay. The encounter exposed indigenous leaders to tribal assemblies in other countries that used the discourse of oppressed classes to discuss their living conditions. Following the conference, chiefs began referring to themselves as victims of national colonization and abuse. Toba at Cerrito for the first time accused missionaries of being "criminals who had destroyed and continue to destroy indigenous people," and one even argued vehemently that "all the whites need to disappear."[135]

With their criticism of integration, the newly organized indigenous leaders and their NGO supporters heightened pressure on the regime to reform the DAI. Münzel's accusations had focused blame on Infanzon for mismanaging the Ache settlement. Samaniego likely had the example of Brazil's failed SPI in mind when, in December 1974, he finally fired Infanzon and replaced him with his nephew, Col. Alberto Samaniego.[136]

The DAI's energetic new director proved a definite asset to the department, the regime, and the indigenous population. After only a few weeks on the job, Alberto Samaniego began to encourage religious missions to provide what he called "comprehensive assistance" to indigenous communities.[137] The new director promptly recommended the delivery of medical services and supplies to native settlements and dramatically increased contacts with indigenous people. In 1974, Infanzon had sent employees to only five indigenous communities.[138] During Samaniego's first year, DAI employees made forty-one trips to twenty-three communities, including weekly visits to the nearby Mak'a village.[139] Staff members of Survival International, an NGO, testified that Samaniego had quickly turned the DAI around and begun to "play a much more active part in trying to improve the situation of many Indian groups in Paraguay."[140] Changes in the DAI's leadership show that NGO advocacy of indigenous rights had influenced and had already started to alter the regime's program for the native people.

While the regime redesigned the presentation of its integration goals, the Marandú Project put leaders in touch with other native organizations. In February, Alberto Santacruz, Nivaklé leader of the new Consejo Indígena (Indigenous Council), and Severo Flores, the western Guaraní secretary, attended the Twenty-fifth Annual Latin American Congress in Florida. Before his departure, Santacruz promised to refute the charges of genocide.[141] In plenary sessions, the leaders praised the Marandú Project for giving native people their first chance to organize but agreed that states must improve conditions for native people. In October, on the way to another meeting in Canada, indigenous delegates stopped in Washington, D.C., where they expanded on the achievements of the Indigenous Council and the Marandú Project.[142] The leaders' references to self-management and respect for cultural diversity show that they had acquired new tools to describe ethnic consciousness and were demanding equal treatment before the law.

Meanwhile, between March and May 1975, the Marandú Project presented courses at seven indigenous communities in the Chaco. In Filadelfia, the project urged Nivaklé to form cooperatives to market their crops and to press the state for documents, property titles, and adequate health care.[143] An elderly Nivaklé, Modesto Gómez, recounted the initial impact of the courses: "Our eyes were opened when we heard what they told us."[144] Listening to non-Indians explain how ranchers had taken over Nivaklé land made an impression, despite communication problems. Gómez had understood Chase Sardi to promise to distribute cows and also to assist his people in reclaiming their land. "But he was only talking," the leader recalled, "nothing ever happened."[145]

In eastern Paraguay, the Mbyá at Jaguá Po'í, near the town of Caaguazú, hoped to gain title to their tribal territory before Mennonite colonists filled the land with soybeans.[146] At the Divine Word mission at Akaray Mí, the Marandú Project encouraged the Avá Guaraní to revive traditional beliefs and strongly criticized religious missions. Catholic priests later abandoned the community as a result, and the Avá began openly to practice tribal religious rituals once again.[147]

At Puerto Casado on the Paraguay River, fifteen hundred native people still worked for the Casado tannin factory. Jobs were so scarce that indigenous people worked only one week out of the month and for only half the minimum wage.[148] Women spoke of receiving short weights on purchases at the company store, experiencing widespread alcoholism, and yearning to return to their ancestral lands.[149]

The Marandú Project, not surprisingly, provoked opposition from the military, landowners, and even the church, who feared that the organization would teach indigenous people to demand labor rights and land. Robert Eaton, the American owner of the largest ranch in the Chaco, forbade native leaders on his land from attending council meetings in the capital.[150] Marandú's days were numbered.[151]

One of the project's most ambitious achievements was to organize the Indigenous Council to lobby on behalf of the native communities. Nine leaders first met in May 1975, and in a letter to Stroessner pledged to "participate in national development, for the growth of the homeland."[152] They maneuvered carefully between honest representation of native goals and compliance with the regime.

It was unfortunate for indigenous leaders that precisely at this time Miguel Ángel Soler Jr., leader of the pro-Moscow wing of the Communist Party in Paraguay, tried to reorganize underground Communist cells. Over two-thirds of the small, splintered Communist Party lived in exile and hardly posed a threat. Nevertheless, security forces responded quickly to Soler's initiative and raided groups suspected of Communist activity. After the rector of the Catholic University reported Communist infiltration of the Marandú offices, police kept a careful eye on the NGO and especially on the Indigenous Council.[153]

Council leaders were well aware that they needed to tread carefully. In August, when delegates met with Minister Samaniego and refuted accusations that their council was a Communist agency, they obviously knew of the current witch hunt for Communists.[154] Indigenous people began to refer to their distinct ethnicity to negotiate specific rights from the government. They had different goals from those of the state: all they requested was toleration for their distinct religious and cultural expressions and the freedom to work for their own communal subsistence.

The new council empowered indigenous people but threatened the state's plans to control integration. Indigenous delegates made so many requests for assistance, however, that they quickly overwhelmed the new organization.[155] Indigenous people became more assertive in expressing their economic difficulties; in the following years, their demands to the DAI increased dramatically.[156] Ultimately, NGOs undermined the regime's attempts to integrate native people into the rural working class because they heightened the indigenous people's ethnic consciousness and encouraged them to organize with other native communities.

The Marandú Project was not the only NGO working to strengthen indigenous organization. In Amambay between 1973 and 1980, the PPT secured land titles for twenty-eight native communities, built a medical facility, and vaccinated native people with very positive effects.[157] The Paï Tavyterã returned from over one hundred small settlements to resettle original communities.[158] Even as they revived *kokueguasú*, or communal farming, they conformed to market demands by raising crops in tribal groups rather than in extended family units.[159] What is more, chiefs redistributed the proceeds to immediate relatives instead of among all community members, as they would have done traditionally.[160] After having tried for years to make a living in small groups, the people realized that communal farming offered the clear benefit of land and credit. The Paï Tavyterã thus re-created traditions to meet current needs, and their perceptions of their heritage helped them unite to defend their land.

As the Paï Tavyterã were reclaiming ancestral territories in Amambay, landless campesinos were also organizing to secure property. Conflicts between native communities and peasants grew in 1975, as peasants became militant and the regime moved against them.[161] By the mid-1970s, throughout the countryside peasants joined to defend land and demand adequate payment for labor. Participation in peasant leagues increased class-consciousness and taught peasants to defend their rights. Campesinos formed cooperatives to market crops and developed more radical forms of

protest. Rural activism, primarily in the form of land invasions and occupations of municipal buildings, grew until 1975, when the regime terminated
the agrarian leagues by torturing hundreds of peasant leaders.

Peasants concentrated their activism in the central areas of eastern Paraguay and in the territories of the Mbyá Guaraní, the Avá Guaraní, and the
Ache. As they occupied more land, they increasingly infringed on native territory. In 1975, peasants in Amambay Department invaded the Paï Tavyterã
communities of Ybypyté, Cerro Acanguá, and Piray Itá, as well as four Avá
Guaraní communities: Paso Cadena, Fortuna, Mboy Yaguá, and Itanaramí.
Canadian Mennonites at the Sommerfeld Colony, in Caaguazú Department,
attempted to expel the Mbyá who had lived on the land that the immigrants
had purchased. Native groups in eastern Paraguay began to lose their land
as non-Indians expanded fields for export crops.

The deteriorating indigenous situation led the AIP, in November 1975, to
launch the Proyecto Guaraní (Guaraní Project), which applied PPT methods
to improving living conditions for the Avá, Mbyá, and Ache south of Amambay Department. The Guaraní Project headquarters in Coronel Oviedo
became a center where indigenous leaders could report land disputes and
where workers could assist the Guaraní in protecting and reclaiming their
properties. Within a few years, the Guaraní Project added medical and educational components that proved of great help to the Guaraní.

NGO projects started to improve the situation of dozens of indigenous
communities. The Marandú Project had informed indigenous people of their
legal right to land and, through the council, had provided their leaders with a
forum in which to voice their concerns. The Paï Tavyterã had started moving
back to their tribal centers, and the new Guaraní Project started to produce
similarly positive effects for the other Guaraní tribes. Finally, the accusations
of violence against the Ache, which refused to disappear, continued to focus
negative attention on the regime's social policies.

Indigenous organization and NGO action on the native population's behalf provoked two reactions from the regime. The first was the formal reorganization of the DAI. Although Alberto Samaniego had improved the DAI,
the agency still bore the blame for having failed to settle the Ache quietly.
As NGOs increased their activity in rural areas and peasants mobilized in
unprecedented numbers, Stroessner and Samaniego created a bureau to replace the DAI. The generals granted the new National Indigenous Institute
(INDI) more resources and authorized it to oversee all agencies that dealt
with native people.[162] In the INDI bylaws, the regime promised to tolerate
the natives' distinct ways of life, including communal landholding, the practice of traditional religious rituals, and tribal government. In the decree that

created the INDI, the dictatorship, in response to the criticism leveled by anthropologists, repeatedly pledged to respect indigenous cultures.[163] The regime had not abandoned plans to integrate the indigenous population, but the accusations of genocide had forced it to promise to do so while respecting basic cultural differences.

There remained an inherent contradiction in this logic, which shows that the decree was actually meant merely to appease the state's detractors. The push for integration and respect for distinctly indigenous cultures were mutually exclusive goals. Still, as native activism grew over the next decade, indigenous people began to pressure the regime to live up to its new promise of toleration.

In addition to improving legal appearances by creating the INDI, the dictatorship also employed force to eliminate NGO intrusions and to obstruct private support for indigenous activism. Throughout 1975, public protests against the regime increased significantly as students, peasants, and political activists demonstrated against the never-ending state of siege. In November, Stroessner responded with more than characteristic brutality. To control growing opposition during the visit of Brazil's president, Ernesto Geisel, security forces arrested hundreds of peasant leaders and political dissidents, expelled radical priests from the country, and imprisoned social scientists and students. Several of those detained belonged to the Paraguayan Communist Party. The party's secretary-general, two committee members, and even pregnant women and children died from torture during one of the regime's most severe crackdowns.

Security forces, however, also took advantage of censorship to cripple the work of the Marandú Project, which had countered the state's plans to smoothly integrate native people and had created animosity on the part of ranchers, the church, and the regime.[164] The rising popularity of the Indigenous Council proved the last straw. On 1 December 1975, immediately following a council meeting, security forces raided project offices at the Catholic University. Police arrested Chase Sardi and three senior staff members, confiscated the agency's vehicle and program documents, and detained Gloria Estrago, the council's native secretary. Security forces charged Chase Sardi with subversion and of operating a Communist cell.[165]

Security forces drugged, beat, and submerged Chase Sardi in human waste. Ironically, prosecutors used letters from the Interamerican Foundation to charge Chase Sardi with spying for the CIA. The difficulty of representing both Moscow and Washington at the same time made the charges all the more preposterous. As a youth, Chase Sardi had participated in socialist activities but had long since foresworn Marxist ideals.[166]

Women associated with the project suffered even greater savagery; one attempted suicide as a result of physical abuse.[167] Chase Sardi suffered a broken rib, permanent hearing loss, and temporary loss of the use of his arms. Not until human rights organizations and individuals such as Noam Chomsky in the United States pressured the regime on Chase Sardi's behalf did security forces release him, seven months after his arrest.[168]

Chase Sardi had studied and worked among indigenous people for over a decade, and security forces could have easily apprehended him at any time. The crackdown was clearly an attempt to end the Indigenous Council and the Marandú Project. Small wonder, then, that many of the indigenous representatives lost jobs near their home communities.

The repression ended the Marandú Project, and council leaders continued to meet only after turning over the oversight of their organization to the new INDI, which compromised their ability to lobby honestly on behalf of the communities. Repression therefore seriously hampered the potential for pan-indigenous organization in Paraguay from the very beginning of native attempts to work across community and tribal divisions.

Censorship of the Indigenous Council marks the clear continuation of a shift within the state from plans for integration to the determined exclusion of native people from national society. As indigenous organization began to pose obstacles to easy development of the countryside and attract negative attention to the regime's policies in the mid-1970s, Stroessner's generals began trying to clear native people from the path of rural development and to limit their efforts to organize.

Conclusion

When Stroessner had a new constitution enacted in 1967, he took advantage of political changes to increase the speed of indigenous integration. Under the assumption that life in closed communities perpetuated distinctive cultural markers, the regime appointed a military officer as DAI director who would not hesitate to destroy native settlements if they obstructed development. Infanzon, in fact, actively helped ranchers dismember indigenous communities and expel native settlers from private property. The new director also sharply reduced the state's medical and nutritional assistance to the indigenous population. Most important, he stepped up attempts to settle the nomadic tribes and make their land available for rural development.

It was the DAI's efforts to settle the Ache, though, that focused negative attention on the regime's policy toward the indigenous population. The regime's most serious error was to tolerate a corrupt manager to settle the

Ache. As a way to hide this egregious mistake, Stroessner's regime forced anthropologist Mark Münzel to leave the country. Instead of silencing him, however, his expulsion only led him to attract negative attention to Stroessner's human rights record. Anthropologists began to pay close attention to both the Ache and the regime's policies.

Scholars in Paraguay took the opportunity to create projects to defend indigenous rights and to secure land for native communities. The Marandú Project informed indigenous leaders of their legal rights and encouraged them to join forces in a pan-indigenous council. In eastern Paraguay, the PPT and the Guaraní Project assisted indigenous communities in securing title to traditionally held territory and improved their health care. The Catholic Church used indigenous human rights as a platform from which to criticize the dictator and focus attention on the negative effects of his development plans.

Criticism from NGOs and anthropologists, at the very time when Stroessner was starting to develop the countryside, began to alter the regime's plans for the indigenous population from integration to exclusion. While the state's goals to influence the natives remained essentially the same, the regime reorganized the DAI and promised to respect indigenous cultures. Indigenous peoples, as a result, improved their bargaining power before the state and private landowners.

Although Stroessner in effect closed down the Marandú Project late in 1975, he could not undo the multiplier effect of political awareness and activism that NGO advocacy had set in motion within native communities. Foreign scrutiny, the rise of NGO activity, and the creation of a pan-indigenous council together altered indigenous communities, helped undermine the regime's public support, and changed the native people's response to the state's policies. Throughout the next decade, as the dictator actively tried to exclude indigenous people, native communities took advantage of these developments to mobilize widely in defense of land and rights.

5

The Indigenous Response to Exclusion, 1976–1987

We need these lands urgently. Our people can no longer continue to exist.

Maskoy leaders from Puerto Casado, in "Nuestro Pueblo"

This law intends to preserve indigenous communities socially and culturally, defend their heritage and traditions, improve their economic conditions, and achieve their effective participation in the process of national development and their access to laws that will guarantee them land ownership and other productive resources with equal rights to other citizens.

Law 904, Statute for Indigenous Communities, 18 December, 1981

Esta Ley tiene por objeto la preservación social y cultural de las comunidades indígenas, la defensa de su patrimonio y sus tradiciones, el mejoramiento de sus condiciones económicas, su efectiva participación en el proceso de desarrollo nacional y su acceso a un régimen jurídico que les garantice la propiedad de la tierra y otros recursos productivos de igualdad de derechos con los demás ciudadanos.

Ley 904, Estatuto de las Comunidades Indídenas, 18 December, 1981

Shaken by the international attention to its human rights record, in the late 1970s and the early 1980s, the regime markedly changed its plans for the indigenous population. Officially, the dictatorship pledged to defend indigenous interests. The 1981 Estatuto de las Comunidades Indígenas (Statute for Indigenous Communities) mandated that Paraguay grant enough land to native groups for people to live according to tribal customs and determine their own future. In practice, however, the state's actions told a different story.

The 1980s saw determined efforts to clear the indigenous population from the path of rural development. To exclude native people from national growth, Paraguay systematically granted less land to their communities than the new legislation called for, thus gradually freeing up territory for ranching or farming and slowly but effectively isolating the indigenous population from national society and development. This unstated policy of gradual exclusion, illustrated by the government's systematic refusal to honor the new indigenous-rights legislation, toleration of peasant land invasions, and outright attacks on indigenous properties and persons, marked a significant shift in plans for the indigenous population. While exclusion might appear to be a totally different goal, given the earlier focus on integration, it really was just another side of the same coin, a different facet of a similar social policy of discrimination toward indigenous minorities. The 1980s, then, began with positive legislation meant to appease critics but saw the implementation of a de facto policy of exclusion still intended to make the indigenous population disappear.

The downturn in the regime's treatment of them provoked a direct response from indigenous communities, which creatively resisted attempts to exclude them. The rise of anthropological and NGO advocacy, as well as foreign attention, encouraged indigenous groups to oppose the state's plans following Münzel's charges of genocide. Throughout the countryside, native groups united and struggled to gain legal ownership of their land, preserve their forests, and recover lost homelands. By organizing widely, communities defended what economic self-sufficiency they had from subsistence production. Indigenous people capitalized on both Catholic and Protestant advocacy to attract popular support for protests and to secure land. The native response to the missions thus creatively took advantage of the very allies on which the regime had initially depended to implement integration.

Indigenous movements to recover land were, in a few isolated cases, successful. In widespread protests against state programs, moreover, native leaders presented a different political plan to the country. Indigenous communities collectively requested toleration of ethnic plurality, equal treatment for minority groups, and national respect for differing ways of life, ideals new in Paraguay's traditional political culture. Still, these goals were neither uniform nor consistent but, rather, fragmented and contested, as were the native settlements themselves. Indigenous communities learned to skillfully and consciously employ their ethnic identities to secure political and economic advantages. Native defense of land and resources highlights new examples of native organization and ethnic consciousness. As civil protest against the regime grew during the 1980s, cooperation between the indigenous population and the missions helped attract, increase, and focus domestic and foreign criticism of the regime's policies.

The Association of Indigenous Groups

Indigenous people in Paraguay organized themselves on two fronts in response to national development and internal colonialism. The most visible was the Indigenous Council, which carried on the activities of the Marandú Project following the crackdown in 1975. In the countryside, far from Asunción, individual communities also mobilized to defend their land and natural resources. Rural settlements attempted to work through the city-based Consejo Indígena (Indigenous Council) and the new INDI, but when they realized that official channels yielded few results, many communities turned elsewhere for support. In the meantime, it was the council that directed early indigenous organization.

It proved relatively easy for the regime to manipulate the Indigenous Council because of the excessive violence security forces had used to close the Marandú Project. After the arrests, the Indigenous Council proceeded with extreme caution. The regime took advantage of the crackdown to further threaten indigenous leaders. While Chase Sardi remained in prison and council members were still greatly intimidated, Samaniego approached Alberto Santacruz, a Nivaklé leader originally from the central Chaco, and convinced him that Chase Sardi was a Communist and to not accept further advice from him. The Inter-American Foundation, though, which had funded the Marandú Project and helped secure Chase Sardi's release, promised future support only if Chase Sardi remained involved.[1] The council agreed to work with him, but its president and the ethnographer cooperated hesitantly in mutual mistrust.

When the council finally cautiously reconvened in April 1976, it was with significant fear. From the start, the dictatorship tried to manipulate the indigenous leaders. First, the regime refused to accept the name that native leaders had chosen for themselves, the Indigenous Council of Paraguay, under the pretext that it was too pretentious. The regime instead forced leaders to adopt Asociación de Parcialidades Indígenas (Association of Indigenous Groups, API), supposedly a less pretentious name. In September 1976, the API formally assumed leadership of the Marandú Project's program, and representatives from rural communities cautiously began to meet every two or three months at the Catholic University.[2]

The API proved to be an indigenous attempt to work within the state framework. Representatives sought better economic conditions through cooperation. The executive committee, especially, comprised a core of leaders who lived in the capital and struggled frequently over salaried positions and regime aid. Strategic accommodation has always been a component of indigenous response to non-Indians; Steve Stern documents such alliances in Huamanga, Peru, as early as the 1540s.[3] Still, cooperating leaders in Asunción were a minority in the new NGO, and the divisions caused crises and split rural communities.

The new Indigenous Council asked settlements to send delegates to larger meetings in Asunción. Since the NGO offered a small stipend, leaders competed for the new posts, causing even more division. Communities, logically, sent delegates with the most experience and who were fluent in Spanish and Guaraní. Precisely because of their greater experience, however, critics called those representatives *acriollados* or *aparaguayados*, "Paraguayan-like" in demeanor. The condescending terms implied that the leaders lived like nationals and did not honestly represent native interests.[4] Some, for instance, were more interested in accumulating personal wealth than in presenting communal requests.[5]

The council soon stopped representing genuine indigenous concerns and, instead, came to resemble native organizations in other states, such as the Comité Pro-Derecho Indígena Tawantinsuyu (Pro-Indigenous Rights Tawantinsuyu Committee), an agency that Peru's president, Augusto B. Leguía, had used to co-opt that country's indigenous movement in the 1920s.[6] In Paraguay, the API, as did native lawyers in Peru, also trod carefully between support for the regime and representation of indigenous demands for land and resources.

The regime's attempts to control the Indigenous Council seriously undermined native organization. The struggle over access to API stipends grew more intense when controversy began over leaders recognized by the INDI and those sent to the council by the communities.[7] By issuing false credentials, the regime divided settlements. As if splitting communities were not enough, in 1976, the INDI offered salaries to council leaders to further control them. State manipulation was largely successful as the API began to rely directly on the INDI for permission to work and even for donations.[8]

Even if the API was almost completely dependent on the regime, during its first years it helped some settlements. By allowing the Indigenous Council to at times channel funds to native communities, the INDI saved the regime considerable expense. For example, in 1975, the API helped Catholic missionaries purchase land and settle Nivaklé at Yichina'chat in the Chaco, and missionaries constructed a school at the Divine Word Catholic mission along the Paraná River. The API also provided health care and aid with funds from U.S. relief organizations. One of the council's greatest successes was its vaccination program. When Misereor, the Inter-American Foundation, and Catholic Relief Services sent enough vaccine for ten thousand injections in

1976, the NGO trained health-care workers who inoculated people in native communities throughout the country.[9]

The API also conveyed requests to the appropriate authorities. Because of its ties to the regime, native communities relied on the API for permission to market lumber, to transport crops, and even to make major purchases such as pickup trucks. The fact that communities needed permission to complete even simple transactions shows why organization was difficult: with colonial tendencies in place, the regime tried to control all political and economic aspects of natives' lives.

Nevertheless, if the state could be manipulative, so could indigenous communities. Savvy leaders used the authorities to gain material and legal benefits. An important component of organization was therefore learning to feign cooperation at appropriate times. Early in 1976, Richard Arens edited *Genocide in Paraguay*, a series of articles about the Ache scandal. Contributors described virtual "manhunts" in which Pereira and, later, the New Tribes missionaries pursued the forest Ache like animals and either killed them or forced them back to the state compound. Elie Wiesel likened the regime's integration policy to the concentration camps he had experienced in the Second World War.[10] Finally, Arens's contributors attributed persecution to the state's deforestation policy, because indigenous people obstructed development. According to Shelton Davis, the state "chose to see Indians as an obstacle to economic development and growth, and became a chief element itself in the massacre and extermination of Indian tribes."[11] The regime's plans for economic expansion in Paraguay were clearly damaging indigenous communities. Comparisons to Hitler's murder of the Jews elicited strong and quick responses. Münzel's books had enjoyed limited circulation; Arens provoked a furious reaction from the regime.[12]

Flagrant accusations by foreigners help explain the regime's severe response, especially after President Jimmy Carter started to examine human rights. In May 1976, Samaniego visited the large Paï Tavyterã community of Ybypyté and in front of reporters asked the natives to deny charges of human rights abuses. Samaniego explained that foreigners, backed by international Marxism, had launched a campaign to defame Paraguay. "The indigenous population rose from 35,000 to 48,000," the minister argued, not citing any dates. "If genocide had occurred, the population would have decreased." At the encounter, the Paï Tavyterã called Samaniego their "big defender," *ruvicha guasú*. They told reporters that "what is being said is pure lies." Neither side mentioned that the Paï Tavyterã lived north of the Ache and did not have the Aches' history of violent encounters with Paraguayans. After recording their approval, the minister distributed food, blankets, and ponchos, the gifts the indigenous people had been eyeing throughout the exchange.[13]

By playing along with the official discourse, indigenous people skillfully turned state coercion to their own advantage.[14] Likely, the Païwere carefully controlling their natural impulse to anger. Such temperance in the interests of loved ones shows the degree of repression that indigenous people endured.

Early Catalysts for Rural Indigenous Organization

Even while native leaders organized their new council and the regime moved to control the agency, rural groups united and pressed the state for improved conditions. Besides meetings with the API, native peoples capitalized on increasing mission activity to secure land, to create a pan-indigenous movement, and to pressure the state. At the same time, the expansion of crops and development projects forced many native communities off their land. Both changes encouraged native people to organize and to begin to pressure religious missions and NGOs to provide them with land.

During the late 1970s, indigenous people took greater advantage of the religious missions. Church agencies hoped for converts, and the regime still meant for proselytism to help change indigenous culture. Native people, though, approached missions as a source of economic, organizational, and religious benefits. They noticed that Mennonites extended credit and land to indigenous people who joined their denomination, so they began to pressure other missions for land as well. Native people also created greater tribal unity as they organized tribal churches and accepted literature in their own languages.

By 1976, Mennonites were overseeing the largest evangelistic effort. The indigenous population in the colonies had grown to ninety-five hundred and outnumbered the Mennonites. Over forty-five hundred native people, though, lived in work camps in poor conditions and pressured Mennonite administrators for land. In 1976, Mennonites created the Asociación de Servicios de Cooperación Indígena-Mennonita (Indigenous-Mennonite Association for Cooperative Services, ASCIM) to settle the indigenous people in permanent locations and "prepare the natives how to survive in a modernizing world, and to become citizens of Paraguay."[15] Mennonites hoped to teach natives their "concept of development and progress . . . based on their view of indigenous people as lazy and passive, [and] not ready to actively develop their own communities."[16]

The new NGO gave landless households a few head of livestock, a plow and cultivator, a wheelbarrow, seeds, and wire to fence fields. By August 1976, indigenous people in the Mennonite colonies were settled in forty-one villages in five "agricultural districts," farmed a total of 695 five-hectare fields, and marketed produce in cooperatives. Villages built schools for nearly seventeen hundred students.[17] Two years later, the colonies purchased 40,000 hectares and settled three hundred more families.[18] Interest in the indigenous situation motivated the settlements, but cheap labor and proselytism also played a part.

Indigenous people took advantage of settler assistance to secure land, jobs, and economic independence. Mennonites encouraged them to increase production and sold them tractors, but the native population stressed self-sufficiency. Mechanization did not increase crop yields. Instead, the number of acres in production actually decreased in direct proportion to the use of the new implements.[19] Indigenous people raised crops for immediate consumption and were slow to embrace outside values of accumulation.[20] Tribal ethics encouraged native people to resist integration into national markets.

Even when many western native communities rejected capitalist production, however, they responded enthusiastically to Mennonite proselytism. During the 1970s, religious fervor produced messianic movements as entire native settlements joined the Mennonite Church at once.[21] Through religious revivals, indigenous people in the Mennonite colonies perhaps sought access to the spiritual forces they believed had given the Mennonites economic success.[22]

The adoption of evangelical practices helped native people resist the regime's pressures for change. Because surrounding nationals were overwhelmingly Catholic, Protestantism offered native people barriers with which to distinguish themselves and reorganize their changing societies. Testimonies show that they felt that *cultos evangélicos* (evangelical church services) strengthened their unity, as baptisms, harvest rituals, and weddings bonded relatives and younger leaders in their new setting. Indigenous people employed the services to strengthen their political and communal fabric.

Indigenous evangelists soon convinced 80 percent of the native adults near the Mennonite colonies to join the native Mennonite Church. Leaders used evangelical Protestantism to unite tribal members, and by 1980, there were seventeen native Mennonite congregations with an adult membership of thirty-five hundred. Both the Nivaklé and the Enlhit tribes created formal church conferences that by the early 1980s had over one thousand adherents each. The Enenlhit United Evangelical Churches had two thousand registered members by 1982.[23] It was these Enenlhit from the Mennonite colonies who later voiced a concerted demand to recover their tribal lands.

Indigenous people also employed Protestant missions to reassert the use of tribal languages. In *Translating the Message*, Lamin Sanneh shows how the reception of scriptures into a vernacular language empowered minority people as it gave value to their languages and cultures.[24] In Paraguay during the mid-1970s, larger Protestant missions translated scriptures into indigenous tongues and emphasized their use. Mennonites had translated much of the New Testament into Nivaklé and Enlhit by the late 1960s. The translations encouraged education; native leaders learned to read and speak publicly to spread the Christian faith.[25] Open use of indigenous languages grew throughout the 1970s, immediately prior to the increasing claims of the western indigenous population to land.

The Anglican mission in 1976 reversed its earlier decision to use only Guaraní and began to encourage the use of the New Testament in the Enlhit vernacular. Soon the Enlhit began to express themselves publicly in their own language, and younger Enlhit started to "show a confidence and dynamism which help[ed] them compete" in local job markets, which could "be attributed in part to their . . . literacy in their own language."[26] During the 1980s, the Enlhit became some of the most militant indigenous people in demanding the return of tribal lands.

It is possible, although not very likely, that the shift in the Anglican program was related to the growing interest in inculturation theology within the Catholic Church. At the 1968 bishops' conference in Medellín, Bishop Ruiz from Chiapas, Mexico, called for recognition of God's presence in civilizations before the arrival of Christianity. In his encyclical "Redemptoris Missio," John Paul II later stressed the Catholic Church's concern for non-European cultures. Anglican leaders in Paraguay were likely aware of growing openness toward other expressions of faith within Catholic sectors, but it is doubtful that their decision to use indigenous languages was directly related, since by the end of the regime there were still no indigenous priests allowed in the Anglican Church in Paraguay. Instead, their decision appears to have been a pragmatic attempt to retain their indigenous members.

Contact with the Marandú Project and the Mennonites led a community of Enlhit squatters in 1975 to pressure Anglicans to help them secure land.[27] Anglican overseers, still hoping to integrate the Enlhit as small ranchers, decided to settle and enable them to raise cattle. They created a new project called La Herencia, or the Inheritance, which, over the next ten years, purchased three properties for a total of 300,000 hectares for three hundred

Enlhit families to settle and farm.[28] The decision to purchase land was, according to one Anglican administrator, a "dramatic reversal that proved very fruitful for the Enlhit."[29]

National Development and Native Resistance

Both religious affiliation and the loss of land led indigenous people to reject integration. Communities organized in unprecedented fashion after 1976, because development directly infringed on their tribal territories. Having crushed the small Communist cadre and peasant activists in 1975, Stroessner turned to developing the economy as a reward for his elite supporters. The largest threat came in the eastern border region, where a surge in peasant land occupations filled the area with cotton, soybeans, mint, and rice. By 1976, the IBR had issued ninety thousand titles to land to peasants from the central zone for four million hectares in eastern Paraguay.[30] New arrivals saw indigenous land as theirs for the taking. Japanese immigrants and 300,000 colonists from Brazil also moved into the eastern border region. Spontaneous Brazilian colonization quickly overwhelmed the settlement program and spilled onto native territories.[31] Perhaps the regime was unable to protect the communities, but, more likely, it allowed the land grabs to boost political support and export-crop production.

During the late 1970s, the regime developed even more along its border with Brazil, a lush territory for farming and cattle ranching. Development projects completely altered the eastern countryside. In 1975, the nation began a US$15 million settlement promotion in Caaguazú Department. By 1980, this effort had displaced five local Mbyá communities—a total of 280 families—from their land.[32] Between 1978 and 1986 Paraguay invested US$4.47 billion in fifteen rural projects to expand export crops.[33] In 1979, the regime put into place a US$54.3 million program in Caazapá to give out titles to land, create health centers, and build roads for small farmers.[34] The regime completely ignored the four hundred Mbyá families in the department, sedentary horticulturists who raised crops or worked on ranches.[35] The Caazapá Project soon proved one of the more violent cases of forced exclusion.

The regime's construction projects also boosted the economy, most significantly, the hydroelectric plants at Yacyretá and Itaipú along the Paraná River. From 1975 to 1982, Itaipú grossed US$1.58 billion for Paraguay.[36] The cost for construction, though, was also enormous. From 1977 to 1980, investors spent over US$250 million in Paraguay each year. The availability of credit, the booming construction industry, and the importation of consumer goods drastically altered the countryside.[37]

Combined, cash crops and construction projects raised support for Stroessner among the elite. The GDP rose by over 10 percent every year between 1977 and 1980. By 1981, Paraguay's GDP was US$4.4 billion and its per capita income had reached $1,372.[38]

Despite praise from foreign bankers, the growth was disastrous for the lower classes, especially in rural areas. Although the GDP grew by 33.5 percent between 1975 and 1981, in the countryside the infant mortality rate was almost 50 percent, and there were only five doctors for every ten thousand people. A full 80 percent of the rural population still lived on dirt floors, and real wages had declined.[39] The projects were a giant "economic co-optation scheme," through which Stroessner retained elite support despite deteriorating rural conditions.[40]

If the dictator traded development for political support, his generals also employed growth to manipulate the indigenous population. Resurrecting the idea that the Guaraní had helped create the glorious homeland, the military described indigenous integration as a part of the larger goal of developing the nation.[41]

Rather than benefiting from economic improvement and social integration, indigenous people suffered from Paraguay's uneven expansion. Development concentrated land in the hands of elite and foreign colonists. Moreover, the boom overvalued the currency, raised domestic prices, and led to a sharp rise in contraband.[42] High-level officials directed this flow of goods, focused largely on the sale of lumber. Soon, hundreds of trucks carried lumber illegally into Brazil, and by 1979, the black-market sale of lumber had destroyed the subtropical forest cover of the northeastern region.[43]

Development projects, the extension of cash-crop farming, and Protestant proselytism all encouraged indigenous people to resist the regime's manipulation. One more event that led to greater indigenous mobilization was the final fall of the API into the regime's clutches late in 1978. This undermined any last hope from the agency and instead pushed rural people to take matters into their own hands.

Renewed Attention to Human Rights

It was again ongoing accusations concerning the Ache that led the regime to manipulate the Indigenous Council. President Carter's probe of human rights abuses uncovered evidence of further violations centered on the crackdown on the Marandú Project and allegations that Stroessner intended to annihi-late the indigenous population.[44] In response, the United States cut military aid from $2.4 million in 1976 to a token $700,000 in 1977, significantly down from $16.7 million in 1971. Economic assistance declined to $3.2 million, down from $5.5 million the year before and $12.6 million in 1971. When the U.S. embassy inquired in 1977 whether the indigenous situation had im-proved, Stroessner tried once and for all to disprove charges and reopen channels of economic assistance.

Early in 1977, the regime invited Richard Arens, brother of Israeli minis-ter of defense Moshe Arens and harsh critic of the settlement of the Ache, to visit Paraguay, hoping to change his mind. In August, General Samaniego himself welcomed Professor Arens by assuring him that "'we love our Indi-ans.' He added immediately thereafter . . . 'it is our policy to integrate them in our society.'"[45] Accompanied by members of army intelligence, Arens vis-ited the Ache, the New Tribes mission to the Ayoreode, and the Maskoy at Puerto Casado. At each community he noted malnutrition, disease, despair, severe depression, and terrible conditions.[46]

Arens's appraisal suggests that the regime had done little to improve conditions. This was exactly what he tried to tell generals at the Ministry of Defense, who refused to listen: "I was guilty of libeling his country and his government. General González's assessment of me as at least a crypto-Communist was swiftly supported by General Bejarano. Pounding on the table with his fist for emphasis, he shouted, 'that the claim that there was genocide in Paraguay was a lie, a communist lie, a diabolical lie.' 'You, as a guest of the Paraguayan government, have soiled its honor.'"[47]

In retrospect, Arens's evaluation may have been too severe. When Har-vard anthropologists David Maybury-Lewis and James Howe evaluated the situation only a year later, in November 1978, they reported a much differ-ent scenario: "The problems faced by the Paraguayan Indians are not caused by unusual actions by General Stroessner's dictatorship and certainly not by any government policy to exterminate them."[48] While this last appraisal is more accurate, it still shows that development policies were damaging indigenous communities. At the very least, Arens's claim to have seen "the Paraguayan version of a 'final solution' directed against forest Indians" seri-ously rattled the regime.[49]

To refute Arens, Samaniego threatened to again imprison Chase Sardi and close the API council unless it countered this new accusation. On 16 February 1978, the API agreed to comply. "We have to please the dictator-ship or else we cannot continue to work," thirty delegates agreed.[50] Under continued threats, the API discredited Arens and denied that the regime intended to exterminate the indigenous population.[51]

Despite attempts to counter Arens' charges, the nagging allegations refused to disappear. On 27 April, the Human Rights Division of the United Nations encouraged Paraguay to "prepare a program of assistance for the Aché-Guayakí by September." The OAS Interamerican Commission on Human Rights took up the investigation of alleged Ache genocide, which led Paraguay's UN envoy to urge his superiors to comply: "I would advise preparation of a letter that would give details of all measures Paraguay's government and pertinent entities that oversee indigenous affairs in our country have taken. I believe you have enough information in the newspapers to prove that the real situation of our indigenous population is not as described in the accusations. Send this note as quickly as possible."[52] The UN investigation forced the regime to consider world opinion and to try to improve its public image.

The Rise of Indigenous Protest Movements in Rural Areas

The desire to maintain independent subsistence has long motivated indigenous resistance to outside threats.[53] Repeated integration pressures have led communities in Latin America to struggle for land and self-sufficiency. As in other places, the indigenous response to national development in Paraguay focused on retention of economic autonomy and tribal territories. The shift toward export crops quickly forced eastern native communities into action.

Meanwhile, poor conditions in the Chaco also led native groups to organize. In 1976, the regime completed the Trans-Chaco Highway from Asunción to Bolivia. Peasants flocked to the western frontier, which raised land prices and made hunting almost impossible for natives. By the late 1970s, the extension of ranching had left indigenous communities completely dependent on wage labor. These conditions directly provoked the western indigenous resistance movements that began in the late 1970s.

The first community to press the state for tribal territory was the Toba-Qom group that Infanzon had expelled from La Gauloise in 1969. Two years after the 1975 visit by staff from the Marandú Project, over 600 Toba in 140 families still lived on 114 hectares at the Franciscan Cerrito Mission at Benjamín Aceval. Surrounding ranchers had forbidden the natives from trespassing to hunt. Unable to farm their swampy mission land, the Toba sold crafts and did odd jobs. For two years, leaders presented their request to the INDI, the AIP, and the API with no positive result. Finally, in February 1977, frustrated chiefs told opposition newspapers that they were desperate to reclaim their "independent lives" and "dreamed of owning their own land once again."[54]

Soon after the Toba-Qom began to press for land, the Maskoy, evicted from Loma Plata late in 1971, lobbied the DAI, and later the INDI, for the land they had occupied at Casanillo. Over the next few years, the Maskoy, living in poor conditions at labor camps near Filadelfia, creatively showed their displeasure—between 80 and 90 percent of Maskoy became intoxicated on weekends and wandered disruptively through the streets. Maskoy women employed an even more severe form of resistance by aborting their unborn children.[55]

At nearly the same time, the Maskoy community at Puerto Casado also began to press the state for its former territories. Originally from eastern Bolivia, this community had earlier gathered and hunted on the western side of the northern Paraguay River along a tributary called Riacho Mosquito. Many of the Maskoy had worked for over half a century for the Casado Limited Liability Company, harvesting quebracho lumber for its tannin factories along the river.[56] By the mid-1960s, when unsustainable extraction had depleted the trees, Casado sold much of its property with total disregard for indigenous communities still on the land. As landowners extended cattle production, they expelled native people, and even more landless natives moved to work for Casado. By 1975, when Casado closed three of its four factories and fired most of its workers, 110 indigenous families, nearly 1,000 people, lived at the so-called *pueblito indio* at Puerto Casado. Living conditions grew worse as the labor surplus meant indigenous people could work only one week out of the month, although machinery ran around the clock.[57]

As the use of tannin declined with the introduction of chemical hide-curing techniques, the company trimmed its labor force and paid employees with company vouchers as late as four months after their services. By 1983, those Maskoy with part-time employment commonly received only alcohol in exchange for their dangerous labor.[58] The curious practice of payment in alcohol at first glance does not make sense, since the company potentially undermined production by poisoning its indigenous workers. Alcoholism certainly, in the long run, would only have cost the company as it broke down the community and created a rootless and alienated mass of workers.[59] While payment in alcohol may have benefited the company in the short term, the practice seems illogical, given the large number of people waiting for jobs at Casado's doors.

Had there been only a few workers available to Casado, it might have made sense for the company to trap them through debt peonage with alcohol. Payment with alcohol in Latin America is not common.[60] But given the tremendous competition for jobs, there should have been no reason for the company to create chemical dependency. It seems most likely that Casado saved money by paying workers in alcohol. Second, given the way that racism and economic advantage reinforce each other, it should not be surprising that managers felt no remorse for using alcohol to pay indigenous workers.[61]

Still, as David McCreery has shown, indebted labor in nineteenth- and early twentieth-century Latin America functioned only when and where the workers saw in it some advantage for themselves.[62] Dependency on the Casado, therefore, must have still been the best option available to landless indigenous workers, who suffered from tuberculosis, alcoholism, hunger, and despair. By 1977, conditions had become so severe that the Maskoy assembled funds and began to send their leaders on the expensive trip to the capital several times a year to press for the return of their land.

The Maskoy and Toba-Qom envoys to the capital spoke both Spanish and Guaraní, not their own languages, to garner public sympathy. When, by 1979, their case seemed to be tangled hopelessly in bureaucratic red tape, chiefs visited opposition newspapers and told reporters that their people would all perish if they did not recover their territory.[63]

The threat of mass extinction played on the regime's fear of further accusations à la Münzel. The chiefs' persistence finally bore fruit in 1979, when INDI director Col. Oscar Centurión promised all three communities that he would work arduously to return their land. The pledge had a dramatic effect on the Maskoy at Filadelfia, who almost immediately stopped their display of drunkenness and began to give birth normally once again.[64]

The three principal communities seeking land strengthened their position by finding allies among opponents of the regime, especially in the Catholic Church but also in higher education.[65] After the 1979 Episcopal Conference in Puebla, Mexico, bishops in Paraguay adopted a pragmatic approach to Stroessner that enjoyed middle-class support.[66] Still, because the regime paid scant attention to indigenous people, the church could support their rights without further endangering relations with the dictator. In August 1979, bishops pressured the regime to respond rapidly to the Toba request for land.[67]

Meanwhile, anthropologists had made plans to assist the native people in the Chaco. During the 1970s, the Ayoreode had abandoned their northern Chaco territory to clear brush for Mennonite ranchers. Concerned for their long-term prospects, in July 1979, German anthropologist Volker von Bremen designed a project to secure enough land to allow the Ayoreode to hunt and gather once again.[68] At nearly the same time, Cristóbal Wallis, an anthropologist formerly employed by the Marandú Project, designed an NGO to improve conditions for the Guaraní-Ñandeva. Most Ñandeva were also day laborers at the Mennonite colonies but had recently drawn together in a religious revival and renewed their efforts to recover tribal lands.[69] Urged on by their requests, the Proyecto Guaraní-Ñandeva (Guaraní-Ñandeva Project, PGÑ) purchased enough tribal territory for three settlements to market their crops because of improved access to water, tools, seeds, and food.[70]

Conscious of growing NGO projects and leery of further human rights scrutiny, the regime addressed Toba demands for land. The Toba successfully garnered public support, and by November 1980, major papers, even those supportive of the regime, were publicizing and supporting the Toba's plight.

But the ranchers played a final trump card. La Gauloise declared that the state should not give land to a "group of natives encouraged by international organizations."[71] The company's attack on Catholic advocates and so-called Communists ultimately defeated the Toba claim.

Still, native pressure was increasing as communities vocalized their opposition to state manipulation. Beginning in 1944, the state had encouraged the Mak'a to sell trinkets and for twenty years had paraded tourists through their village near Asunción and kept the fees, telling visitors what the Mak'a considered to be absurd things about their customs. Finally fed up, in January 1980, the Mak'a evicted the guides from their village. Soon, Mak'a youth were leading tourists through their community for the first time. "The tourists seem pleased to . . . hear from our own mouths what we think and believe," the Mak'a relayed to the INDI when they threatened to make their own decisions.[72]

Increasing collective pressure from indigenous communities and campesinos ultimately gave the Maskoy more success than the Toba. The Maskoy tribes lobbied the INDI steadily, which finally pushed Centurión to negotiate personally with Marcos Casado. At considerable risk to his job, Centurión sided with the Maskoy when Casado offered him land for the Maskoy elsewhere.[73] As publicity grew, in October 1980, Stroessner finally expropriated the property.[74]

The Maskoy movement capitalized on Catholic advocacy, but it was ultimately the Maskoy themselves who forced Casado to comply. Two hundred Maskoy families camped outside of Casanillo and awaited permission to occupy the land. They intimidated the ranchers, so the company posted guards, and the regime cited "the threat of serious social problems" when Centurión finally forced the judiciary to agree.[75] On 26 December, the company begrudgingly opened the gates, and three hundred Maskoy people joyfully rushed in and cleared a road to where they planned to build houses. Father Seelwische recalled their great joy at finally being able to occupy Casanillo.[76] Enenlhit leader Julio Esquivel thanked those who had negotiated on his people's behalf and promised not to disappoint them.[77] By the close of 1980, the Maskoy were the first successful indigenous community to reclaim ancestral lands from a ranching company.

There was no escaping the fact, however, that taking land from a private business to promote indigenous self-support flew in the face of the regime's policies designed to exclude the indigenous people. Since Carlos Casado was Argentine, Gen. Rafael Videla, the dictator of neighboring Argentina, pressured Stroessner to reverse his decision on the grounds that it would not be politically expedient to threaten Argentine interests in Paraguay."[78] Samaniego first fired Centurión and replaced him with Colonel Nestor Machuca Godoy, who had opposed the expropriation and promised to follow the "established line."[79] Native leaders expressed their strong disapproval of Centurión's removal to the media.[80] Severo Flores declared that the indigenous population was part of a "peaceful revolution that claimed land to work and survive."[81]

The regime continued its de facto plans for exclusion on 3 January 1981, when General Samaniego arrived at Casanillo and told the Maskoy that "President Stroessner had found a better place for them to live."[82] Two days later, with the INDI's assistance, soldiers forced the Maskoy onto trucks at gunpoint and drove them fifty kilometers to a plot north of the Mennonite colonies called Kilómetro 220, where the soil was dry clay and completely unsuitable for farming or ranching. In addition, the land was traditional Ayoreode (an enemy tribe) territory. The army posted guards to keep the Maskoy from escaping.

Supporters immediately launched a publicity campaign on behalf of the Maskoy. Bishops denounced the removal as a form of genocide.[83] The Maskoy wisely used the media coverage, and never before had indigenous people attracted so much daily attention in the news. The papers overwhelmingly supported the native group's ancestral right to Casanillo. An intelligent Maskoy leader offered this tear-jerking testimony: "We cannot do anything; we are here and there is no solution. The land is bad; it cannot be cultivated because it is clay and after a rain it is very hard and seeds that have been planted die. But General Samaniego said it is good, and he surely knows much more than we do."[84] His sarcasm indicates a sophisticated attempt to elicit sympathy. Pointed suspicion of the regime's real commitment to indigenous rights, portrayed in almost humorous irony, shows an additional attempt to win over the Paraguayos. The press rallied to the native group's side.

The dictatorship clearly viewed the removal as a chance to refocus integration in the face of indigenous mobilization.[85] Samaniego indicated that Kilometer 220 was only forty kilometers from the Mennonite colonies and therefore it would be easier for the Maskoy to find work and health services.[86] Here the regime was admitting to the most important reason for its dramatic reversal: with its potential for bountiful crops, gathering, and hunting, life at Casanillo would have encouraged indigenous self-sufficiency.

Meanwhile, to draw attention away from Kilometer 220, the regime finally tackled the indigenous census. In January 1981, forty indigenous people trained by the INDI began to collect census data.[87] While the stated goal was to gather information about demographics and land tenure, it soon became clear that officials hoped to discover the degree to which indigenous people had adopted non-Indian ways of life.[88] For a year, census collectors recorded types of housing, kitchen utensils, radios, bicycles, access to education, and whether indigenous people migrated in search of work. When the INDI finally published the census results two years later, the data showed that drastic changes were taking place in most indigenous settlements.

The indigenous census may have distracted human rights workers, but it did not improve conditions for indigenous people directly in the regime's line of fire. The removal from Casanillo was disastrous for the Maskoy. Totally dependent on army rations, the community was soon starving. Three children died from malnutrition in March, and the army hospitalized adults to keep them alive.[89] Still, soldiers prevented the Maskoy from leaving Kilometer 220.[90] Although the INDI dug some wells, by December the papers were predicting that the forced relocation would actually exterminate the Maskoy.[91] Perhaps Münzel had been correct after all. Faced with starvation, by the end of the year over half the Maskoy had escaped and returned to work at the Mennonite colonies.

If the regime saw itself the victor, however, it had not counted on changes in the Catholic Church. Having identified indigenous rights as a social area by which it might secure important public support, throughout 1981 the church lobbied for the Maskoy. First, the CEP filed a suit charging that the removal had been a form of genocide, but the attorney general simply dismissed the suit.[92] Catholic bishops, though, reaffirmed the importance of indigenous cultures and pledged to uphold native land claims.[93] When their actions are viewed in the context of recent Protestant gains, the bishops may have been trying to recover influence within native communities, for they also cited examples of settlements that had found fulfillment in Catholicism.[94]

Legal Changes and Forced Exclusion

When indigenous communities began to press the state for ancestral lands and critics capitalized on these protests, the regime passed an indigenous rights law, Ley 904, in 1981. The regime intended this unique legislation to quiet charges of continued abuse. From the outset, powerful ranchers opposed the bill, fearing that it would force them to remunerate indigenous workers adequately. One influential Mennonite, John Neufeld, personally asked Stroessner to block the legislation.[95]

Though Stroessner initially opposed the law, Samaniego saw its potential political benefits. In the face of ongoing opposition, in the middle of a meeting at the INDI, the general actually slammed his fist down on the table and shouted: "Whether they want it to or not, this law is going to pass!"[96] The draft that finally went to Congress in April 1981, was impressive: it promised indigenous communities the right to exist almost as distinct political entities and a channel through which to legalize their land claims and forbade coercion to force indigenous people to change against their wishes.[97] If passed as proposed, the law would have completely undermined the state's plans to allow development to push native people aside.

Indigenous resistance and demands for land in the interim, especially in eastern Paraguay, continued to attract media attention. An important conflict began at this time when Mennonites at Sommerfeld tried to expel three Mbyá communities from their colony. These conservative and prosperous settlers from Manitoba had, in 1946, purchased thirty-three thousand hectares in Caaguazú. It is vital to distinguish these settlers from the Mennonites in the Chaco; apart from sharing a denominational background, the former was a very different group that had immigrated for economic reasons and had no interest in assisting the indigenous people who worked for them. At first, the native people had helped the Canadian settlers build their farms and later labored in their workshops.[98] By the late 1970s, though, the Sommerfeld Mennonites had grown to fourteen hundred and tried to open farming and ranching areas for their children by evicting the Mbyá. Early in August 1981, administrator Isaac Hildebrand burned Mbyá homes and told the people to leave. Next, the sawmill fired its indigenous workers, and settlers destroyed fifteen hectares of Mbyá crops at Yhovy; the indigenous community of Yhovy completely lost its food supply for the year.

The Mbyá leaders immediately denounced these injustices to their allies in Villarrica, where a sympathetic judge ordered the Mennonites to halt their destruction. Leader Máximo González told reporters: "I have been on this land for over twenty years and it is mine. I will raise crops here, although it may bother the Mennonites. They aren't even Paraguayos, but they carry more weight than a Paraguayo. Even the constable is afraid of them, because they have money. Why their Christ, if they leave their brother without food? This is an evil religion if it teaches wickedness and hatred."[99] In July 1981, the IBR ordered the Mennonites to leave the Mbyá communities in peace.[100]

As conflicts in eastern Paraguay increased, the press took advantage of the deteriorating condition of the natives to criticize the government's development plans. The critical *Tribuna* denounced the regime: "Indigenous people are exposed to constant removal from their lands . . . deprived of the means of subsistence, and the worst of the case is that those responsible are large businesses."[101]

In Congress, meanwhile, a few deputies realized that an indigenous bill might repair Paraguay's image and secure foreign aid.[102] When Stroessner rejected the first version that crossed his desk, Deputy Julio Frutos convinced him the bill could only improve Paraguay's human rights image.[103]

While the law seemed hopelessly stalled in Congress, the Maskoy groups discovered that Casado had offered Casanillo for sale in Europe at a ridiculously low price. With help from local businessmen, in October, the Catholic Church secretly purchased fifteen thousand hectares at Casanillo for the Maskoy and, later, seventy-seven hundred hectares for the Toba group near Paratodo.[104]

For less-fortunate indigenous communities in the Chaco, conditions worsened in 1981, because the labor pool had grown, and Mennonites had mechanized their farms.[105] Like other native people in the Chaco, the Guaraní-Ñandeva had experienced a rise in ethnic pride tied to participation in evangelical religion and conflicts with employers. These people were, in prehistoric times, vassals of the Western Guaraní people and called Tapiete, from Tapy'yete, meaning "servants." There are questions as to their origin, and some scholars believe that they descend from the Chané people, vassals of the Guaraní who migrated to the northern Chaco. Others, such as Nordenskiold, argue that they originated among the Mataco of northern Argentina.[106] By the 1980s, after working among the Mennonites, the Ñandeva tied conversion to improving their living conditions through agriculture. To explain his baptism, one man said: "First Lengua [Enlhit] and Chulupí [Ni-vaklé] grab evangelism, then they receive help; when evangelical, can have land."[107] Working with ASCIM, a new AIP Guaraní-Ñandeva project purchased seventy-five hundred hectares of tribal lands at Laguna Negra, west of the Mennonite colonies, and two groups moved there in December 1981, and planted crops.[108] Over the next two years, the Guaraní-Ñandeva organized five agrarian villages, named Emaus, Bethlehem, Canaan, Timothy, and Damascus, which demonstrates their desire to farm with their widespread conversion to the evangelical Protestant faith.[109]

That December, in the native-rights legislation, national deputies also dramatically increased the INDI's power even as they cut potential benefits to the indigenous population.[110] The new law gave broad powers and ample resources to a reformed INDI, renamed the Instituto Paraguayo del Indígena (Paraguayan Indigenous Institute). The regime eliminated its original pledge to use tax money to purchase land for indigenous communities and to grant land titles to native squatters.[111] On 10 December 1981, the Legislature finally enacted the Estatuto de Comunidades Indígenas (Indigenous Rights Bill, Law 904), to show that it would defend indigenous human rights. The regime used the law to cover the detrimental effects of its integration policy.[112]

The deeper significance of Law 904, however, was the extent to which indigenous communities began to use it to focus their resistance. Catholic activists disseminated the legislation and quickly informed the Maskoy at Puerto Casado; five Maskoy chiefs traveled to Asunción almost immediately to press the INDI for land.[113]

Forty landless Enxet families moved to the gates of El Horizonte ranch, outside their tribal territory, and waited for Law 904 to work in their favor. When I visited this community in September of 1995, leader Felipe Caballero and his people had been camped dangerously close to the Trans-Chaco Highway at Paraje Pirahú. Caballero recalled that his people had known little about legal rights. When they heard about the new law, the chief impressed upon me, "we knew something about our rights and that there was hope. By law [we now] had the right to ask for land where we had been born and lived."[114] Caballero began to visit Asunción in hopes that the new legislation would somehow return their communal territory.

Indigenous leaders soon realized, however, that the regime intended to ignore the new bill, and they began to complain. When one chief learned about the additional power the law gave the new INDI, he exclaimed: "Then we the indigenous population will be in the service of the INDI."[115] Indigenous leaders understood that the regime still intended only to manipulate them, so they employed the legislation over and over as one more tool in their criticism of the state from within its own legislative framework.

Widespread Pan-indigenous Organization and Resistance

In the year that followed the passage of Law 904, native settlements in eastern Paraguay struggled with even more determination to counter the pernicious effects of the state's development programs. In February 1982, the regime began a US$54.3 million program to increase agricultural production in Caazapá Department.[116] Though the regime promised to survey and grant titles to indigenous land, speculators already owned all the land, and the scheme provided no funds to purchase land for native groups.[117]

The regime claimed that only ten indigenous families lived in the difficult-to-locate area and did "not have tribal structures or traditions."[118] Anthropologists, though, knew that over four hundred Mbyá families had long lived there—horticulturists who raised crops in sheltered clearings and kept to themselves. Engineers at the new Itaipú hydroelectric project also found indigenous settlements in their path. Itaipú planned to flood the huge reservoir that was to power the plant in October of 1982. The four Avá Guaraní settlements in its path publicized their plight; the AIP, the API, the INDI, and the Catholic Church pressured the dam project to resettle them. Instead, the company issued US$200 to individual households, far too little to purchase even one hectare of land.[119] The newspapers and NGOs quickly accused Itaipú of attempted genocide.[120] Finally, the CEP and the AIP purchased land and resettled the two Avá communities of Vacaretangué and Kiritó.[121] The INDI, meanwhile, purchased land at Yukyrý and Itavó and in September relocated the two remaining groups.[122] Late in May of that year, though, Itaipú opened a new highway through the middle of one of the newly resettled communities, and peasants stole lumber from the new settlements on four occasions.[123]

In the west, by 1982, the Guaraní Ñandeva who were scattered on ranches throughout the Chaco initiated legal action to gain back their tribal territories. Families at Infante Rivarola and Nueva Asunción requested land titles from the IBR. The Diez Kue community, on Casado property, asked the INDI to purchase their land.[124] The Ñandeva near Mariscal Estigarribia negotiated with the army for property ownership.[125] After a few years, the IBR granted all these communities land titles.

Indigenous mobilization highlights the importance that native people give to their physical territory, both for economic independence and identity and tribal consciousness. In Paraguay, as elsewhere, indigenous people defended their land to continue an economy that allowed them to "still eke out a living from the soil, as long as it was supplemented by other work, work that brought both respect and some traded goods for money."[126] Inseparably tied to economic motives was often the perception of ancestral ties to specific locations. In July 1982, Sommerfeld offered to move native people to Panambí, a property of 306 hectares already being used by other Mbyá. The INDI strongly pressured the natives to comply, because the German Lutheran missionaries already at Panambí might help "develop and integrate [the Indians] into national society."[127] The Mbyá, however, refused to abandon the land because it was their tribal homeland.

Rather than assist indigenous communities in protecting their territory, the INDI focused on ways to obfuscate real indigenous difficulties. Late in 1982, it published the conclusions of its almost-forgotten native census. The state had documented 38,703 indigenous people in the country. The largest group was the Enlhit, with 8,121, followed by the Nivaklé, with 6,667, and the Païˇ Tavyterã, with 4,986.[128] The largest age group was children in their first four years, which shows that the indigenous population was growing.

As soon as the state published the census results, critics charged that the INDI had severely underestimated the number of native people. *Última Hora* had already estimated the number of indigenous people in August 1981, at 70,300, almost twice the census count.[129] Private tallies also suggest that the regime misjudged native demographics.

The INDI admitted that it had encountered difficulties collecting census data. Some people refused to cooperate with state employees. Robert Smith and Ramón Fogel show that most Mbyá people, seven thousand strong and living on land they did not own, did not even figure in the count.[130] Because the United Nations supervised the census, there is no evidence to suggest deliberate deception. Still, in a country where the regime regularly manipulated electoral returns, such a possibility is not out of the question. Reporting a smaller number of native people might have proved that integration was succeeding and hence that the state was less obligated to protect native lands and resources.

What the census failed to indicate, however, was of equal importance. Even as cultures had changed and native people had widely interacted with nationals, the indigenous people had not abandoned their native identities, nor had they automatically identified with national society, as the state had hoped. In 1983, the API president, Severo Flores, explained indigenous organization and identification in a lecture at the Catholic University: "Indigenous persons today know what they want, know what they do, know what they ask for, and with even greater clarity, what they do not want. Every indigenous person always respects another group's culture, and for this reason wants their own culture to be respected."[131] Flores situated indigenous people securely outside of national society. Indigenous leaders had adopted a discourse that presented Paraguayos as oppressors and tied them directly to colonial European depredations. More important, Flores argued that indigenous protests had specific goals that differed markedly from the state's plans.

Indigenous protests notwithstanding, the pace of development continued unabated. In 1983, the Caazapá Project deforested land and built roads, and Paraguayan and Brazilian settlers released cattle and pigs onto native fields to clear them off the land. Hunters and yerba mate collectors overran Mbyá territory in search of quick profits.[132] Unlike the tribes that aggressively countered outside threats, these natives isolated themselves. Such a strategy had allowed two thousand Mbyá to continue living in ten tightly knit communities for centuries, despite relatively close proximity to peasants.[133] As the flow of invaders increased, Ángelo Garay, the eighty-year-old chief of Yukerí Karumbey, threw out project employees who tried to inspect his community and told them never to return, declaring: "They can do what they want in their own nation, but not on Mbyá territory!"[134]

While the Mbyá retreated, other communities actively pressed to reclaim their land. In 1983, the Maskoy at Puerto Casado sent their chiefs on the expensive trip to the capital on six occasions, where they revived stalled negotiations. Chief René Ramírez told me that his people's greatest obstacle was ignorance of Paraguayan law. Mirna Vázquez, the principal lawyer for the Catholic Church who defended the Maskoy, showed Ramírez's people that they would need to learn about the new Law 904. Their difficult economic situation made transportation a burden, so all the Maskoy pitched in to help. Ramírez remembered selling animal skins and fish and doing odd jobs. Most important, tribal elders insisted that they raise funds themselves so no outsiders could intimidate, bribe, or claim the tribe's success as their own.[135] The "whites," Ramírez recounted, also spread rumors that he would fail. Casado tried to turn his community against him, and some of his people gave up hope and left Puerto Casado while others began to mistrust Ramírez because he was away from home so much of the time.[136]

It was the endless legal battle in the capital that presented the greatest obstacle. Ramírez vividly recalled the seeming path he wore between the Chamber of Deputies and the Senate. He was often angered by the legislators' refusal to help and even wondered if the state did in fact hope to eliminate the indigenous population. Finally, in deep frustration, Ramírez threatened to bring his people to camp out in front of the Chamber of Deputies if legislators did not address their desperate pleas for the return of their tribal land at Riacho Mosquito.[137]

The Maskoy's sense of urgency increased in 1983, when they discovered that, even as Casado was negotiating with the regime, it had been trying to sell their land to investors in Europe.[138] This time, indigenous leaders directly addressed high-ranking authorities in the daily newspapers.[139] Their pleas evoked sympathy as they reviewed their critical living conditions and legitimated their land claims while promising to contribute to national crop production. Their determined efforts finally bore fruit. In November, the IBR tried to purchase Riacho Mosquito for the Maskoy. Casado again flatly refused.

The INDI sided with Casado. In March 1984, the agency encouraged the Maskoy to accept an offer that excluded all of their ancestral claims. The chiefs refused the offer and instead outmaneuvered the regime. On one occasion, INDI secretary Doldán arrived in Puerto Casado with a new offer and was surprised when the Maskoy presented him with a copy of the same map he intended to propose, one that again excluded Riacho Mosquito. "In relation to this offer," a leader countered, "we already had our meeting days ago and have rejected it. You have arrived too late."[140]

More aware of social pressure from below than was the INDI, when convenient, the IBR tolerated native interests. This was the case in December 1983, when it authorized the Ayoreode to occupy their new territory at Chovoreca. The NGO that was seeking land for the Ayoreode, the Proyecto Ayoreo, had in August of 1980 purchased twenty thousand hectares of tribal land for communal use at the Chovoreca Hill, several hundred kilometers north of the Mennonite colonies.[141] The regime, though, purposely stalled the titling process and finally, in December 1983, authorized the Ayoreode to occupy Chovoreca but closed the project at the same time.[142]

The attempts to return both the Ayoreode and the Guaraní-Ñandeva to economic self-sufficiency collapsed because of a disagreement over the best interests of the native people. While the AIP supported the state's plans to fully integrate the indigenous communities, foreign anthropologists had tried to restore their economic autonomy and thus had provoked censorship. Following the withdrawal of foreign project directors, the regime built roads, wells, a landing strip, and a communal shed and posted a priest to ensure that the Ayoreode stayed at Chovoreca permanently.[143]

The Ayoreode overwhelmingly rejected state management. Despite the regime's best efforts, by 1990, only fourteen Ayoreode couples had settled on the large property, and they were completely dependent on the AIP for provisions.[144] Perhaps the Ayoreode had discovered that, in a new setting, "gathering" as wage laborers for the Mennonites allowed them greater control over their own affairs than did dependence on state managers at Chovoreca. Guaraní-Ñandeva at Laguna Negra expressed similar views when they expelled the new AIP managers who tried to tell them how to make a living.[145] Unwilling to heed native calls for autonomy, the regime lost the chance to control both groups and finally abandoned the projects.

As in the Chaco, conflicts over land in eastern Paraguay also became more urgent. At Sommerfeld, Mennonites used more and more force to evict the Mbyá. In June 1984, settlers took bulldozers to native homes and fields. Clearly desperate, Demesio Flores denounced the violence and claimed that his people lived in terror.[146] Mbyá protests moved sympathetic authorities, for in August police arrested Mennonite leader Willie Hildebrand and jailed him for burning Mbyá crops.[147] The threat of incarceration cooled the colonists down and gained the Mbyá several years in which to plant crops and rebuild their homes.

The Mbyá protests, while directed specifically against the immigrants, can best be situated within the resistance growing against the dictatorship. In 1982, Paraguay experienced its first balance-of-payments deficit after a decade of growth. Although he was reelected to a seventh consecutive five-year term in 1983, there was little Stroessner could do to maintain public support when the long economic boom slowed. The Itaipú-driven growth ended in 1985, and, as the benefits of Stroessner's rule dissipated, opponents began to demand changes. Unable to deliver economic rewards any longer, the dictator vigorously suppressed opposition. The Catholic Church led the social protests, and in June, hundreds of law students and activists demonstrated in favor of a free press and for an end to state corruption.[148]

As they negotiated and organized resistance to forced exclusion, rural indigenous leaders quickly learned that the regime would ignore Law 904. Felipe Caballero, still camped outside the tribal homeland at Pira'ú, vividly recalled his frustration with the regime and Law 904: "You Paraguayans made and know the law because you yourselves formulated it. We do not know it. But how is it that you who made the law do not obey the law? This cannot be. . . . Now we know we have a right to our land and you do not comply with what you say. What is happening is very unjust."[149] The INDI had taught Caballero to mistrust the law, but he still challenged nationals to comply with their own legislation. Caballero had learned all he wanted to know about national society; by requesting land and autonomy, his people were rejecting life in any closer proximity to outsiders.

The frustrated Enlhit's attempts serve as another example of an indigenous community that took advantage of the religious missions to further their own agenda. Caballero and his people had learned about their right to land while living at Sombrero Pirí, originally an Anglican property. When the regime failed to enforce Law 904, the Anglican Church purchased two more plots for the Enlhit: 22,000 hectares at La Patria in 1983, and 9,474 hectares close by at El Estribo in 1985. Anglicans hoped that owning property would turn the Enlhit into successful farmers: "Our will is to continue to cooperate with the INDI in the line of action defined by the indigenist policies of the Superior Government of the Nation."[150] The Enlhit, however, rejected both Anglican and national plans for development. Rather, they accepted what the missions offered, reorganized their communities, and then demanded more land.

Still, the very process of requesting land increased contact with national society. Trips to the capital exposed indigenous people to NGOs and especially to the Catholic Church, which had increased its public protests against the state. The indigenous population's desperate rejection of the state's practices of exclusion can be fully explained only as part of growing movements to bring down the regime.

As such, in January 1985, the INDI presented a fourth proposal to the Toba Maskoy from Puerto Casado, but the Maskoy discovered that the regime had again craftily excluded their ancestral sites.[151] In April, the Maskoy accused the INDI of siding with Casado to co-opt their leaders and broke off negotiations. By this time, the public had embraced the Maskoy cause, and support had reached unprecedented heights. Never before had an indigenous movement attracted so much attention. Major papers, even those usually proregime, supported the Maskoy and denounced the INDI.[152] The embattled community had forged so many alliances that two hundred citizens, the Paraguayan Lawyers College, and the Catholic University all wrote letters in their behalf.[153]

Although the Maskoy mobilized widespread support, they were facing significant odds. Peasants had by this time become an important national force. By 1985, they had formed over ten groups, including the Movimiento Campesino Paraguayo (Paraguayan Peasant Movement) and the Unión Nacional Campesina (National Peasants Union). Supported by the Catholic Church, these organizations encouraged peasants to use communal marketing to achieve agricultural self-sufficiency.[154] In the first ten months of 1985, peasants invaded thirty-one private properties and forced nearly 300,000 Brazilian settlers back to their country.[155]

Father Pedro Theis arrived in 1986 from Germany to work among the peasants in Itapúa Department. There he found people living in such fear of regime repression that he described conditions as similar to the peace and tranquillity of a cemetery. Peasants responded eagerly to the courses his team offered and organized their own base communities to market crops. Theis vividly recalled the spontaneous and energetic organization of peasants eager for greater freedom and political possibilities.[156]

Heavy-handed Exclusion

Throughout 1985, the Mbyá faced a rush of non-Indian settlers moving onto their land and displacing their communities. The state had surveyed indigenous communities in Caazapá and parceled native lands out to recently arrived settlers from Brazil. Settlers cut fields, strung fences, and brought cattle into the forests.[157] The rush of colonists forced fourteen Mbyá communities to abandon their ancestral land throughout the year.[158]

The most violent indigenous struggle in 1985 occurred in Alto Paraná, near Itakyrý. Over one hundred Mbyá were living at Paso Romero, within the seventy-five thousand–hectare La Golondrina ranch. Owner Blas Riquelme was a powerful industrialist who until 1984 had been president of the Cámara de Industria (Chamber of Industry). For ten years Riquelme had pressured the Mbyá to leave their land. When in July they instead stepped up requests to the government for formal titles to their territory, ranch hands gave sixty-seven Mbyá families twenty-four hours to abandon their homes. Since the men were at work, women, children, and elders escaped across the swollen Acaray River to the woods. One man walked fifty-five kilometers to Itakyrý in search of help; his story made the national newspapers.[159] Riquelme posted soldiers and swore to burn Mbyá houses if the people ever returned. Still, with nowhere else to go, the Mbyá eventually made their way back.[160]

Pressured by the Mbyá and Catholic bishops, General Samaniego himself spoke with Riquelme on behalf of the Mbyá, but the rancher continued trying to evict them.[161] Ranch hands intensified the harassment. One day early in October, ranch manager Antonio Rotelo dragged the tribal shaman, Porfirio Fariña, onto a narrow log bridge over the river, shouting all the while that his people should leave the ranch. The manager hit the healer repeatedly with his rifle butt and even fired shots close to his head. Ripping off Fariña's clothing, Rotelo finally threatened to castrate him with his sharp machete.[162] The following day Riquelme himself arrived with armed thugs on horseback. They beat Mbyá men, raped several of the women, and then pushed over the people's houses with tractors and torched them. The people ran to the adjacent woods. When one couple returned for their possessions, Rotelo forced them into the trees and raped the woman in front of her husband.[163] The entire community fled in terror.

United by their expulsion, the community immediately contacted advocates in Asunción, who denounced the "arrogance, violence, and power of the large landowners" and insisted that the regime honor Law 904.[164] Chief Ignacio Perõ presented their plight to the press.[165] His graphic and emotional testimony provoked a popular outcry that attracted attention even from foreign human rights agencies and forced the INDI to purchase fifteen hundred hectares for the Mbyá next to Riquelme's ranch.[166]

When abuses also continued at Sommerfeld throughout 1986, the Mbyá resorted to desperate measures. In July, campesinos began to cut down the indigenous groups' last trees. Next, they fenced the Mbyá settlements with barbed wire to cut off their access to water.[167] To intensify the harassment, campesinos finally began to rape Mbyá women and girls. The Mennonites had apparently promised to promptly have them freed if by some chance authorities ever arrested them.[168]

These abuses proved to be the last straw; indigenous leaders traveled to Asunción to denounce the violence, but the INDI ignored them.[169] An important change in native consciousness had taken place after years of resistance. Their statement to the press is the first example of an Mbyá person claiming to belong to the Paraguayan nation as a way to demand rights and invoke Paraguayo nationalism.

It was not only foreigners, though, who were drawing public criticism. By 1986, Paraguayos were fed up with the worsening economy, widespread state corruption, and years of constant, heavy-handed repression. Critics used Sommerfeld as an example to denounce regime complicity with wealthy landlords. The Catholic Church asked Stroessner to either expropriate the lands or purchase them from the Mennonites.[170] In January, the church began the Diálogo Nacional (National Dialogue), a popular discussion about greater political participation and a national transition toward democracy. All year, antiregime rallies shook the country. In March and April, hundreds of peasants risked arrest to show support for the opposition Partido Liberal Radical Auténtico (Authentic Liberal Radical Party). The church orchestrated these demonstrations and led four large protest rallies. At the end of May, twenty-five hundred priests and layworkers paraded though Asunción, and in June, thirty-five hundred youth marched to support the Diálogo Nacional.[171]

Protesters again used forced integration to criticize the regime. The Catholic Church launched a national campaign on behalf of the Maskoy, denounced conditions at Casado, and distributed a logo that advocated natives' right to tribal lands. Labor unions, base communities, and peasant organizations all added their support. Nearly ten thousand people signed a statement asking for the expropriation of Riacho Mosquito. Lawyers clinched their case by showing that Casado had defrauded the state of US$3.7 million and never paid for much of the 5.5 million hectares it claimed to own in the Chaco.[172]

Such support of a native group was outstanding. Still, there is no escaping the fact that NGOs also employed native rights to further their own causes and to gain recognition. The regime's response was unambiguous. Stroessner opposed indigenous attempts to secure land, and the INDI helped destabilize indigenous communities. Between 1984 and 1986, the INDI undermined Avá Guaraní and Paï Tavyterã organization as it divided the leadership with bribes, exploited tribal factions, and especially when it extracted and sold native timber reserves.[173]

Even as rural communities protested the INDI's actions, the API continued to operate within regime structures. Early in September, as complaints against the INDI reached a new level, the API praised President Stroessner in a public letter.[174]

Superficially, the API missive expresses a high degree of support for the regime. At a secondary level, though, the letter shows that even native people in the capital were employing what James Scott has called the "hidden transcript," the use of "metaphors and allusions in the interests of safety."[175] The API letter can also be read as a tongue-in-cheek criticism of the dictatorship in which phrases such as "support received" and "in this era of peace in which we all live" stand out. More notably, for the first time, indigenous leaders identified all indigenous people as part of the wider society.

Encouraged by what it interpreted as signs of native compliance, the INDI worked hard to undermine the successful cases of indigenous organization. By 1986, the Paï Tavyterã had regrouped into over thirty communities in Amambay Department and had regained enough economic independence that most no longer depended on peon labor.[176] In December 1986, perhaps because of this success, INDI employee María Elva González moved to Amambay Department and co-opted leaders with gifts and promises to shower settlements with consumer goods, schools, and health facilities if natives abandoned the Proyecto Paï Tavyterã.[177] Then her employees removed dozens of truckloads of timber from indigenous communities.[178] The INDI also moved on Avá Guaraní and Mbyá communities, where state employees also stole timber and yerba mate.[179]

In other cases, the regime simply assisted missions in their attempts to alter native culture. On 25 December 1986, a pilot from the NTM at Campo

Loro spotted a village of Ayoreode known as Totobiegosode ("from the area of the wild pigs"), who were still evading contact with outsiders. Despite past hostility, three days later, missionaries and thirty-four Ayoreode left the mission by truck to search for the Totobiegosode.

On 30 December, the Campolorogosode, as Ayoreode at the Campo Loro mission were known, located the Totobiegosode and ran to touch them, calling out that they came in peace. [180] In Ayoreo tradition, touching an enemy indicated victory in a hostile encounter. In fear, the Totobiegosode killed five mission Ayoreode and wounded four more with spears. After burying the dead, the mission Ayoreode and the Totobiegosode resolved their conflict and celebrated a joyful reunion.[181]

Missionaries took all twenty-five Totobiegosode back to Campo Loro, where they treated them for minor respiratory illnesses and dressed them in Western clothing. The Christian Ayoreo immediately began to preach to the arrivals. A man named Ucarede recounted: "We taught them that the civilized were not bad and that God exists."[182] Missionaries tried to keep journalists out, but the Totobiegosode secretly told the press that they were glad to be at the mission because their lives in the forest had become very difficult.[183]

Other Ayoreode communities had also related violently to one another, and there was a history of conflict between the groups. In 1968 and again in 1971, indigenous people from the New Tribes Faro Moro mission had tried to contact and bring Totobiegosode back to the mission, each time suffering injuries and deaths.[184] The events in December 1986 therefore were the culmination of a tradition of conflict in which missions were directly involved.

News of Ayoreode deaths caused widespread anger. Newspapers labeled the December 1986 encounter as genocide and blamed the deaths entirely on the NTM. They argued that the missionaries were "tied to the purposes of the dangerous expansion of Protestant sects from the U.S., who are spreading like malignant fungi within our traditional Catholic populations."[185] Even the proregime newspaper *Hoy* reported that the NTM "persistently tried to destroy principal Ayoreode values, beliefs, and symbols" and forced converts into hard labor to prepare them as workers for nearby Mennonite colonists.[186] Oleg Vysokolan charged that "the work of New Tribes is an offense to our nation. Their job is an aggressive act toward the state, the INDI, and every citizen."[187]

The regime had encouraged the religious missions to help change indigenous people, but the deaths show that cultural changes were also taking place on indigenous initiative. The Ayoreode had themselves sought out and brought their relatives to the mission. Evangelism was taking the place of earlier intertribal warfare, and knowledge of scriptures was becoming the way the community now tried to control its contact with outsiders. The Ayoreode had adapted their worldview, language, culture, and beliefs to their new economic and social context.[188]

Unlike all the NGO advocates for the indigenous population, only the INDI strongly supported the NTM's choice to settle the Totobiegosode. The regime praised farming and cattle-ranching programs as appropriate for the once-nomadic Ayoreode. Former NTM director Norman Fry explained the mission's congenial relationship with the dictatorship: "Overall we never had any trouble with the Paraguayan government. They have been very cooperative with us and us with them. We've always had a good relationship with the minister of defense, and with the president himself."[189]

Meanwhile, indigenous communities continued to oppose the regime's plans. In January 1987, as Paraguayos staged stronger antigovernment demonstrations, the Maskoy demanded that the IBR expropriate Riacho Mosquito. The embattled tribe appealed directly to the Senate in June, to capitalize on the political turmoil. Outspoken leader René Ramírez attributed their extreme action directly to the INDI's negative posture.[190]

As protests mounted, Stroessner caved to popular pressure. In April, he finally lifted the state of siege that had been in effect almost continuously since 1954, and on 16 July, the Legislature finally promised to expropriate Riacho Mosquito.[191] To accomplish this goal, a large labor union and the AIP championed the Maskoy cause while the Catholic Church presented three thousand additional signatures to Congress. It proved too much for the regime to bear, given the political and economic climate.[192]

By this time, indigenous activism had gained a momentum never before seen in Paraguay. Becoming an informal part of the wider social protest encouraged native people to take daring steps. The Paï Tavyterã communities united to oppose regime intrusion. In July 1987, Paï leaders accused top INDI officials of ignoring earlier promises. They expelled the INDI and forbade regime employees from ever returning.[193] Later, Paï Tavyterã even took INDI workers to court, sending González into hiding. The regime's intrusion had led to alcoholism and disease in Paï communities, not to mention a crisis in tribal leadership and agricultural production.[194] Still, indigenous people from Amambay had defended their tribal lands, resources, and autonomy from government officials.[195]

The popular uprising finally got the best of the weakened regime. On 30 July, the Senate, citing the "long and painful process of the indigenous population," unanimously expropriated 30,103 hectares at Riacho Mosquito from Casado for three hundred Maskoy families."[196]

Although securing land for the Maskoy was another attempt to dampen rising opposition, the campaign still stands as a monument to indigenous organization. By pushing their case against impressive odds, the community came together to repudiate integration and won back some economic autonomy.

The Maskoy success was an unusual victory. Most communities did not score impressive gains even with valiant effort. Still, struggles for land transformed indigenous communities. Most important, resistance tied a collective native allegiance to a distinct way of life and strengthened it. At the end of August 1987, religious and political leaders from eighteen Avá Guaraní communities met at Fortuna after having defeated an INDI attack on their forests. Together the chiefs formulated a response to outside threats:

> We have prayed . . . four days and nights. We have talked much about . . . [the] culture . . . our God and our ancestors have left for our own way of life. We have also seen that we cannot give it up, we the Guaraní, as it is a gift from our God. We also see attempts to introduce another culture among us, which destroys members of our community, our descendants, because it weakens them. Therefore, after much discussion, we have decided these points: In all Guaraní-Chiripá communities we must strengthen our Guaraní culture; we need to revitalize our dances. We the Guaraní need to live like Guaraní if we wish to be authentic.[197]

This declaration demonstrates a strong and united resolve to identify with tribal religious beliefs and communal landholding and to reject state development.[198] Rejecting a Paraguayo or Western way of life, indigenous leaders believed, might ensure that their descendants would still call themselves Avá, that is, "people."

While the Maskoy recovered some of their ancestral lands and the Avá rejected integration, many more communities were unable to turn away outside pressures. Throughout 1987, settlers at Sommerfeld continued to destroy Mbyá fields and forests and to sow them with grass and crops. By this time, the Kilometer 225 community could use only twenty of its earlier four hundred hectares. In October, Juan Gauto, from Yaguarí, denounced their situation.[199]

In Caazapá time had also run out for the Mbyá. Despite a slap on the wrist from the World Bank in 1987, the state continued to build roads, and massive deforestation continued unabated. Logging in Caazapá Department and the destruction of the forest there forced the indigenous population into new productive activities.[200] Guaraní agroforestry had depended on tens of thousands of forest hectares for sustainable extraction, so the loss of land pushed native groups onto increasingly smaller plots, where they lost critical protein from the jungle. As the wildcats and foxes perished, the Guaraní also lost income from the sale of pelts. Without agroforestry, they planted cotton and tobacco. These crops, though, provided only a single product at harvest, so farmers starved during the growing season and went into debt to purchase tools, herbicides, and insecticides, besides food for their families.[201]

Conflicts with the indigenous population only added fuel to the growing number of demonstrations in the capital. The Catholic Church gained mileage in August 1987, when it announced that Pope John Paul II would visit the following year and would meet indigenous people at Santa Teresita mission in the Chaco.[202] The prospect of a papal visit, the worsening economy, and the recently lifted siege raised the number and intensity of demonstrations to an unprecedented level. On 30 August, the church united all of the opposition in a massive show of power as Archbishop Rolón led thirty-five thousand workers, students, laypersons, and priests on a silent march to the National Cathedral. With this demonstration, the largest in Stroessner's thirty-three-year tenure, people quietly demanded an end to repression, corruption, and economic crisis.[203]

Violent encounters in the countryside increased. In November, ranchers attacked eleven Paï Tavyterã who had stopped to rest along a road north of Sommerfeld. Assailants shot the men, raped the women, then hacked them to pieces with machetes and burned the entire group.[204] Police never solved the crime and soon released the suspects, all influential landowners.

Although the regime still supported coercive attempts to limit native autonomy and indigenous people continued to resist integration, the struggle had clearly altered both sides. The Paï Tavyterã victims had been traveling to a neighboring ranch for seasonal work rather than relying on horticulture, as their grandparents had done.

The need to survive and to resist caused momentous changes in native cultures, especially in the form of greater involvement in national affairs. Ironically, just as the Maskoy finally took their appeal for land directly to the Legislature, it was often the very desire to reject national pressures that drew indigenous people even more into Paraguayan society. To secure widespread public support, for instance, the Maskoy, Mbyá, and Avá Guaraní all relied heavily on Catholic legal services. As Catholic authorities must have hoped, such dependence elicited greater sympathy for the church from the indigenous population. In December 1987, indigenous people participated for the first time in the annual pilgrimage to the shrine of the Virgin of Caacupé. Every year thousands of faithful, some on their knees, made the thirty-five-kilometer uphill pilgrimage from Asunción to visit the shrine. This time the church welcomed eight indigenous people to Caacupé, where they read scriptures in their own languages to the entire assembly. An Enenlhit man from Puerto Casado declared his devotion to Catholicism: "I believe in God, the Virgin, we are Catholics. We pray much and have faith. We always pray the rosary and ask to receive our lands, we tried for so many years and for so long that finally we received them."[205] Lucio Alfert, vicar of the Chaco, decried the theft of indigenous land and promised that the unprecedented pilgrimage would show indigenous people that, although in the past they had been excluded, they were now true members of the church and the nation.[206] Bishop Alfert challenged indígenas to help create a new Paraguay, of justice, peace, and liberty.

If struggles against state exclusion and development changed indigenous communities, though, they also altered the regime's plans. Stroessner actually agreed to an indigenous rights law and at least now purported to honor natives' human rights. In December 1987, minister of defense Martínez praised Law 904 as the regime's outstanding achievement for indigenous people and part of Paraguay's contribution to global progress.[207] After indigenous people joined Paraguayos to oppose the tottering regime, the dictator could no longer use force to integrate into or even to exclude native communities from his development scheme. Rather, indigenous protests forced him to promise to respect their distinct ways of life. The struggles of the indigenous population altered their communities and actually focused criticism on the thirty-three-year-old regime.

Conclusion

Indigenous people in Paraguay widely opposed Stroessner's attempts to exclude them from national development. Communities organized on two levels. In the capital, native people formed the Association of Indigenous Groups. While the API channeled some medical assistance and supplies to communities, when rural settlements withdrew their support, they forced API to pay obeisance to the regime to continue its work. With force on his side, the dictator easily controlled formal native organization.

The rural areas saw extensive indigenous mobilization during the 1980s. Communities joined forces to gain ownership of their land, protect resources, and recover their ancestral homelands. Although many communities organized in a united front, they were largely unable to withstand the strength of the forces arrayed against them. Hydroelectric plants and rural development programs inevitably boosted export-crop farming and deforestation and threatened indigenous land by extending peasant settlements.

Native communities formed alliances with NGOs, the Catholic Church, and the media. By adding their demands to growing antiregime protests, the indigenous population helped weaken support for the regime at a critical time.

Indigenous people were creative in their use of religious missions to recover some economic autonomy. Their leaders procured legal advice from the Catholic Church at precisely the time when it had to rely on the lower classes to sustain its anti-Stroessner campaign. Indigenous people in western Paraguay used Protestant organizations to secure land. Thus, while the regime intended for the missions to alter native cultures, indigenous people shaped religious advocacy to meet their own goals.

The ironic and anomalous character of the indigenous struggle was that native organization ultimately succeeded only to the extent to which communities and individuals joined national structures. To defend natural resources and land, indigenous communities appealed directly to an enemy intent on ending their independence and cultural differences. Trips to Asunción, reliance on the media, and cooperation with the church all had an effect. Indigenous leaders who joined nationals in the capital were soon trapped in the regime's economic net. More startling is the degree to which native communities that collectively requested toleration for ethnic plurality, equal rights before the law, and respect for economic independence came to rely on nationals to achieve these goals. The very protests that focused criticism on the dictatorship's social policies actually furthered integration of the indigenous population.

6

Indigenous Mobilization and Democracy in Paraguay, 1988–1992

The communities demand greater respect and better treatment from whites or Paraguayans. The date 12 October [1992] will be a day of mourning because it recalls the beginning of the extermination of our brothers.

Severo Flores and Antonio Portillo, "Indígenas quieren que se respeten sus comunidades"

What I want, from this moment on, is for you to put your shoulder to the wheel and begin to work, so as to gradually move forward and be able to feed all your families.

Pres. Andrés Rodríguez, "Rodríguez inauguró una escuela para indígenas"

[The Constitution] will be a way to guarantee real participation of our country's indigenous communities, which gave us their language—Guaraní—the main pillar of national cohesion and identity of which we are proud.

Celso Velázquez and Julio César Frutos

At first glance, Stroessner's last year in power does not appear to have seen further integration of the native population. Fighting for control, the dictatorship brutally repressed dissent and focused on conflicts within the party. Indigenous groups mobilized as never before to oppose exclusionary policies, keep their land, and retain some economic autonomy. In their mobilization, native people mirrored indigenous activism elsewhere in Latin America. They refined an ethnic discourse and used it to maintain ideological barriers and defend their territories. Strengthened by an increasingly militant consciousness, displaced communities joined other opponents of the regime to call for political and economic changes. When the regime finally collapsed, native people awaited benefits from the new democracy. Integrated far more than ever before, they nevertheless faced a formidable struggle to protect their communities and resources.

In dozens of rural protests, indigenous communities demanded the right to continue a semiautonomous existence on ancestral land. Most of these conflicts resulted from the extension of cash-crop farming, peasant settlements, and development projects into what had been native territories. Indigenous settlements rejected expansion that drastically altered their environment and land. Native opposition obstructed the success of these efforts and helped undermine the regime's control. Indigenous people called widespread attention to human rights abuses and provided ample fuel for Stroessner's critics. By adding their voices to those of the Catholic Church, labor unions, and opposition parties, native people joined the discontent that marked the regime's last years.

Participation in protests, however, did not automatically assure native people equal rights in the government that followed Stroessner. The regime had granted them legal recognition in 1981, and though the new president, Andrés Rodríguez, promised representation and land reform, prejudice still ran deep in Paraguay. Thus, the general who replaced Stroessner revived the integration/exclusion policy regarding natives.

Indigenous people mobilized widely to oppose this disappointing turn and offered Paraguayans their own vision of a multicultural and more democratic state. The INDI, largely staffed by former employees of the Stroessner regime, countered indigenous mobilization in a continuing attempt to make natives disappear through integration. As did native people in other Latin American countries, indigenous groups in Paraguay worked extensively within the state's political structures to force their way onto the national stage. Four years after the Stroessner regime collapsed and following an extraordinary effort, they finally gained a place in Paraguay's new Constitution.

Widespread Indigenous Mobilization and a Declining Regime

Near the end of Stroessner's rule, indigenous struggles became desperate. Especially in eastern Paraguay, ranchers, settlers, immigrants, and lumber companies continued to clear native people off their land. In 1988 alone, peasants tried to displace over two dozen Guaraní communities. Indigenous groups responded by joining forces and securing allies in a concerted effort to defend their property. Their protests drew attention to the regime's decline, corruption, and human rights abuses.

The heightened tension of late 1987 was not a result of increased violence on the part of the regime. Rather, as Cockroft has shown, it was the recent economic downturn that led to new social movements and rising opposition.[1] The economic boom following the building of the Itaipú hydroelectric plant had slowed, and so had the elites' smuggling opportunities along the borders. By 1988, Paraguay also found itself in a deep political crisis as the Colorado Party struggled over the choice of Stroessner's successor. The ruling party was also divided on the best way to handle the growing dissent and turmoil.

Far from the capital, though, native communities still felt the results of the expansion of commercial agriculture and ranching. On 19 January 1988, the Campos Morombí Company tried to evict a small community of Mbyá from Arroyo Mboy, now within the ranch's boundaries. Morombí's owner was none other than Blas Riquelme, and when burning Mbyá homes to the ground did not succeed, the powerful rancher tried to bribe the native people into leaving. This time, though, it was impossible to dissuade leaders with cash or simply to evict the community, even for a rancher as powerful as Riquelme. Instead, the Mbyá chiefs joined the neighboring Toro Pirú settlement and denounced Riquelme to the IBR, the INDI, the AIP, and, finally, their allies in the Catholic Church.[2]

The situation had clearly changed since Riquelme's violent expulsion of Mbyá from La Golondrina in 1985. The regime was now so weak that a brief but intense lobbying effort by Mbyá, Catholic lawyers, and the press forced Morombí to provide twelve hundred hectares from an adjoining property for the forty-four Mbyá families. This time the IBR declared negotiations to have failed and deteriorating Mbyá conditions to amply merit expropriation.[3] If indigenous groups could defeat powerful landowners and even the Colorado elite, the regime was clearly weakened.

In fact, news of rural conflicts and the native people's successful outcomes encouraged opposition groups in the capital. In January 1988, political parties prepared for the national elections in February, when the aging dictator intended to win an eighth consecutive term. The Catholic Church published a final version of the National Dialogue that called for a democratic opening. A distinct call for indigenous rights figured prominently in this document. Native leaders asked for respect and educational opportunities that both tolerated their ways of life and prepared them to function in national society. They again asked to continue independent subsistence on their own land and had, in fact, even asked to be considered legitimate and "authentic nations" within a freer Paraguay.[4] The native vision of a more equitable society that tolerated ethnic plurality shows a clear desire to participate more fully in the national community. Still, their position reflected values and economic goals that differed from Paraguayo norms. Published shortly before the February elections, the National Dialogue demonstrates that indigenous demands for toleration of ethnic plurality were now clearly part of the aging dictator's opposition.

Despite opposition efforts, in February, Stroessner swept the elections for the eighth consecutive time. He became the longest-serving head of state in Latin America and third longest in the world. Instead of campaigning, the dictator merely arrested two hundred members of the Comité Coordinadora Nacional para Elecciones Libres (National Coordinating Committee for Free Elections) and placed opponents under house arrest days before the election. Few were surprised when the seventy-five-year-old president swept the election and pledged to lead the nation through a fifth eight-year term in office.

Official goals notwithstanding, by 1988, many people were questioning Stroessner's chances of serving out another full term. Serious disagreements between the *militantes*, who planned to install Stroessner's son Gustavo when Stroessner was gone, and the *tradicionalistas*, who favored a political opening, divided the Colorado Party. In the February elections the neofascist militantes stacked Congress, the state bureaucracy, and the judicial branch with their political supporters. But in reality, the dictator might indeed have lived out another term had the economy continued to allow the upper classes to engage in corrupt deals. This was not to be the case, however.

Like the protesters in Asunción, indigenous people were not about to quietly allow the regime to continue its usual program of exclusion. On 26 March, fifty Mbyá families from Ka'aguay Poty in Itakyrý decided at an *aty guazú* (a large and unusual meeting) to finally take their demands for titles to property to the national authorities. This community, expelled from La Golondrina in 1985, had lost over 800,000 Guaraníes (US$800) in lumber from their forests to state employees. Tired of continued abuse, the group at last took the INDI to court, which ruled in their favor and ordered the agency to hand over the titles.[5]

The positive resolution showed that desperate indigenous communities were becoming adept at pressuring the regime. In addition, the court's decision indicated that by April the pope's imminent visit had forced the regime to take indigenous demands more seriously. On 19 April, national indigenous heritage day, Día del Indígena, minister of defense Martínez declared at the INDI: "It is only fair, when His Holiness meets with the natives, that the language of truth be spoken, the only valid way to faithfully reflect the great conquests of our autochthonous people, the objects and subjects of the deep Christian conscience of our leaders, especially of the most Excellent Sir Constitutional President of the Republic, and General of the Army, Don

Alfredo Stroessner."[6] Clearly already nervous about the looming encounter between indigenous people and the visiting pontiff, for the first time, Martínez used the term *autochthonous*, a less-pejorative term at the time than *indio* or even *indígena*.

To further polish its record for the papal visit, the regime issued land titles to Itajeguaká, Itaguazú, and Ivytyroví, three Païu Tavyterã settlements that had long awaited legal recognition.[7] Marciano Mendoza, a Païu Tavyterã leader, declared that holding land titles was very important because "that way we have security to work and practice the lifestyle to which we are accustomed."[8] While the regime apparently hoped that token land grants would impress the pope, indigenous people accepted the aid but planned to continue subsistence living.

If the papal visit threatened the regime, the prospect was of even more significance to native peoples. Indigenous communities quickly took advantage of the relaxing political climate to demand greater protection from the state. The Mbyá in Sommerfeld again denounced Mennonite harassment. The prospect of this highly charged case's gaining national attention during John Paul II's visit must have finally pushed the state to action. In April, the IBR at last asked the executive branch to expropriate land from Sommerfeld for the Mbyá. The INDI again promptly blocked the Mbyá request.[9]

Later that month a large poster appeared on walls throughout Asunción. It contained a picture of Stroessner beside an image of the pope as if they were close friends. The poster bore the motto "Blessed are those who sow peace in the name of the Lord—United in faith." Propaganda alone, however, could not quell the state's nervousness over papal attention to human rights abuses. Just a week before the visit, Stroessner tried to cancel the pontiff's meeting with four thousand political and social activists, but the pope refused to meet the dictator if he forbade this gathering.[10] Clearly in a difficult spot, Stroessner not only agreed to the meeting but also promised, overriding the INDI's wishes, to allow the encounter between indigenous people and the pope.[11]

The church had arranged the encounter between activists and the pope to capitalize on media attention for the indigenous people's benefit and as a way to criticize the regime. Papal nuncio Jorge Sur rejected the initial copy of the native presentation and instead made plans for a Communion service. On 17 May, Bishop Lucio Alfert welcomed John Paul II to Mariscal Estigarribia, an army outpost and mission in the dry western Chaco. In front of several thousand indigenous people, rather than delivering a homily, the bishop quickly took his seat and instead René Ramírez took his place at the podium. Ramírez told the surprised pontiff that there was more land available for cows than for natives. "We wish to be respected and treated as people," Ramírez emphasized. The pope began to cry when he realized he was unprepared to respond to the poignant and unexpected native statement. He greeted the gathering in Guaraní and asked if the people could understand him. When they shouted yes, John Paul responded that he then could be a missionary in the Chaco and won the crowd's sympathy. After calling on those in power to respect indigenous people and land, the pope invited the Catholic missionaries to the platform and gave them his hand in friendship.[12]

This unexpected turn of events made a significant impression on the indigenous population and church workers alike. Indigenous people from around the country used the encounter to meet each other and discuss their situation. Dances, speeches, and festivities lasted long into each of the three nights.[13] Church workers view this event as an important catalyst for the popular uprising that culminated in the regime's collapse.

The INDI tried immediately to discredit the indigenous message. Minister of defense Martínez accused the church of forcing Ramírez to read a dictated script and declared that, on the contrary, "all is well. We are doing everything possible to improve their living standards, even though there is much still to do."[14] Given the death threats against Ramírez and his eight-month flight to the woods near Riacho Mosquito, state reassurances rang hollow.

Indigenous people themselves drew inspiration from the pope's message. They had heard the pontiff call on the state to improve their land-tenure situation. Time and again they recalled this message, especially when tensions over land ran high. Félix Cabrera, an Mbyá from Sommerfeld, declared: "I really like the part where he emphasized that indigenous people should be given the lands they need." His friend Anuncio Duarte appreciated the pope's concern: "The pope came to see all the indígenas because he loves them. He said that we live oppressed in our communities. This affirmation pleased me because it shows his concern for us." Santiago Centurión, also from Sommerfeld, hoped his people's land claims would now carry more weight: "We have hope of securing titles for our lands and that what we say will carry more weight." Silvio Flores, from Ybý Ybaté in Caaguazú, recalled: "I really liked when he affirmed that we are owners of these lands and that we are all equal. Our truth is the need to have more lands to raise crops. . . . We also desire respect for our authorities and persons." Other native people predicted that the papal visit would improve their situation. "If the pope had not come we would have remained as we have been until now, without support. The father of the church asked that we be given land, though only a bit, but that it be ours, so we can cultivate it. That is most important for us."

The pope's message additionally encouraged indigenous people to demand their legal rights. Finally, the occasion provided indigenous people with another chance to publicize their struggle for land: "[The pope] came out of love for us. We went to him so that he might know that we live broken lives. It is urgent that they return land and forests to us."[15] While indigenous people drew strength from the pope's message, the Catholic Church used their testimonies as weapons in its struggle against the regime.

If indeed the pope's visit encouraged indigenous people, it should not be surprising that they promptly intensified their struggles. Indigenous requests following the papal encounter took on a desperate character. Leaders from the Paï Tavyterã community of Takuaritiy arrived in Asunción on 7 June 1988 and asked the INDI and the IBR to grant title to their five hundred hectares. Instead, they learned that the IBR had recently divided their communal land and sold it to foreign settlers without having notified the Paï Tavyterã, the very people who lived on the property. This explained why Brazilian immigrants had recently occupied the territory and were harassing the indigenous people to leave. In the capital the Paï told the press they were ready to die on their land as their ancestors had and would never abandon it.[16]

The Mbyá in Sommerfeld also renewed their case against the Canadian immigrants. This time, in desperation, the three native communities took the INDI to court for not defending their interests. Mbyá leader Nemecio Flores declared that Mennonites had already demolished six communities on the colony's land. "We can no longer live in peace because they are constantly harassing us. Not long ago they opened a ranch and put cattle on the land one of us used. They cut down all the trees and planted grass, because they say they are the owners and can do what they wish. But we also have rights here. . . . We realize that Law 904 does not serve the indígenas but only the Mennonites, because it seems like only they have rights here."[17] Indigenous people were calling into question the legal foundation of Paraguayan society and again showing their disagreement with the regime's goals.

Those few native communities that had recovered territory provided successful examples to other settlements. In June, René Ramírez reported that the Maskoy recently settled again at Riacho Mosquito had successfully begun to farm their land: "We grow beans and corn, which has benefited many families. The land is dry due to the climate, but we are organizing ourselves little by little. . . . Moreover, our nutrition has improved since the time when we lived close to the factory. But the most important of all is that we now find ourselves on our land. All of this is especially important because we were able to overcome different obstacles to be able to settle definitively on the place where our ancestors lived."[18] The occupation of Riacho Mosquito showed other native groups the benefits that owning land might provide, that is, greater tribal organization, agricultural self-sufficiency, and improved living conditions.

The rise of indigenous demands and the pope's visit challenged the declining regime's ability to oppose native rights. Early in June 1988, after persistent lobbying by the Mbyá from Morombí, the dictator ordered the expropriation of land for the community evicted by Riquelme in January. Congress complied and granted twelve hundred hectares to the Mbyá, citing "disturbances of this population, which, because of the owners, endures desperate situations." When he left the following day to speak on disarmament at the United Nations, Stroessner carried with him a recent and ready example of his action in behalf of indigenous land rights.[19]

While the dictatorship made occasional concessions, more often it failed to act in behalf of the indigenous population in the interests of economic growth. The Mbyá in Sommerfeld, for instance, still suffered continued attacks. On a daily basis, Mennonites harassed the natives at Kilometer 220, one of the last remaining indigenous communities in the colony. Early in August, immigrants again torched native fields and homes, leaving the people desperate. Santiago Centurión, who lost eight hectares of crops in the attack, promptly denounced the depredations in Coronel Oviedo.[20]

Native settlements in Caaguazú, north of Sommerfeld, denounced the additional expansion into their territories. On 16 August, Mbyá from Y'paú and Pindo'í told reporters that Mennonite settlers were destroying their forests and crops. Farther south, in Caazapá, indigenous communities also denounced Mennonite settlers from nearby colonies who extended export crops into indigenous territory, again destroying part of the natives' forests.[21] With growing urgency, the Mbyá from Caazapá added their voices in protest.[22] In swift and vocal protests, the Mbyá disagreed with state projects and instead asked to make their own choices about natural resources.

Development programs devastated many indigenous communities throughout eastern Paraguay. As intended, state projects led to a sharp rise in the area's population. Hunters and trappers overran Mbyá territory, and immigrants competed with native groups for food and land. As the demand for labor declined, natives faced increasing difficulty finding work.[23] By 1988, no Mbyá settlements in Caazapá had secured property titles, in spite of the state's promises. Instead, all of the communities had lost at least part of their forests and fields.[24]

Rather than protecting indigenous people, the INDI actually swindled US$18,000 donated by the World Bank to secure land for the Mbyá.[25] The bank suspended loans in 1987 to force protection of the Mbyá's forests; it promptly reinstated the loans when the regime promised to comply. In the end, the regime demarcated only seventy-two hundred hectares for the Mbyá, a fraction of the forty thousand needed to protect their communities.[26] The once unseen and voiceless Mbyá now added their protests to those of other native groups and denounced the regime's economic goals.

Desperate Resistance

By mid-1988, indigenous peoples were organizing themselves as never before and using class-based analysis as well as an ethnic discourse to demand basic human rights and respect for their land. Indigenous leaders joined forces and created alliances with other critics of the regime, especially the Catholic Church. Native groups themselves also changed as they countered outside threats to their land and independence in terms of production.

Although indigenous communities had become very vocal about protecting their territory and way of life, the regime continued trying to dismember them. On 18 August 1988, a cavalry division suddenly appeared at the Paï Tavyterã settlement of Takuaguy Oygue, the location of the largest and last remaining virgin forests in Amambay. Col. Lino Oviedo and eight camouflage-suited soldiers with automatic weapons threatened to shoot anyone who fled the community to seek help. Oviedo was an ambitious and ruthless rising military star who ten years later tried to overthrow Paraguay's new democratic state. After securing the area and setting up a camp, peons who worked for the army used chainsaws and bulldozers to cut down the Paï Tavyterã's trees. Soon, five army trucks were transporting lumber, twice a day, to the town of Pedro Juan Caballero.[27]

Under cover of darkness, native leaders defied Oviedo's threats and denounced the invasion locally at first, but soldiers blocked an INDI investigation. The chiefs then took their case to the minister of defense, but Martínez argued that the problem was outside his jurisdiction.[28] By this time, sixty army employees were cutting the last of the trees and the remaining corn, manioc, and beans.[29]

Finally, the Paï Tavyterã found allies in other communities. On 27, 28, and 29 September, leaders from sixteen neighboring native communities met and, out of sheer desperation, "affirmed, 'either ourselves or the end of the world,' and given the state's indifference . . . decided to expel the invaders."[30]

The show of solidarity on behalf of Takuaguy Oygue was not an isolated incident. By this time, the Paï Tavyterã had discovered that, as the best-organized and most cohesive indigenous group in eastern Paraguay, by acting together they could influence the regime. During the last months of the regime they repeatedly challenged the state's plans to deforest their land and hasten their disappearance.[31]

South of Amambay in Alto Paraná, the Avá Guaraní had also heightened communal organization and bonds. Between 25 and 27 August, religious and political leaders from nine Avá communities met at Paso Cadena and together concluded: "All the members of the Alto Paraná communities have come together . . . so that we can live in our traditional system as our God and our grandparents have left us our way of life. . . . We have prayed much and have talked about our way of life. We have also debated . . . the needs we have to secure our lands. We have seen that no outsider to our communities can stay with us because they influence us negatively. All the Chiripá communities . . . need to live as true Guaranís by our traditional way of life. . . . In sacred dances, white perfumes and decorations should not be used."[32]

There were actually very few visible racial or linguistic differences between these people and the peasant majority. Still, the struggle to preserve resources and production had encouraged the Avá to perpetuate what they felt were important cultural distinctions. They identified these differences primarily as religious and ritualistic, but this time they rejected details as seemingly insignificant as non-Indian perfumes. By limiting outside influences these communities actually believed themselves to be preserving the original essence of "Guaraníness," the cultural practices that represented the true indigenous character of their land and which they believed to be a superior way of life.

What exactly were these cultural practices that the Guaraní so jealously protected? Traditional life among the Guaraní centered on agroforestry, that is, harvesting trees without destroying lowland ecosystems. Indigenous people had for at least two centuries sold forest products for cash while they gathered, gardened, hunted, and raised domestic animals for subsistence. To live in this way required collecting crews, bulking centers, and processing facilities, a complex organization built on kin groups that provided groups of laborers. Men worked the forests alongside brothers and cousins and delegated labor by consensus rather than coercion. The workers then divided profits equally. Production strengthened relational ties among families. Products went to central marketing areas in the forest, which solidified kin-based links among settlements.[33] Unlike the national practice of cash-crop production, the traditional Guaraní economy not only strengthened communities, but as centuries of use had proven, it could be sustained over an indefinite period of time without destroying the environment.

Other cultural markers were perhaps less visible but no less important. Instead of the linguistic differences that often distinguish natives from national populations elsewhere in Latin America, in eastern Paraguay the principal markers of ethnic identity were religion and place of residence. Despite years of Catholic proselytism, the Avá Guaraní still considered attending Mass and following orders from a priest to be a national way of life. Instead of using language or skin color as identity markers, Guaraní referred to peasants as "*cristianos*," using a religious term to distinguish them. When Avá leaders identified what made them different, they referred to the way "our God and our grandparents have left us our way of life" and described long prayers about the changing times. To the Avá, all Guaraní were "people of the forest" (*ka'aguyguá*) while Paraguayans were "people of the outside" (*okapeguá*). Both religion and place of residence strengthened Guaraní determination to maintain a native identity and way of life.

Nevertheless, indigenous people had changed as relations with outsiders intensified. The Avá Guaraní engaged in many commercial relationships with outsiders, including the gathering of *esencia*, a citrus oil from the leaves of orange trees, and selling skins from peccary, fox, caimans, and snakes.[34] While commercial relations intensified, not only did natives adopt Western products, but nuclear families also gradually replaced extended kin as the principal units of residence and production.[35] Despite such changes, as elders had concluded at Paso Cadena, it remained critical to the Avá Guaraní that their people retain the kinship affiliations and political and economic networks of forest communities.

As had the Avá at Paso Cadena, other indigenous communities also changed culturally due to contemporary pressures and forged their identity in response to local conditions. Along the northern Paraguay River, the Ïshïro people largely abandoned fishing, hunting, and gathering in favor of wage labor on ranches or the extraction of hardwoods. In an interview, Ïshïro chief Bruno Barras explained to me that his people changed as the need arose but still continued to identify with an indigenous heritage.[36] Barras was aware that native cultures had changed with greater outsider contact. Still, for him it was important that his children and grandchildren also be familiar with ancestral ways of raising crops and collecting food, for at some point they might need to depend again on such survival skills. Thus, he could feel assured that his descendants would be true Ïshïro, that is, "people." Still, awareness of tribal practices did not mean forgoing Western clothing. It was perfectly feasible, in Barras's view, for his children to be familiar with indigenous traditions while using outside conveniences.

Similarly concerned about their future, the PaïꞮ Tavyterã from Takuaguy Oygue, where Oviedo had overrun their community, received assistance from neighboring indigenous settlements. The crisis in the capital gave indigenous people more freedom to organize. Finally, on 3 October, seventy Pai Tavyterã men with neighboring relatives painted themselves for battle and fell on the soldiers and peasants still clearing their forest. Most of the soldiers fled in disarray, frightened by the sight of indigenous warriors armed with bows and arrows bearing down on them. The Pai Tavyterã took several prisoners but released them when the army removed its equipment and promised to leave the community in peace.[37]

But the regime's promises proved once again illusory—mere attempts to defuse indigenous protests. Even in its weakened state, the ruling party elite was not about to simply give up a chance to enrich itself at the expense of another indigenous community. Six days later, a militia troop entered Takuaguy Oygue once again, this time firing into the air indiscriminately with automatic weapons. The soldiers detained seven indigenous men and threatened to kill the community leaders who had notified outsiders if they were ever able to apprehend them. Next, the invaders destroyed the plantations and burned down the natives' homes. The entire Pai Tavyterã group fled to the woods in fear, never to return. The soldiers again brought in heavy equipment and, by the end of October, had leveled the community forest and sold the remaining lumber, worth an estimated US$400,000, to Brazilian businesses across the border.[38] The community's efforts came to naught; the people of Takuaguy Oygue lost their communal property to another violent act ordered by officials to enrich themselves at the expense of the native people.

If the occupation of Takuaguy Oygue was disastrous for the Pai Tavyterã, it gave other communities additional incentive to cling even more tenaciously to their own land. The Mbyá in Sommerfeld reported that they were determined to stay on their ancestral property and tried to play Paraguayan nationals against the immigrants. Ignoring their own historical exclusion, Máximo González reminded Paraguayans that Mennonites were recent arrivals: "This place has always been our place. My grandparents and my parents have lived here since time immemorial. . . . It should not be possible to give priority to the Mennonites who moved here long after we did, but instead we should be considered as equals."[39] This developing consciousness, through which indigenous people claimed greater rights than recent immigrants to land, was clearly geared to appealing to those nationals who resented the Mennonites' success and wealth.

When the Catholic Church appealed the Mbyá case directly to the Legislature in early November, in fact, lawyers borrowed this new indigenous strategy, claiming that "these privileges today create an irritating inequality for the impoverished masses submerged in backwardness and misery . . . we think that the Mennonites should be incorporated immediately into the class that contributes to the nation, to begin repaying Paraguayan society for all the benefits they have received from it."[40] By casting indigenous people as part of the larger group of the lower class, the Catholic Church tried to show that the Mbyá were in fact integrated enough to deserve full legal protection and rights. Rather than worry about impoverished indigenous people and peasants, the church argued, the regime should further integrate the Mennonites and thus take advantage of the wealth that these immigrants had reaped from Paraguayan soil.

This logic was not lost on the dictatorship, by this time unraveling from the inside and under widespread attack. In December, Martínez again used indigenous rights to flatter the declining dictator: "The indigenous people of the country are active subjects of a governmental policy that proceeds from a patriotic and nationalistic government, led by Gen. Alfredo Stroessner."[41] Indigenous people were in fact now more a part of national society than ever before. Curiously, however, as native testimonies indicate, they allowed this to happen in order to perpetuate what they understood as distinct cultural and spatial boundaries between themselves and the majority. Thus, even as they continued to demand titles to land and economic autonomy, they were forging a wider pan-indigenous unity and sense of ethnic distinction, which would be the foundation for future struggles.

The Indigenous Population and the Collapse of the Dictatorship

The indigenous population contributed to the political instability by challenging the state's exclusionary practices, demanding their ancestral lands, and calling attention to human rights abuses. These protests took place amid more widespread discontent with endemic corruption and Stroessner's failed economic program. Indigenous protests also led the dictatorship to monitor carefully how it portrayed its economic and social goals. Growing indigenous organization alone, however, was certainly not capable of overthrowing the regime. Ultimately, it was the internal disintegration of the Colorado Party structure that brought down the *tiranosaurio* (tyrannosaurus), as critics privately referred to the aging tyrant.

In September 1988, Stroessner underwent prostate surgery, and his declining health spurred a flurry of negotiations about a successor. The principal threat to the militante faction was Gen. Andrés Rodríguez, the dictator's second-in-command, whose daughter was married to the dictator's son Alfredo. Rodríguez had enriched himself through contraband and owned the nation's largest foreign-exchange house, farms, ranches, and a brewery, as well as shares in banks and construction companies.[42]

As if to distract from the political turmoil, the end of 1988 saw a flurry of state-led repression. In October, police raided the offices of Misereor in Asunción and arrested priests who worked with peasant leagues. Security forces imprisoned Theis and his team at the Técnica detention center, and it was only the German embassy that kept Theis's torture from being as terrible as that of other prisoners. The regime later expelled him from the country.[43] The crumbling regime lashed out against any opponent in a final attempt to keep control.

In January 1989, a nervous Stroessner reorganized the command structure to ensure maximum allegiance. To chastise the power-hungry Rodríguez, he retired his strongest supporters and closed down his businesses in the capital.[44] When these measures failed, he tried to maneuver Rodríguez into early retirement. To counter this threat, the large group of junior army officers who supported Rodríguez drove forty tanks into the capital and captured Stroessner, giving the militante faction a victory. Several days later, the former president, with two suitcases, allegedly containing US$8 million, flew to exile in Brazil. Three hundred opponents chanted "assassin" and burst into cheers as his jet finally lifted off the runway.[45]

Andrés Rodríguez assumed power and promised to preside over a transition to full democracy. He scheduled elections for May, restored freedom of speech and assembly, and lifted the restrictions on the press and opposition parties that had been in place for so many years. The new president freed political prisoners and stacked the entire military command with his supporters. Finally, he promised to enact a new constitution.

The indigenous population immediately expressed interest in the upheaval and a desire to influence new policies that might affect their communities. The day after the coup, an indigenous woman asked: "Can it be that now they will respect us and our rights?" While indigenous people largely considered the coup "an event among the Paraguayans that did not directly concern them," indigenous leaders visited Asunción to inquire about the political changes.[46]

The indigenous population quickly began to pressure the new government to allow them greater participation in the new state. First, they encouraged Rodríguez to alter indigenist policy. Indigenous leaders expressed hope that the new state would leave their communities in peace and honor tribal organizations, regulations, and those few land titles that the regime had granted. "Indígenas desire to participate in a multicultural Paraguay," leaders conveyed, but "nevertheless, are conscious that such participation can only be achieved by living and strengthening their cultural values."[47]

The process of lobbying to protect and recover land opened new space for subaltern expression in Paraguay. As Enenlhit chief René Ramírez explained: "We wanted liberty in democracy, and for indigenous people to be considered human, as they are the nation's original people."[48] As Ramírez made clear, within the climate of political change, native people sought the freedom finally to be viewed as fully human. In Ramírez's view this was their right by virtue of having had ancestors in the area prior to the arrival of the Europeans. The recognition, education, and experience he had gained during the Maskoy's long struggle for land served him well. Once his people were safely resettled at Riacho Mosquito, the Enenlhit leader continued actively to represent indigenous rights before national society.

The indigenous population's requests indicate a high degree of political sophistication and a keen awareness of the national situation. Individual communities immediately tried to use the momentous political change to their own advantage. The Mbyá from Sommerfeld arrived in Asunción only a month after the coup and presented a request for land. "The former authorities never worried about our problem," declared Felipe Centurión, "but now we have much hope for the new authorities and believe they will keep us in mind and find a solution. Mennonites wish to evict us from our property at all costs, and we say that there is no foreigner who can throw us Paraguayos off our land."[49]

After a decade of fruitless struggle, the Mbyá now identified themselves as full members of the national population when they attempted to sway public sentiment against the Sommerfeld immigrants. In response, Mennonites offered two thousand hectares outside the colony's boundaries if the Mbyá agreed to move. Although the INDI strongly pressured them to accept, the three communities again flatly refused the Mennonite offer.

The new government even made a feeble attempt to reform the INDI. While creating his new cabinet, in February Rodríguez appointed Numa

Alcides Mallorquín as president of the INDI.[50] Even critics admitted that, because he held a bachelor's degree in sociology and was the first civilian to lead the INDI, Mallorquín was probably the best-prepared person ever to have assumed the post.[51]

The new government almost doubled the budget of the new INDI, to US$730,000 in the first year, with a 160 percent increase in funds allocated to reimburse landowners. One year later, the INDI budget was increased again by another 243 percent.[52] Freed from the jurisdiction of the Ministry of Defense, Mallorquín and the INDI finally convened the advisory council of private indigenist agencies and the API, as Law 904 had required years before.[53] Because Stroessner's other appointees remained in place, though, the INDI did not improve or alter its practices. Change would depend on the indigenous people to define their role in the new system.

In his campaign speeches, Rodríguez made promises to respect indigenous cultures.[54] To support the presidential candidate as the country prepared for elections, minister of defense Samaniego promised additional assistance to indigenous communities. Mallorquín pledged to "effectively support . . . all the indigenous brothers of the country, who are as Paraguayan as all of us." Ache leader Luis Duarte, an API official, responded that "a new perspective of understanding, justice, and welfare was opening for all indigenous people in Paraguay."[55]

Such political rhetoric, notwithstanding the prevailing democratic discourse, revealed an intransigent pejorative attitude toward the indigenous population. Underlying the candidate's pledges to improve the living conditions of the native population still ran a desire to see them disappear into the peasant class by moving them out of their former communities. The elevation of indigenous "brothers" to an equal plane, while resonating with the current democratic discourse, was simply a continuation of the former policy to integrate and, in the process, exclude native people.

In the end, though, such speeches attracted voters. In May 1989, in the "freest" elections ever documented in Paraguay, Rodríguez won the presidency with 73 percent of the popular vote.[56]

The indigenous population, however, saw through the hollow campaign speeches and recognized the new regime for what it really was: a continuation of most of Stroessner's policies in democratic trappings. In June, Mbyá leaders from Sommerfeld grew tired of negotiating with the new INDI and sent a detailed version of their ten-year struggle directly to the president of the Chamber of Deputies, Alberto Nogués. "The lands under Mennonite power were ours. These were sold in 1948 with us inside and no one consulted us. We make our request with deep confidence in today's changed situation, which we hope favors a just consideration of our request. Mr. President, the survival of our communities is in your hands, for the land you could recognize for us."[57] The Mbyá put the burden of proving that the new government was a true democracy firmly on the shoulders of the new administration. It would prove difficult to ignore the challenge.

In July, Rodríguez set in motion a plan to stimulate agricultural and cattle production nationwide. The state development project included a specific indigenous component for the first time.[58] The INDI began to assist the new "Plan Nacional de Desarrollo Económico y Social 1989–1990" (National Plan for Economic and Social Development 1989–1990) to extend health care, education, social security, housing, and technical assistance to indigenous communities, as well as to "preserve them, culturally and socially."[59] The state promised to educate nationals about indigenous people and called for their "progressive integration into Paraguayan society."[60]

The continuation of Stroessner's policies became even clearer when Mallorquín pledged that assistance to indigenous settlements would gradually, but inevitably, pave the way for native *transculturación*, or cultural change.[61] Clearly, it was impossible for indigenous people to remain in their former habitats, the director reminded the media, and to live by hunting, as had their ancestors.[62]

The only change from the former regime's plan was the promise to allow native people to choose the way in which they would integrate their communities into national society. The state cast the indigenous population's wish to influence politics as evidence that they wished to be more fully a part of national society.[63]

Promises to respect indigenous cultures were part of a discourse of political openness that the new administration avidly encouraged to distance itself from the former regime. Interest groups quickly appropriated promises of toleration and used them when lobbying the state for favors. It did not take long, however, for indigenous people to realize that the new administration would also use its laws to obfuscate any failure to protect indigenous rights and lands, as the Stroessner regime had with Law 904, or failure to honor distinct tribal laws and traditions.

In April 1989, shortly after the Colorado and Liberal party conventions, seventeen indigenous communities came together to jointly request honest political representation and to encourage the state to stand by its promises to improve the living conditions of the native population. The leaders' statement sheds light on changing indigenous goals:

Many things have happened, many changes, the politics of democratic opening in the country, the government appears to be sincere, but there is one thing that we must make clear: no political leader, even General Rodríguez . . . has remembered and remembers the indígena. We remind you that in Paraguay we are fifty to sixty thousand Indians who demand our fundamental rights: rights to life; rights to land; rights to culture; rights to ideology, philosophy, and politics. Many call for liberty, but it seems that liberty serves to continue oppressing or discriminating against people on the periphery, in this case, indigenous groups. We Indians need sincere participation and proposals; we also desire an opportunity in Congress in the future to show national and international society the indigenous capacity for self-management. We also ask, Who is the indigenous representative in the national Congress?[64]

Only indigenous representation in the legislative branch, natives concluded, would help remedy obvious omissions.

Indigenous people clearly saw through the state's promises of economic development and recognized Stroessner's age-old, but hollow, goal of exclusion through integration. Still, to convey their message, tribes had relied on and appealed to the API Council and leaders in the capital, which were still tied closely to the INDI. The process was therefore contradictory. To request equal representation and the freedom to practice tribal ways of life, indigenous communities had to appeal to the very structures that they were denouncing as unfair.

Additionally, the process of identifying and presenting needs to the new government produced a reaffirmation of ethnic pride. Mak'a chief Andrés Chem'hei told reporters: "We do not deny we are indígenas, because that is how God created [us]. There is no reason to be ashamed of being indios." Chem'hei blamed problems in his community, such as alcoholism, on the "bad influence of Paraguayans." He went on: "But even though we live with the Paraguayos, we will not lose our customs."[65] Ïshïro leader Pablo Barboza reaffirmed his people's vitality: "We are finding favorable solutions, and the indigenous population is not extinct; on the contrary, it is growing."[66] He reminded reporters that native people could live in Western society and still identify themselves as indigenous.

Leaders strategically employed the new political terminology along with the judicious use of a distinct ethnic discourse to influence the new government.[67] Taking full advantage of the state's promise to restore democratic freedoms, indigenous people developed a powerful tool to express their rights as minorities and to repudiate the state's plans for social integration. In August, the Maskoy conveyed their rejection of integration through a missionary: "Integration for them is a type of discrimination. They call integrated Indians Paraguayos and isolate themselves from them . . . because they yell, get angry, hit their women and get drunk like Paraguayos. The Maskoy do not want to be Paraguayos but recognize that it is necessary to learn Spanish to get documents . . . and to defend themselves from dishonest persons."[68]

The democratic opening encouraged indigenous people to become more politically and ethnically aware, but in August a Colorado politician also hailed the successful and complete integration of the indigenous population: "Indigenous integration, in my judgment, is complete from the perspective of indigenous insertion into the national community. They are interacting profoundly in every moment and place."[69] The politician was partially correct: native people were interacting to a greater degree with outsiders, and their lives had changed markedly. What he ignored, however, was of equal importance. Despite greater interaction with and reliance on nationals, the struggle to defend their land, resources, and political rights had encouraged native people to reject closer and further identification with the wider society.

Regardless of greater contact, then, indigenous people continued to strongly defend independent production and communal landownership. When the Mbyá refused to drop claims against Sommerfeld late in August, the INDI pressured the communities of Yaguary and San Juan de Yjhovy to remain fenced in by Mennonite fields. The INDI urged the group at Kilometer 220, however, to resettle outside of Sommerfeld.[70]

The Mbyá immediately refused yet another "final" offer and instead charged the INDI with having consistently opposed their interests.[71] To show that they meant business, the next day the Mbyá again asked the Senate to expropriate nineteen hundred hectares for them from Sommerfeld and denounced the Mennonites in the press.[72]

The press release was a judicious use of the media to sway the political powers, given the political climate. By contrasting their frustrations with the former regime and their hopes regarding the new government, indigenous people capitalized on the prevailing anti-Stroessner feeling. The formerly atomized Mbyá communities now presented themselves as a single bloc, with clear desires and a need for autonomy.

The campaign attracted the attention of legislators, who saw the chance to capitalize politically on the indigenous requests. Early in October, leaders from six Mbyá settlements at Sommerfeld met with national deputies and again asked them to expropriate their ancestral lands from Sommerfeld. Chief Gauto passionately told the legislators: "For some time, we the Mbyá have not been able to live peacefully, because of the worries to which we are subjected by the owners of our settlements. We live in a place that is ours and not the strangers'."[73] So important was hunting and gathering for their subsistence that the Mbyá again argued that the total destruction of their forests would lead to their physical extinction.

The Mennonites blamed continued indigenous resistance on the Catholic Church. Óscar Tuma, the Mennonites' lawyer, promised to prosecute Catholic workers if they crossed Mennonite property again to visit the Mbyá: "I don't care if they are priests, bishops, or missionaries. This has finished. Do they want war? They will have war. We will finish with all those indigenists."[74] The Sommerfeld attack shows that the immigrants were unwilling to recognize Mbyá initiatives and their successful use of church allies against the Protestant immigrants. The prosperous foreign enclave may have served Stroessner's economic goals but, by threatening the Mbyá, Mennonite actions now came face to face with the new democratic ideals.

During the Stroessner regime, indigenous requests for land had usually met with a cold shoulder. On 29 October 1989, however, the Senate finally expropriated 1,457 hectares from Sommerfeld for the three Mbyá communities.[75] Mbyá leaders, present for the expropriation, applauded the vote that ended an eighteen-year campaign for the return of their land.[76]

The Mbyá struggle with Sommerfeld highlights the way in which indigenous people used the democratic opening to improve their leverage. The Mbyá took full advantage of the state's new tolerance to engage the press with greater success, publish their position, and collect signatures to bolster their cause. The native people had even counterpoised officials at the INDI against those in the Legislature and the IBR.

Even more than the colonists, the clear loser in the conflict was the INDI. "For the indígenas," Oleg Vysokolán reaffirmed in September, "the Stroessner regime continues to exist."[77] Catholic missionary Wayne Robins told the press that the INDI was clearly continuing the policies of the former regime and had ignored indigenous interests.[78] Only two days later, comptrollers proved that all levels of the INDI, including Minister of Defense Martínez himself, had embezzled state funds. Stroessner had tolerated the corruption to build his cadre of supporters, increase rural production, and move native people off their land.

Political Changes for Indigenous People?

In the first year of democracy, indigenous people created a space for themselves in the new political framework. Natives forced the elite to pay attention to their claims for land, forged allies within and outside the administration, and reminded politicians that true democracy should include rights for everyone, even indigenous people. Native leaders, especially in the capital, saw themselves, more than ever before, as participants in the political changes but continued to remind nationals that they proudly distinguished themselves from the majority.

General Rodríguez had promised to replace Stroessner's Constitution of 1967 with a new code of law that would enshrine democracy in Paraguay forever. When the political parties began to prepare for a 1992 constitutional convention, indigenous leaders expressed active interest in being represented there, for the first time, as a minority people.

In February 1991, the INDI formally asked the government for permission to allow indigenous contributions to the new constitution. Natives called on the state to acknowledge the minorities that "form part of the multicultural and multiethnic population" of Paraguay.[79] Indigenous people were now using sophisticated language that situated them alongside other minority groups in a country of many immigrants. For the INDI, it was an opportunity to rise in the new bureaucracy.

On 19 April 1991, National Indigenous People's Day, indigenist agencies took native requests to the constitutional convention and lobbied for the inclusion of their rights in the new constitution. The INDI and the Comisión Congresional sobre Derechos Humanos (Congressional Commission on Human Rights) encouraged deputies to make the protection of native rights and land part of Paraguay's supreme law.[80] Serafina de Álvarez, from the ENM, argued that the country should use this opportunity to guarantee natives the right to a distinct identity, land, bilingual education, and religious freedom.[81]

Indigenous people themselves, distrustful after years of working with the INDI and NGOs alike, mobilized as never before to request participation. On 29–31 May, 134 representatives from 64 indigenous settlements gathered at Coronel Oviedo to agree on a collective request to the constitutional convention. This encounter was the largest gathering of native leaders from different communities ever in Paraguay.[82]

Despite many differences, their shared history of resistance allowed indigenous representatives, together, to call for respect for their distinct cultural systems and tribal laws, the return of native lands in sufficient measure to guarantee their survival, and participation in the development of the nation from the perspective of their own worldview. Leaders also requested permanent exemption from all military duty and conscription for their youth. Finally, they suggested that the state owed them free social services and exemption from taxation.[83]

The leaders sent their conclusions to the deputies who were already drafting the Constitution. Father Wayne Robins served as intermediary. The indigenous communiqué asserted the right to reclaim sacred sites and added: "The state should provide us with as much free land as we need. . . . The new constitution should clearly state that national unity is constructed on a foundation of respect for the cultural diversity of the autochthonous people of the country."[84] For the first time, indigenous leaders were asking the state to repay what they called a "historical debt" occasioned by the theft of their land and resources since the beginning of colonization. All seventeen indigenous tribes declared themselves united in their demands and grievances. The petition made it clear that native people would contribute to the economy only when treated as equal human beings and as indigenous peoples, rather than as part of the larger peasant class.

In case this first gathering had not sent a clear enough message, even more indigenous delegates met a second time, on 11 and 12 September. Robins positioned the Catholic Church firmly behind the indigenous effort: the Catholic Missions Team provided structural organization and lobbied Congress to secure indigenous representation.[85] Over seventy communities called for land reform and asked, as a minimum reparation, that they be given title to their land and that the communal properties not be sold to "foreigners or strangers."[86] Indigenous leaders capitalized on the antiquincentenary movement that had gained strength in Brazil during the 1987–1988 constitutional assembly, when a massive indigenous lobby spearheaded by the Kayapó people forced legislators to include a section on indigenous rights.[87] Elsewhere, at the Primer Encuentro Continental de Pueblos y Naciones Indígenas (First Continental Encounter of Indigenous Nations), in Quito in 1990, indigenous nations from the Americas strongly denounced ongoing and violent abuse of their human rights. When indigenous delegates also won recognition of their communal *cabildo* (town hall) organizations and *resguardo* ("protected") land rights in Colombia's 1991 constitutional reform, they contributed to the growing support for indigenous rights and demands.[88] Indigenous people in Paraguay had access to these events through the media, which encouraged them to apply a neoblack legend to their own situation. Natives built a strong case that must have tugged emotionally at legislators and formally requested, for the first time, that four of their own representatives be allowed to participate directly in the constitutional convention.[89] This was a risky gamble, since delegates from other minority groups could participate only as members of political parties. Not only did Paraguay's native people again distinguish themselves from Paraguayos but, incredibly, they requested that the constitutional convention include a new cabinet-level ministry, at the same level as Defense or Education, in the new constitution to represent their interests.

On 21 November, representatives of fourteen of the seventeen tribes marched to the Chamber of Deputies to demand a reason for the continuing congressional opposition to their requests. By this time, the Liberal Party had named René Ramírez one of its delegates to the convention, and deputies were finally considering allowing native people to attend the convention as observers and consultants.

The long struggle with the state had led to the creation of a pan-indigenous identity in Paraguay. Indigenous people had identified themselves as nations prior to the Europeans' arrival, and, as the product of a concerted multiethnic bloc, they now called themselves "the indigenous people of Paraguay" rather than claiming to be small individual tribes. No more would the state be able to divide tribes to diminish their call for social justice.

Persistent indigenous lobbying finally bore fruit. In October, indigenous leaders secured the assistance of Julio César Frutos and Celso Velázquez, two Colorado deputies, who agreed to lobby for native participation in the constitutional convention and asked their chamber to amend the law to include indigenous people. "They are part of the people and have the same right to be represented," the advocates told the press.[90] Deputies again argued that native people had given Paraguay its distinct unifying element, the Guaraní language.[91]

Frutos and Velázquez clearly realized the unifying potential of the Guaraní language and the importance of a shared indigenous legacy for the country. What is more, they plainly foresaw that including native representatives would in effect be a way of further incorporating the indigenous people.[92] Not only would greater participation by indigenous groups formalize their inclusion as equal citizens, but formal recognition of minorities would also show the world, in their view, that Paraguay was finally a true democracy.

Despite the uphill battle, native people refused to give up. By this time indigenous leaders were far too caught up in political maneuvers to simply abandon their original goals. In January 1992, delegates began the first deliberations. Indigenous tribes declared their participation critical if they were to successfully "defend their cultural heritage and lands" and again requested that four native representatives be allowed to participate fully in deliberations.[93] When the convention continued to exclude them, in February, indigenous people presented eight articles they hoped to introduce in the new constitution. After a tense debate legislators finally agreed to include native rights in a chapter of the Constitution and to allow four indigenous delegates to speak on the convention floor.[94] Over the next months the Colorado delegates composed most of the indigenous rights chapter and overrode proposals contributed by the other parties.

On 30 April 1992, the convention agreed in plenary session to include a chapter on native rights in the new constitution. The four indigenous delegates participated actively, explaining in emotional language how the proposed articles would protect indigenous people from "predators who destroy their habitat." Western Guaraní leader Severo Flores thanked politicians for excluding indigenous people from military conscription, which, he argued, freed them from a "heavy load, because our society is eminently pacifist."[95] Long rounds of applause punctuated each indigenous statement.

René Ramírez participated in the convention as a delegate for the Liberal Party. The recognition he had gained from the successful bid for Riacho Mosquito allowed him to represent Puerto Casado in the capital. Despite requests from the local Colorado chapter, after careful consideration, Ramírez finally affiliated with the Liberal Party because of his dislike of the Stroessner regime. Liberal Party members respected him highly, Ramírez recalled, because he held them to party regulations and prevented dishonesty.[96] For the Enenlhit leader, there seems to have been no contradiction in representing a political party instead of the indigenous bloc. His own political ambitions were not, in his view, inconsistent with his former advocacy of communal land claims. Ramírez's willingness to participate in politics shows the degree to which some indigenous people had joined national society.

The six articles that compose the fifth chapter of the new constitution mark a significant achievement for the indigenous population. The Constitution recognizes the existence of indigenous pueblos, defined as "groups with cultures that predated the organization of the Paraguayan state." They are guaranteed the right to "preserve and develop their ethnic identity within their respective habitats" and freely practice their own political, social, economic, cultural, and religious organization. Indigenous groups can own land communally, and the Constitution promises them enough property to secure a living however they choose. Indigenous people can now freely participate in national society, markets, and politics, but the state will respect their "cultural peculiarities," especially in relation to formal education. Finally, the Constitution pledges to defend indigenous people from economic exploitation and exempts them from any social or political duties such as compulsory military service.[97] Indigenous people thus achieved the bulk of their demands for greater legal rights and recognition.

During the following days, the four indigenous representatives, celebrities for a brief time, reiterated their people's need for "more respect and better treatment" from the people they still referred to as Paraguayos and *blancos* (whites).[98] The entire constitutional struggle had reinforced the indigenous sense of autonomous identity. Delegates once again built on the quincentenary anniversary to underscore their plight: "The twelfth of October will be for the indigenous groups . . . a day of mourning because it recalls the beginning of the extermination of our brothers. The eleventh of October of 1492 was our final day of independence." Despite complaints about continued injustices, indigenous delegates clearly regarded the new constitution as a significant victory.[99]

The extent to which indigenous representatives coupled contemporary democratic discourse to a critical examination of the European conquest shows how aware they were of current issues and the national political agenda. In fact, the entire constitutional process had only drawn them farther into politics and the non-Indian sphere.

Their greater interest in national politics does not invalidate the long struggle that indigenous people waged to retain their autonomy and to protect their resources. In fact, constitutional success in Paraguay was a milestone that paved the way for efforts by indigenous people elsewhere. After a monumental struggle that culminated in the election of one of their leaders as vice-president of Bolivia, the Aymara successfully reformed the first article of the country's Constitution in 1993. The nation acknowledged for the first time that is was a multiethnic and pluricultural democracy founded on the union and solidarity of all Bolivians.[100] Later, in 2005, Evo Morales even became Bolivia's first indigenous president. Paraguay also stands as an early example in the period that Charles Hale has termed "El Indio Permitido" (The Tolerated Indian), in which states used native legislation to position themselves as inclusive and politically correct.[101] The struggle by indigenous people in Paraguay thus was a step toward the forging of a state that respects cultural differences and autonomy, at least in written law. They became an example of minorities who, as had the French in Canada and the Basques in Spain, expanded the framework of democracy by demanding autonomy within the nation-state.[102]

While indigenous people celebrated their inclusion in the Constitution, deputies also praised the chapter on indigenous rights, though for different reasons. Colorado politicians emphasized instead the new constitutional guarantees of greater indigenous participation in national society as well as access to education and state assistance.[103] Delegates to the constitutional convention were aware that, much like Law 904, the new legal document would not carry much weight in everyday events. Politicians would continue to exclude indigenous people from the benefits of development even as they worked to erase their ethnic distinctions through integration. By the conclusion of the legal process, the government clearly regarded the new recognition of indigenous people as another important step toward making them disappear into the peasant lower class. For Colorado politicians, Paraguay seemed to have had finally completed the elusive goal of complete indigenous integration.

Conclusion

Greater indigenous participation in national politics was not a result of improved living conditions, additional land security, or even more respect for indigenous people in Paraguay. The Stroessner regime's last year saw only a rise in the many threats to indigenous lands and resources. The regime's collapse provided no relief. Living conditions for most indigenous communities continued to be difficult long after Stroessner fell and, if anything, competition for land and natural resources only increased in the early years of the democracy. The indigenous population's successful inclusion in the Constitution, therefore, did not mark an indigenous victory over the former regime. Instead, their participation in the constitutional convention highlighted only the significant way in which the struggle had altered both the country and indigenous people to a degree neither had foreseen. The latter made allies with forces that opposed the regime, but their participation in national events at the same time drew their communities closer to the very national structures they opposed.

During Stroessner's last year in office, indigenous people sharpened and refined their struggle against the aging dictator. They capitalized on alliances with opposition forces and drew strength from the pope's timely visit to press the regime for land titles, legal protection, and greater autonomy. Indigenous struggles, such as the lengthy Mbyá conflict with Sommerfeld, focused criticism on the government's attempts to clear indigenous communities from the path of national development. At times, indigenous resistance provoked severe repression, as occurred at Takuaguy Oygue. More often, the dictatorship simply allowed peasants to overrun indigenous lands or state employees to enrich themselves at the natives' expense. These attacks destroyed many indigenous settlements, especially in the area of development programs such as the Caazapá Project. Despite obvious losses, though, the native struggle led to a pan-indigenous movement, greater NGO activism in behalf of indigenous people, and several important victories in the struggle for indigenous land. Combined, these helped focus criticism on the regime's social policies at a critical, national-political juncture.

By the time Rodríguez's administration legislated a constitution, indigenous people were united enough to force their way into the new law. They seized the chance to participate more fully in the non-Indian political system, despite their long attempt to reclaim greater independence within the national framework. The very law that granted more political and cultural autonomy to indigenous people than to any other minority group also represented greater integration than ever before. Indigenous communities and the national government had both won and lost their struggles and in the process changed the outcome of one another's goals and future.

Conclusion

Everyday Forms of Exclusion

The Stroessner regime attempted to exclude Paraguay's indigenous people from the benefits of development and the most basic human rights. The dictator tried to use religious missions to alter indigenous cultures. By limiting their self-sufficiency, the regime increased native participation in wider markets. Indigenous resistance, however, simultaneously influenced national events at a critical time. Native people challenged the regime's economic policies with their own vision of independent, subsistence-based production. Ultimately, they helped point the nation toward a more complete democracy by demanding greater respect for ethnic plurality and the natural resources that made their lifestyles viable.[1]

From the perspective of indigenous policy, one can see important but often overlooked aspects of the Stroessner regime and the ambiguous nature of his social and economic goals. Stroessner's plans for the indigenous population, framed as integration but in effect exclusionary, show the degree to which he encouraged economic development to reward upper-class supporters at the expense of marginal groups.

An examination of indigenous-government relations extends the scope of the indigenist strategy within South America. Scholars have described the importance of indigenism in Mexico, Brazil, Ecuador, and Peru, areas of previous colonial administration with large native populations.[2] Even in Paraguay, though, long seen as isolated, politicians went out of their way to conform to foreign indigenist guidelines. Paraguay used these policies as part of its struggle to join the league of more developed Latin American nations. The Stroessner regime employed the country's indigenous legacy to present a positive image to foreigners even as it tried to clear natives out of the path of economic development. The façade of integration thus masked exclusionary goals. Indigenism in Paraguay was a strategy that lacked indigenous perspectives and participation, and thus led to the same controversial, ambiguous, and even scandalous results that occurred elsewhere.[3]

The effects of the passage of time is clear in the Paraguayan struggle. New means of communication allowed indigenous people to forge alliances with opponents of the Stroessner regime and denounce attacks on their resources and lands. The coerced settlement of the Ayoreode and Ache people took place in a very different climate from that of earlier examples of forced relocation. Working in the highly charged environment of the 1970s, human rights advocates quickly drew attention to indigenous conditions and regime abuses in Paraguay. Foreign scrutiny forced the dictatorship to change the presentation of its social policies.

While goals, per se, had not changed, the government promised in 1981 to respect native cultures, which profoundly affected indigenous people. Communities demanded that the government honor its promise of toleration, especially after the Catholic Church and NGOs embraced their plight and allied with them against the regime. NGO advocacy contributed to widespread native mobilization in the 1980s.

Stroessner's treatment of indigenous people was often brutal as he attempted to enforce exclusion. But I have shown that critics also exaggerated charges of ruthless repression because of the period in which they operated. A closer look dispels the widely publicized version of a purposeful plan of genocide.[4] While development programs often had negative effects, the regime made token efforts to protect indigenous people from settler abuse. Although loosely enforced and often ineffective, state paternalistic legislation did protect some indigenous lives and lands.

The Stroessner regime's use of native issues to project an overly positive image was possible at first because the indigenous population had few venues in which to express their own views. As indigenous people quickly noticed, Law 904 of 1981 led to few tangible improvements. Stroessner instead used the law to portray himself as a beneficent *patrón* who protected his indigenous population, while his generals used the natives' rising popularity in anthropological circles to improve their own political image. As native people organized, however, they rejected such misrepresentations and changed the situation.

Colorado Party policies regarding the indigenous population thus highlight frequently overlooked aspects of the regime. Scholars have emphasized the ruthless nature of Stroessner's rule, and his repressive tactics were certainly no secret. To stress his severe brutality, though, observers claimed that he made few concessions to U.S. pressure.[5] On the contrary, a study of indigenous affairs shows that foreign criticism did influence the regime's policies. It was precisely the threat of declining U.S. foreign aid that compelled Stroessner to re-create the INDI and pass an indigenous-rights bill unique at the time in the Americas, one that other nations soon imitated. Paraguay presents an early example of the move to a "multicultural" public sphere in

Latin America, a project that uses cultural rights to divide and domesticate indigenous movements.[6] While Stroessner often employed brutal force, he also gained foreign support by championing his own social policies.

Social programs notwithstanding, the Stroessner regime's interaction with native people shows that Stroessner seriously overlooked the rural population. He was indeed a skillful strategist, as evidenced by his careful management of party, employees, and military officers to ensure the support of the elite.[7] But he clearly viewed indigenous people as ignorant, inept, and uninformed, for he underestimated their ability to focus opposition through their claims for land and equal rights.[8] As the indigenous population pushed for different developmental goals, they challenged traditional views of nationalism and the very concept of the nation-state.[9] By bringing their goals to the public's attention, indigenous people showed Paraguay that it would have to recognize their rights and growing influence. Mobilized indigenous people played a role in the country's social awakening in the late 1980s.

Without this ethnohistorical perspective in mind, scholars have argued incorrectly that Stroessner's development plans created rising prosperity, even for the lower classes, and thus perpetuated his time in power.[10] A look at indigenous protests shows, on the contrary, that the state's economic programs actually made rural conditions worse by undermining self-sufficiency and land tenure.

One theme that underlies indigenous resistance in Paraguay and occasionally bursts through in clear testimonies—to employ Gavin Smith's useful analogy of an underground stream—is the strong native critique of the regime's economic policies. The indigenous rejection of the state's economic and social programs was a reflexive cultural critique that stood in "implicit judgment of the expansionist state."[11] Native people in this way communicated their separation and disengagement from the encompassing state program as well as from surrounding peasant values. As Ronald Stutzman has paraphrased in his study of indigenous people in Ecuador: "We do not agree on the values of the system, and want to be left alone, with enough resources to pursue our own ends, whatever you may be doing. We will treat you [national peasants] as if you are pursuing different values from those we have."[12] By claiming the right to use resources and land as they saw best, indigenous people showed their disapproval of the expansion of cash-crop farming at a high cost to their subsistence. Time and again indigenous people set what they called in Guaraní "*ñande reko*" (literally, our way of being) in opposition to the enveloping capitalist system and values of material accumulation.[13] Ultimately, as Haas recapitulates, land was of vital importance to indigenous communities because it guaranteed them a "still viable means of subsistence," especially for natives who worked as wage laborers on farms owned by non-Indians.[14]

Collective activism in defense of natural resources and territory united indigenous people against outside forces and thus helped perpetuate rather than eliminate barriers between them and the Paraguayans. Defense of ecological or economic niches may contribute directly to indigenous identity and mobilization, especially in response to changed environmental situations and new forms of domination.[15] Native ethnic and even cultural identities in Paraguay were inherently political, formed by perceptions of their own "threatened cultures" and their aspiring to greater access to economic resources.[16] Indigenous identity was therefore, to some degree, conscious and chosen, even while grounded in the idea of common ancestors and shared with members of a linguistic and kinship group. More important, indigenous people formulated a collective identity based on their different understanding of ethnic, cultural, and economic choices.

Dwelling solely on resistance as the source of identity, however, presents a false image of national-indigenous relations in Paraguay. Without addressing the indigenous struggle for inclusion in the 1992 Constitution, history might project an image of noble savages bravely resisting a brutal regime by clinging to their land and ways of life. As do other ethnohistorical country studies, such as Seth Garfield's examination of the Xavante in Brazil, the Paraguayan case shows that such a view is too simplistic and entirely inaccurate. Within the historical and material perspective of constantly changing cultures, such a view diminishes indigenous resilience and obfuscates the choices made by native people in Paraguay.

The indigenous struggle for inclusion in the new Constitution of 1992 helps correct an erroneous view of cross-cultural interaction and demonstrates the widespread indigenous desire for participation in political events and the new democratic process.[17] The Paraguayan case thus helps counter an essentialist view of indigenous people, one that might view "Indianness" as the product of a singular period, bound to "wither away with the emergence of individualism and the transformation of agrarian class relations that accompany capitalist development."[18] Instead, native resistance in Paraguay suggests that societies that undergo cultural contact with outside groups do not inevitably disappear. Indigenous attempts to secure recognition in Paraguay's Constitution show that native people were already a part of national society to an extent that even they were not ready to admit and seized the opportunity for greater political representation when it arose.[19] Instead of withering away, Paraguay's native people adapted to drastic cultural changes while continuing to identify as indigenous.

Indigenous participants in the creation of a new constitution attributed their desire for legal recognition to the need to protect their communal lands and distinct ways of life. The very images they presented, however, of "extremely impoverished ethnic cultures upholding non-economic and non-pragmatic values," show that they had partly internalized a Paraguayo vision of the native "other." As Guidieri and Pellizzi have argued: "The non-Western world can be said to have succumbed to progress only to the extent to which it accepts and incorporates this alienating contradiction."[20] The dictatorship's plan to integrate and thus exclude indigenous people had succeeded to a significant degree.

The conflict between indigenous people and Stroessner's regime was therefore primarily an attempt by the former to retain their ancestral lands and enough independent control over their labor to guarantee some measure of autonomous subsistence. Indigenous identity, in this context, was a way to resist total incorporation into an economy and cultural world always under national domination.[21] This struggle supports the view that modern indigenous identity is created and sustained as a result of native struggles with the state. By the late twentieth century, indigenous people in Paraguay had asserted their ethnic identity almost entirely in opposition to the surrounding culture of the people they referred to as "blancos" or "Paraguayos."

This book adds to the growing work on the influence that religious missions and NGOs have had on indigenous people. Those organizations that assisted indigenous communities in reclaiming their lands and opposing state control provided the opportunity for indigenous people to express their distinctiveness.[22] Rather than furthering the goal of integration, indigenous initiatives often turned mission work to their own benefit. Mission activities at times strengthened indigenous resistance and made independent subsistence more feasible by helping indigenous communities recover their land.[23] This conclusion challenges the criticism that religious missions have always been detrimental to indigenous cultural identity. Instead, the Paraguayan case highlights the vitality that native people exhibited by using outside organizations to buttress their own cultural and economic choices vis-à-vis the law.

By the time Paraguay enacted a new constitution in 1992, indigenous people were participating in national society and politics to a greater extent than ever before. They did so, however, from the vantage point of a program for national society that ultimately buttressed their own ethnic distinctiveness. By encouraging legislators to include the idea of a pluralistic society in the Constitution of 1992, indigenous groups contributed their vision of a multiethnic state that respected minorities not only in law but also in reality. As native people did throughout the Americas, native groups, in effect, encouraged Paraguayans to stop building governments on a centralizing party structure and to, instead, substitute a coalition that respected cultural diversity and autonomy.[24]

Stroessner tried to ignore this native request even as his regime tried to make the troublesome indigenous people disappear into the peasant class and to exclude them from the benefits of economic expansion. Nevertheless, native people at last forced their way into a democratic Paraguay.

Appendix

Paraguayan Newspaper Sources

ABC Color (ABC)
El Diario
Hoy
Noticias
Nuestro Tiempo (Nuestro)
El País
Patria
El Pueblo
El Radical
La Tarde
La Tribuna
Última Hora

Notes

Chapter 1. Introduction

1. Ramírez, "Discurso de bienvenida," 17 May 1988, addressed to pope at Mariscal Estigarribia. All translations are mine unless otherwise noted.

2. Horst, "Catholic Church, Human Rights," 741.

3. Carter, *Papel*, 123.

4. "Le hicieron leer," 10.

5. Langer, *Contemporary Indigenous Movements*, xxvii.

Chapter 2. A Racially Mixed Nation and an Authoritarian Political Culture

1. Melià, *Guaraní conquistado*, 174.

2. Ganson, *Guaraní under Spanish Rule*, 108.

3. Ibid., 187.

4. Reed, *Prophets of Agroforestry*, 49.

5. Susnik, *Aborígenes del Paraguay*, 110–112.

6. Whigham, "Paraguay's Pueblos de Indios," 179–180.

7. Whigham, *Politics of River Trade*, 50; see also Métraux, "Guaraní," 80.

8. Ganson, *Guaraní under Spanish Rule*, 64.

9. Barrett, *Dolor paraguayo*, 125, 130–131.

10. Reed, *Prophets of Agroforestry*, 50.

11. Williams, *Rise and Fall*, 435; Reed, *Prophets of Agroforestry*, 50.

12. See Ganson, "Evueví of Paraguay," 486.

13. Susnik, *Aborígenes del Paraguay*, 158.

14. Susnik, "Apuntes de etnografía," pp. 40–41, cited in Chase Sardi, Brun, and Enciso, *Situación sociocultural, económica*, 110.

15. Renshaw, *Indígenas del Chaco*, 51.

16. H. Warren, *Rebirth of the Paraguayan Republic*, 65.

17. P. Lewis, *Paraguay under Stroessner*, 32.

18. Cominges, *Exploraciones al Chaco del Norte*, cited in Susnik, *Aborígenes del Paraguay*, 157.

19. Grubb, *SAMS Magazine (1908/9)*, cited in Kidd, "Religious Change," 60. *SAMS Magazine* is the publication of the South American Mission Society (Anglican).

20. Ibid., 61.

21. Kidd, "Religious Change," 67–68.

22. Vázquez, "Historia de la legislación," 102.

23. Albospino, "Caza del Guayakí," 6. The name Paraguayans use for the Ache—Guayakí—means "rabid dog."

24. Vellard, *Civilisation du miel*, cited in Melià and Münzel, "Ratones y jaguares," 126.

25. Ibid., 125.

26. Zook, *Conduct of the Chaco War*.

27. Stahl, *Escenario indígena chaqueño*, 20–21.

28. Ibid., 27.

29. Ibid., 65.

30. Hanratty and Meditz, *Paraguay*, 36.

31. Prieto and Rolón, *Estudio legislación indígena*, 15.

32. Turner and Turner, "Role of Mestizaje," 146.

33. Ibid.

34. Knight, "Racism, Revolution, and Indigenismo," 98–101.

35. Bertoni, *Civilización guaraní*, cited in Robins, "Importancia de la cultura indígena," 23; González, *Proceso y formación*.

36. Robins, "Importancia de la cultura indígena," 18.

37. *Anales de la Asociación Indigenista*, 5.

38. de la Cadena, *Indigenous Mestizos*, 76, 78.

39. Robins, "Importancia de la cultura indígena," 18.

40. Knight, "Racism, Revolution, and Indigenismo," 100–102.

41. Vázquez, "Historia de la legislación," 102.

42. The Ache pronounce their name without emphasis on the last syllable, unlike its pronunciation in Spanish (Hill and Hurtado, *Aché Life History*, 41).

43. Cadogan, "Guayakí," 7.

44. Miraglia, *Gli Avá, I Guayakí*, 343, cited in Chase Sardi, Brun, and Enciso, *Situación sociocultural, económica*, 214. Kim Hill claims that there is no evidence from the Ache that they were sold at San Juan Nepomuceno. Rather, they were held there once after being captured but escaped. Ache also worked there for ranchers they liked (Kim Hill, anthropologist, interview by author, 10 July 1996).

45. The Vatican's *Anales Lateramensis* of 1940 reported that in eastern Paraguay it was not a crime to kill a "guayakí," and people were proud of the act, thinking it akin to killing a tiger (Albospino, "Caza del Guayakí," 6).

46. Chase Sardi and Almada, "Encuesta para," 166–167.

47. Prieto and Rolón, *Estudio legislación indígena*, 15.

48. *Anales de la Asociación Indigenista*, 11.

49. Corvalán, "Política lingüística," 123–124.

50. P. Lewis, *Paraguay under Stroessner*, 63–72.

51. P. Smith, "Search for Legitimacy," 91.

52. P. Lewis, *Paraguay under Stroessner*, 64.

53. Nickson, "Tyranny and Longevity," 239.

54. Graber, *Coming of the Moros*, 24. "Ayoreode" is the plural designation for the Ayoreo people.

55. Reed, *Prophets of Agroforestry*, 65.

56. Hanratty and Meditz, *Paraguay*, 114.

57. Verdecchia, *Algunas consideraciones*, 24.

58. Hill and Hurtado, *Aché Life History*, 49.

59. Abente, "Foreign Capital," 67.

60. Reed, *Prophets of Agroforestry*, 26.

61. Melià and Münzel, "Ratones y jaguares," 125.

62. Hill interview.

63. P. Lewis, *Paraguay under Stroessner*, 240.

64. Hicks, "Interpersonal Relationships," 102.

65. Miranda, *Stroessner Era*, 66.

66. Ibid., 109.

67. Cockcroft, "Paraguay's Stroessner," 340.

68. Ibid., 339.

69. Anderson, *Imagined Communities*, 16, 37, 140. See also Arens, *Genocide in Paraguay* and "Forest Indians."

70. Stephen Kidd, anthropologist, interview by author, Asunción, 24 May 1995.

71. Rafael Trinidad, interview by author, Asunción, 10 January 1995.

72. René Ramírez, interview by author, Asunción, 23 May 2001.

Chapter 3. A State Policy of Integration, 1958–1966

1. Oliveira, "Indian Movements and Indianism," 12.

2. Van Cott, *Indigenous People*, 190.

3. Stavenhagen, "Challenging the Nation-State," 429.

4. Cerna, "Beginning," 2.

5. Deloria, *Behind the Trail*, 231–232.

6. Swepston, "Latin American Approaches," 181.

7. Cadogan, "Carta a Ñandé," 26; idem, "Guayakí," 7.

8. Casement, in Taussig, *Shamanism*, 20.

9. Taussig, "Culture of Terror," 480, 492.

10. Reed, *Prophets of Agroforestry*, 15.

11. "Circular de la Corte Suprema," cited by Cadogan in "Tragedia guaraní," 272.

12. P. Lewis, *Paraguay under Stroessner*, 90.

13. Cadogan, *Extranjero*, 93.

14. Cadogan, "Tradiciones," cited in Melià, "Obra," 21.

15. Cadogan, "Tragedia guaraní," 270. *Curar de* can mean "to look after" as well as "to cure."

16. Cadogan, "Guayakí," 7.

17. Melià, "Obra," 19.

18. Cadogan, "Tragedia guaraní," 273.

19. Cadogan, "Torno a la aculturación," 148.

20. Cadogan, "Tragedia guaraní," 272.

21. See P. Lewis, *Paraguay under Stroessner*, 116–117. Marcial Samaniego passed away on 24 August 1990.

22. Graciela Ocariz Penoni, sociologist, interview by author, Asunción, 14 August 1995.

23. John Renshaw, economist and consultant, phone interview by author, 9 May 1996.

24. Decreto no. 1, 343, *Por el cual se crea*, 1958, 1, 20, Instituto del Indígena library (hereafter cited as INDI), Asunción; see also the appendix to Decreto no. 1, INDI.

25. P. Lewis, *Paraguay under Stroessner*, 89.

26. Ibid., 221.

27. Hanratty and Meditz, *Paraguay*, 180.

28. Maybury-Lewis, "Becoming Indian," 207ff.

29. Bejarano, *Solucionemos*, 143.

30. P. Lewis, *Paraguay under Stroessner*, 131.

31. Porfiria Zarza de Gómez, interview by author, Asunción, 15 March 1995.

32. Borgognón, *ABC*, 25 February 1968, cited in Bejarano, *Solucionemos*, 136.

33. Hill and Hurtado, *Aché Life History*, 49.

34. Pikygi, who led other Ache to the ranch, worked for Pereira after the rancher captured him but later escaped and returned to his people in the forest (Melià and Münzel, "Ratones y jaguares," 137).

35. Münzel, *Aché Indians*, 20.

36. "Grupos de indios."

37. Juan Borgognón to Dr. Estrellita Linz, 27 August 1959, file 110, 1958–1969, Departamento de Asuntos Indígenas (hereafter cited as DAI), Asunción.

38. Chase Sardi, Brun, and Enciso, *Situación sociocultural, económica*, 218.

39. Ibid., 219.

40. The congress provided an outline for inclusion; see Bejarano, *Solucionemos*, 135–139.

41. Ibid., 137.

42. Ibid.

43. Borgognón to "Señores Comité de 'Cáritas Paraguaya,'" 20 June 1959, file 110, 1958–1969, DAI, Asunción.

44. Gestolín Sanabria to Borgognón and Paso Yobai, 6 January 1960, file 110, 1958–1969, DAI, Asunción.

45. Monsignor Ángel Muzzolón, apostolic vicar of the Chaco, to Samaniego, 25 January 1960, file 122.2, 1959–1973, DAI, Asunción.

46. Samaniego to Dionisio Torres, minister of public health and social welfare, 1961, no. 8, file 110, 1958–1969, DAI, Asunción.

47. Dora Cáceres to Borgognón, 6 July 1959, file 122.2, 1959–1973, DAI, Asunción.

48. Borgognón to Juan S. García, 14 September 1960, file 110, 1958–1969, DAI, Asunción.

49. Zárate to Eladio Aquino, police chief of General Artigas, 1 June 1966, no. 46, file 110, 1958–1969, DAI, Asunción.

50. José Vera to Borgognón, 17 August 1959, file 122.2, 1959–1973, DAI, Asunción.

51. Ercilia Portillo de Vigo, director of the Liceo Nacional, to Zárate, 23 May 1966,

file 122.2, 1959–1973, DAI, Asunción; see also de la Cadena, *Indigenous Mestizos,* 177–182.

52. Father A. Saralegun, O.F.M., to Borgognón, 8 July 1959, file 122.2, 1959–1973, DAI, Asunción.

53. Cadogan to Marcial González, Villarrica, 13 September and 29 December 1959, file 122.2, 1959–1973, DAI, Asunción.

54. "Ataque de Indios."

55. Borgognón to Mr. J. J. French, president of the Food and Agriculture Organization of the United Nations (FAO) Mission in Asunción, 9 September 1959, file 110, 1958–1969, DAI, Asunción; see also Samaniego to French, 30 September 1959, file 110, 1958–1969, DAI, Asunción.

56. Samaniego to French, 30 September 1959, file 110, 1958–1969, DAI, Asunción. See also "Memoria del ejercicio de 1961," Memorias, 15 January 1962, DAI, Asunción; "1963 Memoria Annual Report," Memorias, DAI, Asunción; Borgognón to Francisco Facetti, director, National Health and Chemistry Department, 8 April 1963, file 110, 1958–1969, DAI, Asunción.

57. Borgognón to Fábrica Paraguaya de Alpargatas y Afines "America," 8 July 1960, file 110, 1958–1969, DAI, Asunción.

58. Reed, *Prophets of Agroforestry,* 32–73.

59. Borgognón to Bruno Müller, Misión Paso Cadena, 8 September 1961, file 110, 1958–1969, DAI, Asunción. See also Mörner, *Political and Economic;* Borgognón to Adán Godoy, Concepción and Asunción, 1 September 1961, file 110, 1958–1969, DAI, Asunción.

60. Regeher, "Teorías," 5; von Bremen, "Fuentes," 82.

61. "1963 Annual Report," 1.

62. Borgognón to M. Louet, French ambassador, 6 June 1962, file 110, 1958–1969, DAI, Asunción.

63. Münzel, *Aché Indians,* 21.

64. Clastres, *Chroniques,* 78, cited in Münzel, *Aché Indians,* 21.

65. Borgognón to Pereira, 26 November 1962, file 110, 1958–1969, DAI, Asunción. See also Pereira to Borgognón, San Juan Nepomuceno, 7 December 1962, file 122.2, 1959–1973, DAI, Asunción.

66. Münzel accuses Pereira of abusing Ache girls and providing them to visitors in *Aché Indians,* 29.

67. Monsignor Maricevich to Marcial Samaniego, Villarrica, 28 February 1962, and the response, file 110, 1958–1969; file 122.2, 1959–1973; both in DAI, Asunción.

68. Muntzel and Radelli, *Homenaje a Leonardo Manrique,* 38.

69. Samaniego to Dr. B. Gorostiaga, 7 October 1961, file 110, 1958–1969, DAI, Asunción.

70. "Que planes tiene el DAI," ca. 1958, M. Samaniego to Volta Gaona, director, Correos, 11 October 1960, no. 75, file 110, 1958–1969, DAI, Asunción.

71. Borgognón to Alejandro Cáceres Almada, director, Radio Nacional del Para-

guay, 30 May 1962, file 110, 1958–1969, DAI, Asunción; María González, Escuela Normal, San Lorenzo, to Borgognón, 10 July 1959, file 122.2, 1959–1973, DAI, Asunción.

72. Borgognón to Felix Urquhart, 5 May 1959, file 122.2, 1959–1973; Borgognón to Dr. Juan Bogarín Argaña, 3 August 1960, file 110, 1958–1969; Elías Hernández, director, Centro Cultural Paraguayo Americano, to Borgognón, 18 October 1962, file 122.2, 1959–1973; all in DAI, Asunción.

73. "Memoria 1961," "1962 Memoria Annual Report," 2; both in Memorias, DAI, Asunción.

74. Ministerio de Defensa Nacional, "Resolución ministerial no. 479," S3; no. 215, 17 September 1962, in "1963 Memoria (Annual Report)," 1, Memorias, DAI, Asunción.

75. Klassen, *Mennonites*, 143.

76. Stahl, *Escenario indígena chaqueño*, 91.

77. Hack, "Indios y mennonitas I," 219; idem, "Indios y mennonitas II," 237.

78. Hack, "Indios y mennonitas III," 64.

79. Loewen, "From Nomadism," 27.

80. Ibid., 29.

81. Ibid., 28–29.

82. Hack, "Indios y mennonitas I," 220.

83. Loewen, "From Nomadism," 28.

84. Ibid.

85. Klassen, *Mennonites*, 84.

86. Mennonite Central Committee, *1962 Workbook*, A12; Samaniego to Snow, U.S. ambassador, 7 June 1962, file 110, 1958–1969, DAI, Asunción; Graber, in Hack, "Indios y mennonitas," I, Spring and Winter, 1978, 225.

87. Hack, "Indios y mennonitas," I, Spring and Winter, 1978, 222.

88. "Parte semanal de actividad del DAI," 24 September 1962, in "1963 Memoria [Annual Report]," 1, Memorias, DAI, Asunción.

89. Borgognón to E. Nelson y Cía, Buenos Aires, Argentina, 6 March 1962, file 110, 1958–1969, DAI, Asunción.

90. Klassen, *Mennonites*, 139.

91. Loewen "From Nomadism," 36.

92. For years the military in the Chaco had released nationals from military service for killing a "moro." A nonviolent encounter with Ayoreode took place for the first time in 1958. See file 110, 1958–1969, DAI, Asunción.

93. Regeher, "Tierra y población," p. 6.

94. Von Bremen, "Ayoreode cazados," p. 4.

95. Bishop Ángel Muzzolón, apostolic vicar of the Chaco Paraguayo, to Borgognón, 29 August 1962, file 122.2, 1959–1973, DAI, Asunción.

96. See the Salesian Missions Web page, http://www.salesianmission.org/aboutus/index.html, accessed on 17 April 2006.

97. Regeher, "Tierra y población."

98. Hill, "Aché del Paraguay oriental," 150.

99. Cadogan to Dr. Alsina, minister of agriculture, Villarrica, 7 August 1962, file 122.2, 1959–1973; Borgognón to Alfredo Sacchetti, 9 March 1962, file 110, 1958–1969; both in DAI, Asunción.

100. "1963 Memoria Annual Report," Memorias, 19 December 1963, 7, DAI, Asunción.

101. Hill and Hurtado, *Aché Life History*, 49.

102. Laíno, *Familias sin tierra*, 47.

103. Ibid., 48.

104. Galeano, "Transformaciones agrarias," 51.

105. Verdecchia, *Algunas consideraciones*, 30–31.

106. *Censo de población y vivienda 1962*, cited by Nickson, "Brazilian Colonization," 114.

107. Hanratty and Meditz, *Paraguay*, 116.

108. Ibid., 115.

109. Law 854, Agrarian Statute, Art. 16, cited in Prieto and Rolón, *Estudio legislación indígena*, 55.

110. Robins, *Etnicidad*, 146.

111. "1964 Memoria Annual Report," Memorias, 30 January 1965, 4, DAI, Asunción. See also correspondence from Zárate to ministers of all seven departments, 7 November 1963, no. 130, file 110, 1958–1969, DAI, Asunción.

112. "1964 Memoria Annual Report," Memorias, 30 January 1965, 4, DAI, Asunción.

113. Chase Sardi, Brun, and Enciso, *Situación sociocultural, económica*, 428.

114. "1964 Memoria Annual Report," Memorias, 30 January 1965, 5, DAI, Asunción.

115. Ibid. See also Borgognón to Samaniego, 27 May 1963, file 110, 1958–1969, DAI, Asunción.

116. "1963 Memoria Annual Report," Memorias, 6–7, DAI, Asunción.

117. "1964 Memoria Annual Report," Memorias, 30 January 1965, 1, DAI, Asunción.

118. Zárate to Gen. Eligio Torres requesting travel expenses for Avá chief Juan Pablo Vera and a companion to return to Hernandarias, n.d., file 110, 1958–1969, DAI, Asunción. See also Wanda Jones, N.T.M., to Zárate, 18 May 1964, file 122.2, 1959–1973, DAI, Asunción.

119. "1964 Memoria Annual Report," 2, Memorias, DAI, Asunción.

120. Chase Sardi, "Monumento al indio."

121. "1963 Memoria Annual Report," Memorias, 9, DAI, Asunción.

122. Hanratty and Meditz, *Paraguay*, 44.

123. Zárate and Dr. Ezequiel Alsina to Monsignor Victor Righi, papal nuncio, 11 January 1965, file 110, 1958–1969, DAI, Asunción.

124. CEP bishops to archbishop of Asunción, 25 March 1965, Equipo Nacional de Misiones (ENDEPA [formerly AENM]), Asunción.

125. Dr. Fleitas to Dr. Fracchia, Asunción, 14 October 1967, AENM, Asunción.

126. Muratorio, "Protestantism," 520, 522.

127. Rappaport, "Misiones protestantes," 122.

128. Horst, "Breaking Down Religious Barriers," 69–70.

129. Kidd, "Religious Change," 111.

130. Ibid.

131. Ibid., 112.

132. Ibid., 116–117.

133. Ibid., 118.

134. Horst, "Breaking Down Religious Barriers," 71.

135. Edward Brice, administrator, Anglican indigenous program, personal correspondence with author, 31 October 1996.

136. Wallis, "Cuatro proyectos," 30.

137. Ibid., 41.

138. Miller, *Tobas argentinos*, 131, 154ff.

139. Regeher, "Mennonite Economic Life," 37.

140. Hill and Hurtado, *Aché Life History*, 50.

141. "1966 Memoria Annual Report," Memorias, 25 February 1967, 3, DAI, Asunción.

142. Juan Benítez, caretaker of natives, Caaguazú Department, to DAI director, 25 June 1962, file 122.2, 1959–1973, DAI, Asunción.

143. Hill and Hurtado, *Aché Life History*, 53.

144. "1966 Memoria Annual Report," Memorias, 25 February 1967, 3, DAI, Asunción.

145. Nickson, "Brazilian Colonization," 120.

146. "1966 Memoria Annual Report," Memorias, 25 February 1967, 2, DAI, Asunción.

147. Ibid., 6.

148. "Brief History."

Chapter 4. Integration Turns to Exclusion, 1967–1976

1. P. Lewis, *Paraguay under Stroessner*, 98–99.

2. Hanratty and Meditz, *Paraguay*, 162.

3. Cockcroft, "Paraguay's Stroessner," 340.

4. Borgognón to C. Achucano, 20 February 1968, no. 20, file 110, 1958–1969; Borgognón to J. Rojas, 26 March 1968, no. 32, file 110, 1958–1969; Infanzon to C. Oviedo, chief of police, 8 July 1968, no. 52, file 110, 1958–1969; all in DAI, Asunción.

5. Neighbors of "Cerro Sarambí" to Samaniego, Concepción, 25 March 1967, file 122.2, 1959–1973, DAI, Asunción.

6. N. Lewis, *Missionaries*, 143.

7. P. Lewis, *Paraguay under Stroessner*, 109, 113.

8. Mirna Vázquez, lawyer and professor, interview by author, Asunción, 20 October 1994.

9. Infanzon, "Política indigenista."

10. Ibid.

11. Chase Sardi, "Situación actual"; see also *Suplemento Antropológico* Vol. 6, 1971: 9–55.

12. Borgognón, "Panorama indígena paraguayo," 347.

13. Ibid., 348.

14. Ramos, *Indigenism*, 13–59.

15. Mainwaring and Wilde, *Progressive Church*, 10.

16. Ibid., 12.

17. CEP to Archbishop, 25 March 1965; Dr. Fleitas to Dr. Fracchia, 14 October 1967; both in AENM, Asunción. See also Horst, "Catholic Church, Human Rights," 724.

18. Minutes from meeting of Catholic leaders and Borgognón, 14 December 1967, AENM, Asunción.

19. Seelwische, "Misioneros," manuscript, AENM, Asunción, p.4.

20. Infanzon to E. Torres, director of Digetren, Asunción, 1 July 1969, no. 31, file 110, 1958–1969, DAI, Asunción.

21. Hill and Hurtado, *Aché Life History*, 49.

22. Pereira to Infanzon, 13 August 1968, file 122.2, 1959–1973, DAI, Asunción.

23. Münzel, "Manhunt," 23.

24. Chase Sardi, "Situación Actual," 221.

25. Pereira to Infanzon, 13 August 1968, file 122.2, 1959–1973, DAI, Asunción.

26. Infanzon to Dr. Riveros, *La Libertad*, no. 58 (18 July 1968), file 110, 1958–1969, DAI, Asunción.

27. Pereira to Infanzon, 13 August 1968, file 122.2, 1959–1973, DAI, Asunción.

28. The name Cerro Morotí is also significant, since the Ache had whiter skin color than many nationals. See Infanzon to General Ávila, director, Servicio de Intendencia, Fuerzas Armadas, 30 August 1968, file 122.2, 1959–1973, DAI, Asunción.

29. Pereira to Infanzon, 17 December 1968, file 122.2, 1959–1973, DAI, Asunción.

30. Ibid.

31. Hill and Hurtado, *Aché Life History*, 50.

32. Caulfield, "Culture and Imperialism," 186.

33. Ibid., 209.

34. Dostal, *Situation*, 12.

35. "Jornada nacional de pastoral," in Carter, *Papel*, 67.

36. Ibid., 59.

37. Langer and Muñoz, *Contemporary Indigenous Movements*, xxvii ff.; see also Churchill, *Struggle for the Land*.

38. Infanzon to General Aquino, IBR, 24 April 1969, no. 13, file 110, 1958–1969, DAI, Asunción.

39. Ibid.; Infanzon to Frutos, IBR, Asunción, 26 February 1969, no. 3, File 110 DAI-INDI.

40. La Gauloise Enterprise to Infanzon, 8 April 1969, file 122.2, 1959–1973, DAI, Asunción.

41. Francisco Cáceres, Toba-Qom leader, interview by author, Cerrito, 6 July 1995.

42. Ibid.

43. Atilio Velázquez to Infanzon, 22 February 1972, file 122.2, 1959–1973, DAI, Asunción.

44. Infanzon to Jorge Brugada, editor, *Farolito* (17 October 1969), file 110, 1958–1969, DAI, Asunción.

45. Hill and Hurtado, *Aché Life History*, 50.

46. Ibid., 52, 54.

47. Ibid., 51.

48. Interview, November 1984, by Kuchingi, found in Hill and Hurtado, *Aché Life History*, 52.

49. Ibid., 52.

50. Infanzon to Albospino, AIP, 10 December 1970, DAI-INDI A-2; "1971 Memoria Annual Report," Memorias, 21 January 1972, 3, DAI, Asunción.

51. Münzel, *Aché Indians*, 58.

52. Infanzon to the CAI, 6 April 1971, file 110, 1970, DAI, Asunción.

53. Melià and Münzel, "Ratones y jaguares," 143.

54. Hill and Hurtado, *Aché Life History*, 54.

55. Verdecchia, *Algunas consideraciones*, 32.

56. Carter, *Papel*, 70.

57. Ibid., 76.

58. NORMA Mission to Infanzon, Ypacaraí, 4 November 1971. file 122.2, 1959–1973; Federico Sammons, NTM, to Infanzon, 5 August 1970, file 122.2, 1959–1973; both in DAI, Asunción.

59. Deutsche Indianer Pionier Mission to L. Cabello, minister of defense, 10 November 1971, file 122.2, 1959–1973, DAI, Asunción.

60. L. Peterson, NTM, to the IBR and DAI, requesting fifteen hundred hectares of land to settle "los Manjui" [Yofauxa] in western Paraguay, 11 March 1971, file 122.2, 1959–1973, DAI, Asunción.

61. "Ejercicio del año 1971," no. 6, Memorias, 21 January 1972, 5, DAI, Asunción.

62. Maybury-Lewis, "Becoming Indian," 222.

63. Dostal, *Situation*, 12.

64. Ibid.

65. Colombres, *Por la liberación*, 31.

66. Chase Sardi, "Present Situation," 178, 180.

67. Colombres, *Por la liberación*, 21–30.

68. "Ejercicio del año 1971," no. 6, Memorias, 21 January 1972, 8, DAI, Asunción.

69. Redekop, *Strangers Become Neighbors*, 147.

70. Münzel, *Aché Indians*, 52; idem, "Manhunt," 29.

71. Münzel, *Aché Indians*, Extracts from 50, 51, 52.

72. Ibid., 32.

73. Ibid., 22, 28–29.

74. Ibid., 60.

75. Chase Sardi, Brun, and Enciso, *Situación sociocultural, económica*, 41.

76. Steve Herrick, former Peace Corps volunteer, telephone interview by author, 26 February 1999.

77. Ibid., 225.

78. "Habrá reunión," 8; "Concluye hoy," 26; Colombres, *Por la liberación*, 38–39.

79. Herrick interview.

80. "Persigue hoy conferencias."

81. Chase Sardi, "Situación actual," 37.

82. Melià and Münzel, "Ratones y jaguares," 145.

83. Kowalski, "Aceptar al otro como constituyente," 37–39.

84. Melià, *Guaraní conquistado*, 9.

85. Chase Sardi, Brun, Enciso, *Situación sociocultural, económica*, 278.

86. See appendix in Chase Sardi, "Situación actual," 37; Miraglia, "'Señuelos' guayakí cazan," and idem, "Melià: Los indios están," cited in Münzel, *Aché Indians*, 61.

87. Münzel, *Aché Indians*, 55.

88. Ray, Guggenheim Memorial Foundation, to Garret Sweany, consul, U.S. Embassy, 25 August 1971, file 122.2, 1959–1973, DAI, Asunción.

89. Chase Sardi to the CAI, 1 February 1972, Miguel Chase Sardi, personal files, Asunción (hereafter referred to as ACHS); also see appendix in Chase Sardi, "Situación actual," 41.

90. Münzel, *Aché Indians*, 73; "La CEP estudia," 6.

91. Bejarano, AIP, to Infanzon, 20 August 1972, file 122.2, 1959–1973, DAI, Asunción. See also Münzel, *Aché Indians*, 61.

92. Chase Sardi, Brun, and Enciso, *Situación sociocultural, económica*, 225.

93. "Informe," 30. "When a scientist takes many pictures of people who often do not wear clothes, it is easy to charge sexual misconduct" (Miguel Chase Sardi, interview by author, Asunción, Paraguay, 16 August 1995).

94. "Informe."

95. "1972 Memoria Annual Report," Memorias, 24 January 1973, 7, DAI, Asunción.

96. Milan Zeman, CAI, to NTM, 28 June 1972, file 122.2, 1959–1973, DAI, Asunción.

97. "Annual Report" (hereafter cited as NTM).

98. "1972 Memoria Annual Report," Memorias, 24 January 1973, 3, DAI, Asunción.

99. Hill and Hurtado, *Aché Life History*, 54.

100. Proyecto Paï Tavyterã, "Recuento histórico-analítico," 7.

101. Ibid., 23.

102. Renshaw, "Paraguay, the Marandú Project," 15.

103. Chase Sardi and Susnik, "Indios del Paraguay," 312.

104. Münzel, *Aché Indians*, 5.

105. Ibid., 63.

106. Department of Ethnology, University of Bern, to the Consulate-General of Paraguay, 4 June 1973, in Arens, *Genocide in Paraguay*, 6–7.

107. Münzel, *The Aché*, 28.

108. Ibid., 21.

109. Ibid., 29.

110. Carter, *Papel*, 75–76.

111. Marvin Cole, NTM, to Infanzon, 7 July 1973, file 122.2, 1959–1973, DAI, Asunción.

112. "Ejercicio 1973 Memoria (Annual Report)," no. 3, 3, Memorias, 8 January 1974, DAI, Asunción.

113. John Battman, Anglican Mission, to Infanzon, 18 June 1973, file 122.2, 1959–1973, DAI, Asunción.

114. Infanzon to Lars Forland, NORMA, 8 March 1974, no. 30, file 110, 1970 , DAI, Asunción.

115. Abourezk, "Genocide Activities." 5941.

116. Hanratty and Meditz, *Paraguay*, 196.

117. Arens, *Genocide in Paraguay*, 13.

118. Foreign Relations Ministry to Samaniego, no. 085, 23 May 1974, 10 February 1975, file 122.2, 1973–1988, DAI, Asunción.

119. Infanzon to Melià, 17 April 1974, file 110, 1970 , DAI, Asunción; "No hay genocidio," 7.

120. Bartomeu Melià, interview by author, Asunción, 19 April 1995.

121. Infanzon to J. María de Mahieu, Buenos Aires, 11 May 1974, file 110, 1970 , DAI, Asunción.

122. "No hay genocidio."

123. Ibid.

124. "Proyecto Marandú," 9.

125. Llorente and Carmona, "Parte crónica," 21.

126. Ibid., 21–23; "Tobas reclaman," 16.

127. Münzel, *The Aché*, 14.

128. Ibid., 26.

129. Hill and Hurtado, *Aché Life History*, 54.

130. Herrick interview.

131. Miguel Chase Sardi, interview by author, Asunción, Paraguay, 10 October 1994.

132. "Se inició," 14; Colombres, *Por la liberación*, 248.

133. Colombres, *Por la liberación*, 253.

134. "Parlamento indio," 9.

135. Llorente and Carmona, "Parte crónica," 24.

136. See the analogous case of Brazil's Fundação Nacional do Índio (National Foundation for Indians, FUNAI) in Maybury-Lewis, "Becoming Indian," 222.

137. "Determinaron problemas," 10.

138. "1973 Memoria Annual Report," Memorias, 8 January 1974, 7, DAI, Asunción.

139. "1976 Memoria Annual Report," Memorias 1 and 2, pp. 1-2, DAI, Asunción.

140. Renshaw, "Paraguay, the Marandú Project," 17.

141. "Dos aborígenes," 6.

142. "Retornaron indígenas," 11.

143. Llorente and Carmona, "Parte crónica," 28; "Finalizó," 14.

144. Modesto Gómez, interview by author, New Halbstadt, Paraguay, 9 May 1995.

145. Ibid.

146. "Marandú."

147. Llorente and Carmona, "Parte crónica," 25.

148. Renshaw, "Paraguay, the Marandú Project," 16.

149. Ibid., 17.

150. Llorente and Carmona, "Parte crónica," 30.

151. Colombres, *Por la liberación*, 244, 246.

152. Ibid., 43.

153. Ibid., 3. On Communist activities, see P. Lewis, *Paraguay under Stroessner*, 221.

154. "Consejo indígena," 9.

155. Llorente and Carmona, "Parte crónica," 45.

156. Renshaw interview.

157. Proyecto Païr Tavyterã, "Recuento histórico analítico," 35. See also Hans-Rudolf Wicker, "Informe semestral," 6 January 1978; and Pedro Juan Caballero, PPT; both in Asociación Indigenista Paraguaya (hereafter AIP), Archives, Asunción.

158. Proyecto Païr Tavyterã, "Recuento histórico analítico," 24.

159. B. Bentley, *Projects*, 8.

160. Wicker, "Informe semestral," January–June 1977, 2, AIP, Archives, Asunción.

161. Kokueguara, *Experiencias campesinas* (*Peasant Experience*), 48–49, written for the Comisión Nacional de Rescate y Difusión de la Historia Campesina (National Commission for the Rescue and Diffusion of Peasant History).

162. Decreto no. 18, 365, *Por el cual se crea*, 1975, 20 October 1975, DAI, Asunción.

163. Ibid.

164. Llorente and Carmona, "Parte crónica," 30.

165. Renshaw, "Paraguay, the Marandú Project," 15.

166. Chase Sardi interviews.

167. Ibid. See also Arens, *Genocide in Paraguay*, xii.

168. Chase Sardi and Susnik, "Indios del Paraguay," 316.

Chapter 5. The Indigenous Response to Exclusion, 1976–1987

1. Chase Sardi interviews.

2. Llorente and Carmona, "Parte crónica," 48.

3. Stern, *Peru's Indian Peoples*, 27.

4. Reed, *Prophets of Agroforestry*, 181.

5. Sinforiano Rodríguez, physician with the Marandú Project, interview by author, Asunción, 21 February 1995.

6. de la Cadena, *Indigenous Mestizos*, 91.

7. Reed, *Prophets of Agroforestry*, 182.

8. "Sesiones diarias de la Comisión Ejecutiva API," Act 3, 7 January 1975, Asociación de Parcialidades Indígenas (hereafter API), Archives, Asunción.

9. Smith, "Evaluación de API," in Chase Sardi and Susnik, *Indios del Paraguay*, 317.

10. Wiesel, "Now We Know," in Arens, *Genocide in Paraguay*, 165.

11. Davis, "A Lawyer's Summation," in Arens, *Genocide in Paraguay*, 145.

12. Robins, *Etnicidad*, 117.

13. "Desmienten rumores," 14.

14. Scott, *Domination*, 36–37.

15. Stahl, "Chaco Native Economies," 13; Wallis, "Cuatro proyectos," 39.

16. Regeher, "Mennonite Economic Life," 38–39.

17. "Los indígenas del Chaco"; "Las comunidades indígenas," 15.

18. Klassen, *Mennonites*, 204.

19. Wallis, "Cuatro proyectos," 45.

20. Regeher, "Mennonite Economic Life," 38–39.

21. Miller, *Tobas argentinos*, 131.

22. Wallis, "Cuatro proyectos," 41.

23. Stahl, *Escenario indígena chaqueño*, 102.

24. Sanneh, *Translating the Message*, 124.

25. Stahl, *Escenario indígena chaqueño*, 99.

26. Edward Brice, interview by author, Asunción, Paraguay, 23 March 1995.

27. Wallis, "Cuatro proyectos," 28.

28. Ibid.

29. Brice interview.

30. Baer and Birch, "Expansion of the Economic," 786.

31. Ibid., *787*. See also Nickson, "Brazilian Colonization," 111.

32. Fogel, *Proceso de modernización*, 54.

33. Ibid., 31, 135–136.

34. "Se prepara," 16.

35. Fogel, *Proceso de modernización*, 62.

36. Prieto, *Entre la resignación*, 144.

37. Baer and Birch, "Expansion of the Economic," *787*.

38. Ibid., *795*; "Estamos canalizando," 10.

39. "Los ricos," 3; Baer and Birch, "Expansion of the Economic," 795; Arens, "Forest Indians," 1–11.

40. Miranda, *Stroessner Era*, 109.

41. "Samaniego."

42. Baer and Birch, "Expansion of the Economic," 792.

43. Ibid., *790*.

44. Teltsch, "UN Body Accuses U.S.," 5.

45. Arens, "Forest Indians," 7.

46. Ibid.

47. Ibid, 9.

48. Maybury-Lewis and Howe, *Indian Peoples*, 110.

49. Arens, "Forest Indians," 13.

50. Chase Sardi interview. 10 October 1994.

51. "Aclaración a la opinión pública," 16 February 1978, API, Archives, Asunción.

52. Luis G. Arias, Paraguayan mission, to Dr. Alberto Nogues, minister of foreign relations, UN–New York, 27 April 1978, Instituciones Oficiales–1982 file; Arias to Nogues, 3 May 1978, 252/78/MR (Memorandum Received); both in INDI, Asunción.

53. Stern, *Peru's Indian Peoples*, 138–139. See also G. Smith, *Livelihood and Resistance*, 59.

54. "Tobas-lenguas," 20.

55. José Seelwische, missionary and former director of the AENM, interview by author, Asunción, 29 June 1995; see also Bush, *Slave Women*, 141–149.

56. Casaccia and Vázquez, La lucha por la tierra en defensa de la vida, 17.

57. Renshaw, "Paraguay, the Marandú Project," 16.

58. Ibid., 24–30.

59. Bauer, "Rural Workers," 63.

60. On payment with alcohol, see Zogbaum, *B. Traven*, 164, 167; Muratorio, *Life and Times*, 154; Barrett, *Dolor paraguayo*, 125, 130–131.

61. Chase Sardi and Almada, "Encuesta para," 166.

62. McCreery, *Sweat of Their Brow*, 125.

63. "Tobas piden," 12.

64. Seelwische interview.

65. Stunnenberg, *Entitled to Land*, 105.

66. Carter, *Papel*, 110.

67. Ibid.

68. See von Bremen, "Ayoreode cazados," 5.

69. Wallis and Lincoln, "Propuesta," 10; "Proyecto Guaraní-Ñandeva," ca. 1985, AIP, Archives, Asunción.

70. "Acompañamiento básico a las comunidades guaraníes fuera de las colonias mennonitas," Proyecto Guaraní-Ñandeva, ca. 1981, housed at Servicios Profesionales Antropológicos y Jurídicos (hereafter SEPSAJ), file "Informes, Proyecto Guaraní-Ñandeva."

71. "La Gauloise."

72. Mak'a to INDI, 9 January 1980, file 122.2, 1973–1988, DAI, Asunción; "Guías," 8; "Maká," 13.

73. Óscar Centurión, former director of INDI, interview by author, Asunción, 13 March 1995.

74. "Decretan ocupación," 11.

75. "Tobas-maskoy," 18.

76. Seelwische interview.

77. "Tobas-maskoy podrán," 6.

78. Robins, *Etnicidad*, 121.

79. "Asumió," 12.

80. "Se hizo cambio."

81. "Nos preocupa cambio."

82. "Casanillo está disponible," 21.

83. "INDI," 13

84. "Nadie quiere," 18.

85. Rubén Osorio, general auditor of war, correspondence received 14 January 1981, file 122.2, 1973–1988, DAI, Asunción.

86. "Casanillo es un potrero," 13.

87. "En marcha 4;" R. Bejarano, AIP, to Centurión, 19 August 1980, correspondence received, file 122.2, 1973–1988, DAI, Asunción

88. "Buscar," 16.

89. "Extranjero," 7.

90. "Difícil sobrevivencia," 11.

91. "Asentamiento," 21.

92. "La CEP," 11; "Gobierno," 11; "Caso toba-maskoy," 12.

93. Seelwische, "Una interpretación del indígena," 23–25; "Indígena como persona," 7; "Indígena es una persona," 15; open letter from the Catholic Church to its congregations, "Carta de los misioneros católicos a todos los pueblos indígenas del Paraguay," 1 December 1981, 7, AENM, Asunción.

94. "Carta de los misioneros católicos a todos los pueblos indígenas del Paraguay," 1 December 1981, 7, AENM, Asunción.

95. Vázquez interview.

96. Penoni interview.

97. Anteproyecto de ley que establece, July 1980, Asunción, 3ff, INDI, Asunción; Ester Prieto, attorney, interview by author, Asunción, 20 February 1995.

98. Fretz, *Pilgrims in Paraguay*, 48, 50.

99. "Desalojo," 16.

100. Chase Sardi, Brun, and Enciso, *Situación sociocultural, económica*, 373.

101. "Los indígenas siguen," 3.

102. "Existiría premura," 27.

103. Julio César Frutos, Colorado Party deputy, interview by author, Asunción, 20 February 1995.

104. Seelwische interview.

105. "Proyecto Guaraní-Ñandeva: Informe de actividades, 9/81–2/82," Filadelfia, February 1982, AIP, housed at SEPSAJ, Asunción.

106. Renshaw, *Indígenas del Chaco*, 55.

107. Wallis, "Las expectativas," 3.

108. Wallis, "Cuatro proyectos"; biennial report "Proyecto Guaraní-Ñandeva: Informe semestral, 7–12," 1982, SEPSAJ, Asunción.

109. Chase Sardi, Brun, and Enciso, *Situación sociocultural, económica*, 188–193.

110. Frutos, "Estatuto del Indígena," 74.

111. "Anteproyecto de ley que establece," July 1980, 11, 13, INDI, Asunción.

112. Samaniego to Bishop Olevar, 27 January 1982, SI no. 019, file 122.2, 1973–1988, DAI, Asunción.

113. Vázquez interview; "Estatuto," 10.

114. Felipe Caballero, Enlhit leader, interview by author, Paraje Pirahú, 28 September 1995.

115. "Proyecto de ley," 14.

116. "Se prepara," 16.

117. Fogel, *Proceso de modernización*, 64.

118. Ibid., 62.

119. Ibid., 43.

120. "Reasentamiento," 15.

121. "Indígenas pedirán indemnización."

122. Samaniego to Francisco Almada, 2 May 1982, file 110, 1970 , DAI, Asunción; see also "Itaipú ubicará," 28.

123. "Itaipú ensanchó," 11.

124. "Proyecto Guaraní-Ñandeva."

125. Ibid.

126. Haas, *Conquests*, 38–39, 90–91.

127. Col. Anrés Zaracho, "Comisión efectuada en la Colonia Mennonita," Occasional Report, 4, INDI, Asunción.

128. *Censo y Estudio de la Población Indígena*, INDI, 97–103.

129. "Y se mueren," 9.

130. Smith and Fogel, "Invisible Guaraní," 2.

131. Flores, "Las comunidades," 98–99.

132. "Proyecto de desarrollo," 13.

133. Prieto, *Entre la resignación*, 48.

134. Smith and Fogel, "Invisible Guaraní," 67.

135. Ramírez interview.

136. Ibid.

137. Ibid.

138. Casaccia and Vázquez, *Lucha*, 40.

139. "Nuestro pueblo," 10.

140. "Los indígenas maskoy," 32.

141. Biennial report, "Proyecto Ayoreo: Informe semestral, 7–8," January–June 1983, AIP, housed at SEPSAJ, Asunción.

142. Biennial report, "Informe final del Proyecto Ayoreo," February 1984, 10, 13, 15, AIP, housed at SEPSAJ, Asunción.

143. Chase Sardi, Brun, and Enciso, *Situación sociocultural, económica*, 47.

144. Ibid., 46.

145. Cristóbal Wallis, telephone interview by author, 8 August 1996.

146. "Continúan presiones," 6; "Mennonitas ingresaron," 19.

147. Chase Sardi, "Situación," 424.

148. Nickson, "Tyranny and Longevity," 248.

149. Caballero interview.

150. Correspondence from Anglican Church, API, and Equipo Nacional de Misiones (ENM), to INDI, 19 December 1980, Paraguayan Anglican Church, Archives, Correspondence (hereafter AIAP), Asunción.

151. "Nuevo rechazo," 11.

152. "Maskoy," 13.

153. Correspondence from two hundred Paraguayan citizens to General Martínez, INDI, 4 October 1984, AENM, Asunción.

154. America's Watch Report, *Paraguay*, 38–39.

155. Ibid., 27.

156. Pedro Theis, peasant organizer, interview by Berta Horst, Resistencia, Argentina, 24 September 1999.

157. Reed, *Forest Dwellers*, 83.

158. Smith and Fogel, "Invisible Guaraní," 91.

159. "Denuncian desalojo," 41.

160. Horst, "Catholic Church, Human Rights," 736.

161. "Denuncian quema," 19; "Armados," 18.

162. *Paraguay*, 59.

163. Ibid., 60.

164. "A la opinión pública," *El Diario*, 6.

165. "Líder mbyá," 21.

166. "Comunidad 'mbyá,'" 16.

167. "Mennonitas," 41.

168. "Prosigue conflicto," 4.

169. "Comunidad mbyá-apyteré," 16.

170. "Menonitas hostigan," 10.

171. Williams, "Paraguay's Stroessner," 26.

172. "Más firmas," 11.

173. "Denuncian que el INDI," 26.

174. "Indígenas agradecen," 9.

175. Scott, *Domination*, 165.

176. Grünberg, "Estudio," 4.

177. Proyecto Païi Tavyterã, "Recuento histórico analítico," 88.

178. "Denuncian venta," 23.

179. Crispín Torres, Yvykatú, to Dr. Gadea, Coronel Oviedo, Project Guaraní headquarters, 3 September 1987, PG files, AIP, Asunción.

180. Campolorogosode were Ayoreode who lived at the Campo Loro mission.

181. "Informe de la Comisión de Entidades Privadas," report, 4 February 1987, 11, SEPSAJ, Asunción.

182. Ibid., 13.

183. Ibid.

184. Perasso, *Crónicas*, 105.

185. "Genocidio."

186. "Inícua explotación," 23.

187. "Piden investigación," 19; see also "Más acusaciones," 18.

188. Von Bremen, "Ayoreode cazados."

189. Norman Fry, NTM director, interview by author, Asunción, 29 May 1995.

190. "Los sufrimientos," 11.

191. "Los maskoy solicitan," 26; "Pueblo maskoy," 11.

192. "Nuevas muestras," 21; "Otras 3,000," 16.

193. Grünberg, "Estudio," 24.

194. Proyecto Païi Tavyterã, "Recuento histórico-analítico," 95.

195. Horst, "Consciousness and Contradiction," 121.

196. "Senado," 11.

197. "Debemos vivir," 12.

198. Taussig, *Devil and Commodity*, 10.

199. "Se agudiza," 26.

200. Reed, *Forest Dwellers*, 84, 89.

201. Ibid., 93–98.

202. "El papa estará," 18.

203. "Miles," 10.

204. "Esto pasa."

205. "Emotiva presencia," 8–9.

206. Horst, "Catholic Church, Human Rights," 740. See also Lucio Alfert, bishop, Apostolic Vicariate of Pilcomayo, interview by author, Mariscal Estigarribia, 18 May 2005.

207. "Hemos labrado," 12.

Chapter 6. Indigenous Mobilization and Democracy in Paraguay, 1988–1992

1. Cockroft, "Paraguay's Stroessner," 338.

2. "Reclaman cese," 20.

3. "IBR," 14.

4. "Conclusiones," 16.

5. "Finiquitado juicio," 41.

6. "En el Día del Indígena," 12.

7. "Nuevos y más," 15.

8. Ibid.

9. "Posiciones encontradas," 22.

10. Carter, *Papel*, 122.

11. "INDI no organiza," 15.

12. Miguel Fritz, priest, Apostolic Vicariate of Pilcomayo, interview by author, Mariscal Estigarribia, 18 May 1995.

13. Alfert interview.

14. "Le hicieron," 10.

15. "El papa trajo," 11.

16. "Indígenas denunciaron," 44.

17. "Ésta es," 19; "Nos quieren."

18. "Los maskoy cultivan," 5.

19. "Expropian tierras para indígenas," 10.

20. "Mbyá denuncia," 16.

21. "Nuestro hábitat," 18.

22. "Los mbyá denuncian," 21.

23. Smith and Fogel, "Invisible Guaraní," 79.

24. "Conflictos sin solución," 26.

25. "Proyecto Caazapá," 6.

26. Reed, *Forest Dwellers*, 84.

27. Comisión de Solidaridad con los Pueblos Indígenas, "Denuncia del ecocidio," 225.

28. "Chiripá se reunen," 3.

29. Comisión de Solidaridad con los Pueblos Indígenas, "Denuncia del ecocidio," 226.

30. Ibid.

31. "Solidaridad," 18.

32. "Chiripá se reunen," 9.

33. Reed, *Forest Dwellers*, 128–129.

34. Reed, *Prophets of Agroforestry*, 139–147.

35. Ibid., 16–17.

36. Bruno Barras, Ïshïro leader, interview by author, Asunción, 11 March 1995.

37. "Se saben," 28.

38. Comisión de Solidaridad con los Pueblos Indígenas, "Denuncia del ecocidio," 227.

39. Reed, *Prophets of Agroforestry*, 15.

40. "Privilegios," 21.

41. "Un saldo," 16.

42. "Paraguay Coup," A5.

43. Theis interview.

44. Carter, *Papel*, 134.

45. "Paraguay General," A9(B).

46. "Después del golpe," 15.

47. FEPI to Gen. Adolfo Samaniego, 10 February 1989, file 122.1, INDI, Asunción; "Nos preocupa la situación," 19; "Inquietudes," 5.

48. Ramírez interview.

49. "Autoridades," 23.

50. Mallorquín to Chase Sardi, 14 April 1989, P.C. no. 22/89, file 46, INDI, Asunción. See also Executive Decree no. 998, 12 April 1989, which names Mallorquín as president of the INDI.

51. Chase Sardi and Susnik, "Indios del Paraguay," 339.

52. Reed, "New Rules," 315.

53. "Después del golpe," 15.

54. "Discurso," 8.

55. "Samaniego con indígenas," 14.

56. Carter, *Papel*, 138–139.

57. "Piden expropiación," 5.

58. Fernando Ramírez, CONCORDER, to Mallorquín, INDI, 10 July 1989, file 122.1, INDI, Asunción.

59. Dr. Federico Mandelburger, presidential secretary, to Mallorquín, 10 July 1989, S.E. no. 651, 393, file 122.1, INDI, Asunción.

60. Ibid., 393–394.

61. "Transculturación," 16.

62. "Mantenerlos," 16.

63. "S.E. no. 651," correspondence, 394, file 122.1, INDI, Asunción.

64. "Indígenas quieren un lugar," 25.

65. "Estamos muy orgullosos," 19.

66. "Población indígena," 20.

67. Diskin, "Ethnic Discourse," 157.

68. "Los indígenas saben," 18.

69. "Está dada," 18.

70. "Posición final," 18.

71. "Posición del INDI," 20.

72. "A la opinión pública," *Hoy*, 21.

73. "Indígenas denunciaron acoso," 15.

74. "Menonitas endurecen," 24.

75. "Sanción," 20.

76. "Exprópian tierras de Sommerfeld," 3.

77. "Para los indígenas," 60.

78. "Culturas indígenas," 15; "Auditoría," 13.

79. "La constitución," 25; "INDI y la futura constitución," 21.

80. "Indígenas y la reforma," 7.

81. "Carta Magna," 22.
82. "Constituyente," 22.
83. "Primer encuentro," 32. See also "Nativos analizaron," 12.
84. "Nativos presentan," 16.
85. Robins, *Etnicidad*, 132.
86. "Indígenas desean," 2.
87. Ramos, *Indigenism*, 257–259.
88. Kloosterman, "El derecho a la tierra," in Varese, *Pueblos indios*, 208.
89. Frutos and Velázquez, Colorado deputies, to Dr. Antonio Ruffinelli, 19 September 1991, Paraguay, Congress, Archives (hereafter referred to as APNC), Asunción.
90. "Buscarán," 8.
91. Frutos and Velázquez, Colorado deputies, to Dr. Antonio Ruffinelli, 19 September 1991, APNC, Asunción.
92. Ibid.
93. "Voz," 7.
94. "Implementarán," 2.
95. "Dan fin," 3.
96. Ramírez interview.
97. Constitución nacional, 1992, 14, 15.
98. "Indígenas quieren que se respeten," 2.
99. "Satisfacción," 2.
100. González Casanova, Roitman, and Albó, *Democracia*, 54.
101. See Hale, "Rethinking Indigenous Politics," 17–19.
102. Polanco, *Indigenous Peoples*, 94, 116.
103. "Analizarán," 2.

Chapter 7. Conclusion: Everyday Forms of Exclusion

1. Mallon, "Indian Communities," 52.
2. See Alan Knight on Mexico, Antonio de Souza Lima on Brazil, Blanca Muratorio and Ronald Stutzman on Ecuador, and Stefano Varese on Peru.
3. Gutiérrez, *Nationalist Myths*, 90.
4. See, for example, all of Münzel's publications and, more recently, Cockcroft, "Paraguay's Stroessner," 341.
5. Cockcroft, "Paraguay's Stroessner," 344.
6. Hale, "Rethinking Indigenous Politics," 17.
7. See P. Lewis, *Paraguay under Stroessner*, 226.
8. Ibid., 227.
9. Stavenhagen, "Challenging the Nation-State," 440.
10. P. Lewis, *Paraguay under Stroessner*, 228.
11. Stutzman, "Mestizaje," 76.
12. Ibid., 76.
13. Varese, "Multiethnicity and Hegemonic Construction," 73–74.

14. Haas, *Conquests*, 90.

15. G. Bentley, "Ethnicity and Practice," 45.

16. Guidieri and Pellizzi, "Smoking Mirrors," 31.

17. Ibid., 27.

18. K. Warren, "Transforming Memories," 203–204.

19. See "Agrarian Structure and Ethnic Resistance," in Guidieri, Pellizzi, and Tambiah, *Ethnicities and Nations*, 101.

20. Ibid.

21. Muratorio, *Life and Times*, 204.

22. Muratorio, "Protestantism"; Miller, *Tobas argentinos*.

23. Horst, "Breaking Down," 65–92.

24. Mallon, "Indian Communities," 53. See also Van Cott, *Indigenous People*, 16.

Bibliography

Archives and Primary Sources

Asociación de Parcialidades Indígenas (Association of Indigenous Groups, API). Archives. Minutes and reports. Luque.

Asociación Indigenista Paraguaya (Paraguayan Indigenista Association, AIP). Archives. Correspondence and papers. Asunción.

Centro de Estudios Paraguayos (Center for Paraguayan Studies, CEPAG).

Chase Sardi, Miguel (ACHS). Personal files. Asunción.

Conferencia Episcopal Paraguayo (Episcopal Conference of the Paraguayan Catholic Church, CEP), Asunción.

Departamento de Asuntos Indígenas (Department of Indigenous Affairs, DAI). Archives. Instituto Nacional del Indígena Library. Asunción.

———. Correspondence sent, file 46. Instituto del Indígena Library. Asunción.

———. Correspondence sent, file 110, 1958–1969, 1970 . Instituto del Indígena Library. Asunción.

———. Correspondence received, file 122.1, 1989. Instituto del Indígena Library. Asunción.

———. Correspondence received, 1959–1973, 1973–1988, file 122.2. Instituto del Indígena Library. Asunción.

———. Memorias, 1961–1981. Instituto del Indígena Library. Asunción.

Equipo Nacional de Misiones (Catholic Missions Team, ENDEPA [formerly Archives of the Equipo Nacional de Misiones (AENM), currently Coordinadora Nacional de Pastoral Aborígen (CONAPI)]. Catholic Diocese Archives. Asunción.

Instituto de Bienestar Rural (Rural Welfare Institute, IBR). Asunción.

Instituto Nacional del Indígena (National Indigenous Institute; after 1989 called Instituto Paraguayo del Indígena (Paraguayan Indigenous Institute), INDI). Asunción.

———. Instituciones Oficiales–1982 file. Instituto Nacional del Indígena Library. Asunción.

New Tribes Mission (NTM). Archives. Reports, correspondence. Asunción.

Paraguay. National Congress. Archives (APNC). Correspondence and reports. Asunción.

Paraguayan Anglican Church (Iglesia Angelicana Paraguaya, AIAP). Archives. Correspondence. Asunción.

Paraguayan Episcopal (Catholic) Conference. Asunción.

Proyecto Païˉ Tavyterãˉ (Païˉ Tavyterãˉ Project, PPT). AIP and SEPSAJ. Asunción.

Regeher, Walter (AWR). Personal files. Neu Halbstadt, Neuland Colony, Paraguay.

Servicios Profesionales Antropológicos y Jurídicos (Professional Anthropology and Legal Services, SEPSAJ). Correspondence and records for AIP. Asunción.

Interviews

Alfert, Lucio, bishop, Apostolic Vicariate of Pilcomayo, interview with author, Mariscal Estigarribia, 18 May 2005.

Barras, Bruno, Ïshïro leader, interview with author, Asunción, 11 March 1995.

Brice, Edward, interview with author, 23 March 1995.

Caballero, Felipe, Enlhit leader, interview with author, Paraje Pirahú, 28 September 1995.

Cáceres, Francisco, Toba-Qom leader, interview with author, Cerrito, 6 July 1995.

Centurión, Óscar, former director of INDI, interview with author, Asunción, 13 March 1995.

Chase Sardi, Miguel, interview with author, 10 October 1994, Asunción, 16 August 1995.

Fritz, Miguel, priest, Apostolic Vicariate of Pilcomayo, interview with author, Mariscal Estigarribia, 18 May 1995.

Frutos, Julio César, Colorado Party deputy, interview with author, Asunción, 20 February 1995.

Fry, Norman, NTM director, interview with author, Asunción, 29 May 1995.

Gómez, Modesto, interview with author, New Halbstadt, Paraguay, 9 May 1995.

Herrick, Steve, former Peace Corps volunteer, telephone interview with author, 26 February 1999.

Hill, Kim, anthropologist, telephone interview with author, 10 July 1996.

Kidd, Stephen, anthropologist, interview with author, Asunción, 24 May 1995.

Melià, Bartomeu, interview with author, Asunción, 19 April 1995.

Penoni, Graciela Ocariz, sociologist, interview with author, Asunción, 14 August 1995.

Prieto, Ester, attorney, interview with author, Asunción, 20 February 1995.

Ramírez, René, interview with author, Asunción, 23 May 2001.

Renshaw, John, economist and consultant, telephone interview with author, 9 May 1996.

Rodríguez, Sinforiano, physician with the Marandú Project, interview with author, Asunción, 21 February 1995.

Seelwische, José, missionary and former director of the AENM, interview with author, Asunción, 29 June 1995.

Theis, Pedro, peasant organizer, interview with Berta Horst, Resistencia, Argentina, 24 September 1999.

Trinidad, Rafael, interview with author, Asunción, 10 January 1995.

Vázquez, Mirna, lawyer and professor, interview with author, Asunción, 20 October 1994.

Wallis, Cristóbal, telephone interview with author, 8 August 1996.

Zarza de Gómez, Porfiria, interview with author, Asunción, 15 March 1995.

Secondary Sources

Abente, Diego. "Foreign Capital, Economic Elites and the State in Paraguay during the Liberal Republic (1870–1936)." *Journal of Latin American Studies* 21, no. 1 (February 1989): 61–88.

Abourezk, James. "Genocide Activities in Paraguay." *U.S. Senate Congressional Record* (8 March 1974): 5941–5945.

"Acompañamiento básico a las comunidades guaraníes fuera de las colonias mennonitas." Unpublished manuscript. In file "Informes, Proyecto Guaraní-Ñandeva," SEPSAJ, Asunción, ca. 1981.

"A la opinión pública." *El Diario* (3 November 1985).

"A la opinión pública." *Hoy* (24 September 1989).

Albospino, Luis. "La caza del Guayakí." *Ñandé* 1, no. 22 (February 1960): 6.

America's Watch Report. *Paraguay: Repression in the Countryside.* New York: America's Watch Committee, 1988.

Anales de la Asociación Indigenista del Paraguay 1, no. 1 (October 1945).

"Analizarán capítulo referente." *Hoy* (6 June 1992).

Anderson, Benedict R. *Imagined Communities: Reflections on the Origin*

"Annual Report of the New Tribes Mission in Paraguay." Asunción: New Tribes Mission Offices, 1991.

Arens, Richard, ed. "The Forest Indians in Stroessner's Paraguay: Survival or Extinction?" *Survival International Report.* London: Survival International, 1978.

———. *Genocide in Paraguay.* Philadelphia, Penn.: Temple University Press, 1976.

"Armados desalojaron a los indígenas." *Hoy* (19 October 1985).

"El asentamiento corre un serio riesgo de fracasar." *Hoy* (5 November 1981).

"Asumió director del INDI. Extrañeza y malestar en indígenas." *Última Hora* (23 December 1980).

"Ataque de Indios: Hubo 8 muertos." *El País* (20 November 1960).

"La auditoría constató irregularidades en el INDI." *ABC* (30 June 1989).

"Las autoridades nunca se preocuparon por nosotros." *Última Hora* (7 March 1989).

Baer, Werner, and Melissa Birch. "Expansion of the Economic Frontier: Paraguayan Growth in the 1970s." *World Development* 12, no. 8 (August 1984): 783–798.

Barrett, Rafael. *El dolor paraguayo.* Caracas: Biblioteca Ayacucho, 1978.

Bauer, A. J. "Rural Workers in Spanish America: Problems of Peonage and Oppression." *Hispanic American Historical Review* 59, no. 1 (1979): 34–63.

Bejarano, Ramón César. *Solucionemos nuestro problema indígena con el INDI.* Serie Estudios Antropológicos, no. 6. Asunción: Centro de Estudios Antropológicos de Asunción, 1977.

Bentley, Barbara, ed. *Projects with the Indigenous Peoples of Paraguay: Past and Future.* New York: Survival International, 1980.

Bentley, G. Carter. "Ethnicity and Practice." *Comparative Studies in Society and History* 29, no. 1 (1987): 24–55.

Borgognón, Juan Alfonso. "Panorama indígena paraguayo." *Suplemento Antropológico* 3, nos. 1–2 (October 1968): 347–348.

"Brief History of the Work of New Tribes Mission." Sanford, Fla.: New Tribes Mission, ca. 1993.

"Buscarán dar representación a los indígenas." *Hoy* (17 September 1991).

"Buscar medidas que permitan integrar al nativo." *Última Hora* (24 November 1980).

Bush, Barbara. *Slave Women in Caribbean Society*. Bloomington: Indiana University Press, 1990.

Cadogan, León. "Carta a Ñandé." *Ñandé* 1, no. 24 (1960): 26.

———. *Extranjero, campesino y científico: Memorias*. Biblioteca Paraguaya de Antropología, vol. 9. Asunción: Centro de Estudios Antropológicos, Universidad Católica, 1990.

———. "Los Guayakí." *Patria* (26 May 1957).

———. "Los Mbyá-Guaraní del Guairá." *América Indígena* 22, no. 2 (April 1960): 147–148.

———. "Torno a la aculturación de los Mbyá-Guaraní del Guairá." *América Indígena* 20, no. 2 (April 1960): 133–150.

———. "Tragedia guaraní." *Suplemento Antropológico* 2, no. 2 (June 1969): 269–283.

"La Carta Magna debe asegurar los derechos de los nativos." *Última Hora* (18 April 1991).

Carter, Miguel. *El papel de la iglesia en la caída de Stroessner*. Asunción: RP Ediciones, 1991.

Casaccia, Gladys, and Mirna Vázquez. *La lucha por la tierra en defensa de la vida: El pueblo maskoy frente a Carlos Casado*. Asunción: Equipo Nacional de Misiones, 1986.

"Casanillo está disponible pero buscamos sitio mejor." *Hoy* (7 January 1981).

"Casanillo es un potrero." *ABC Color* (9 January 1981).

"Caso toba-maskoy; fiscal aconsejó el rechazo del amparo." *ABC Color* (20 January 1981).

Caulfield, Mina Davis. "Culture and Imperialism: Proposing a New Dialectic." In *Reinventing Anthropology*, edited by Dell Hymes, 182–212. New York: Vintage Books, 1974.

"La CEP estudia informe sobre masacre de indios." *La Tribuna* (30 June 1972).

"La CEP pide amparo para los tobas." *Hoy* (14 January 1981).

Censo y Estudio de la Población Indígena del Paraguay, INDI, Asunción, 1982.

Cerna, Carlos. "The Beginning of the Inter-American Program on Behalf of the Indians." *Boletín Indigenista* 1, no. 1 (August 1941): 1–4.

Chase Sardi, Miguel. "Monumento al indio . . . pero mueren de viruelas." *Comunidad* 10, no. 381 (March 1965): N.p.

———. "The Present Situation of the Indians in Paraguay." In *The Situation of the Indian in South America*, edited by Walter Dostal, 178, 180. Geneva: World Council of Churches, n.d.

————. "La situación actual de los indígenas del Paraguay." *Suplemento Antropológico* 6 (1971): 9–98.

————. "Situación de los indígenas en el Paraguay." *América Indígena* 49, no. 3 (July–September 1989): 419–429.

Chase Sardi, Miguel, Augusto Brun, and Miguel Ángel Enciso. *Situación sociocultural, económica, jurídico-política actual de las comunidades indígenas en el Paraguay.* Asunción: Universidad Católica, 1990.

Chase Sardi, Miguel, and Marcos Martínez Almada. "Encuesta para detectar la actitud de la sociedad ante el indígena." *Suplemento Antropológico* 8 (1973): 163–170.

Chase Sardi, Miguel, and Branislava Susnik. "Indios del Paraguay." Unpublished manuscript, n.d.

"Los chiripá se reunen." *Diálogo Indígena Misionero* 9, no. 30 (October 1988), 9–11.

Churchill, Ward. *Struggle for the Land: Native North American Resistance to Genocide, Ecocide and Colonization.* San Francisco: City Lights, 2002.

Cockcroft, James D. "Paraguay's Stroessner: The Ultimate Caudillo." In *Neighbors in Turmoil: Latin America*, by James D. Cockcroft, 335–348. New York: Harper and Row, 1989.

Colombres, Adolfo, ed. *Por la liberación del indígena.* Sáenz Peña: Ediciones del Sol, 1975.

Comisión de Solidaridad con los Pueblos Indígenas. "Denuncia del ecocidio cometido en el Tekoha Paï Tavyterã de Takuaguy-Oygue." *Suplemento Antropológico* 23, no. 2 (December 1988): 223–227.

"Las comunidades indígenas cuentan con 41 escuelas." *ABC Color* (4 August 1976).

"Comunidad 'mbyá' aceptó el asentamiento de 1.500 has." *Última Hora* (30 May 1986).

"Comunidad mbyá-apyteré denuncia a menonitas." *Última Hora* (23 July 1986).

"Conclusiones del Diálogo Nacional: Indígenas aspiran a que se reconozca su presencia." *Última Hora* (21 January 1988).

"Concluye hoy Consulta Indígena." *ABC Color* (10 March 1972).

"Conflictos sin solución en Caazapá." *Hoy* (21 October 1988).

"Consejo indígena rechazó acusaciones." *ABC Color* (1 August 1975).

"La constitución y el indígena." *Última Hora* (12 February 1991).

"Constituyente: Indígenas quieren participar." *Última Hora* (7 June 1991).

"Continúan presiones para desalojo de los mbyá." *Diálogo Indígena Misionero* 5, no. 13, p. 6-7 (June 1984).

Corvalán, Graziella. "La política lingüística y su implementación en el Paraguay." *Suplemento Antropológico* 18, no. 1 (June 1983): 107–135.

"Las culturas indígenas no están en agonía." *Última Hora* (16 December 1989).

"Dan fin a discriminación de los pueblos indígenas." *Noticias* (1 May 1992).

"Debemos vivir." *Diálogo Indígena Misionero* 8, no. 27, pp. 12–13 (December 1987).

"Decretan ocupación de tierras para asentamiento de indígenas." *Última Hora* (11 October 1980).

de la Cadena, Marisol. *Indigenous Mestizos: The Politics of Race and Culture in Cuzco, Peru, 1919–1991.* Durham, N.C.: Duke University Press, 2000.

Deloria, Vine, Jr. *Behind the Trail of Broken Treaties.* New York: Delacorte Press, 1974.

"Denuncian desalojo de 100 indígenas de una estancia." *El Diario* (8 August 1985).

"Denuncian que el INDI reconoció a falso líder." *La Tarde* (22 September 1987).

"Denuncian quema de capueras en Paso Romero." *Hoy* (24 September 1985).

"Denuncian venta ilegal de madera de colonos indígenas." *El Diario* (21 March 1987).

"Desalojo de mbyá en Sommerfeld. Le rezan a su Diós pero nos dejan sin pan." *Hoy* (9 September 1981).

"Desmienten rumores de genocidio indígena." *ABC Color* (26 May 1978).

"Después del golpe de estado." *Diálogo Indígena Misionero* 10, no. 32, pp. 15–16 (April 1989).

"Determinaron problemas sociales y logros de las misiones indígenas del Chaco paraguayo." *ABC Color* (8 December 1974).

"Difícil sobrevivencia toba-maskoy en km. 220." *Última Hora* (28 March 1981).

"Discurso de Presidente Rodríguez en Concepción." *Última Hora* (22 April 1989).

Diskin, Martin. "Ethnic Discourse and the Challenge to Anthropology: The Nicaraguan Case." In *Nation-States and Indians in Latin America*, edited by Greg Urban and Joel Sherzer, 156–177. Austin: University of Texas Press, 1991. Paperback, Tucson, Ariz.: Hats Off Books, 1994.

"Dos aborígenes paraguayos participarán." *ABC Color* (11 February 1975).

Dostal, Walter, ed. *The Situation of the Indian in South America: Contributions to the Study of the Inter-Ethnic Conflict in the Non-Andean Regions of South America, Symposium on Inter-Ethnic Conflict in South America.* Geneva: World Council of Churches, 1972.

"Emotiva presencia de indígenas hubo en Caacupé." *El Diario* (7 December 1987).

"En el Día del Indígena el INDI destaca aspectos de su actividad de apoyo." *Última Hora* (19 April 1988).

"En marcha primer censo nacional indígena." *Diálogo Indigena Misionero* 1, no. 3, p. 4 (September 1980).

"Está dada la inserción indígena en la sociedad." *ABC Color* (2 August 1989).

"Ésta es nuestra tierra y no queremos mudarnos." *Última Hora* (29 June 1988).

"Estamos canalizando la vida del país por el camino del progreso." *Última Hora* (20 October 1980).

"Estamos muy orgullosos de ser indios." *Última Hora* (28 July 1989).

"Estatuto de las comunidades indígenas, ¿un instrumento válido?" *Diálogo Indígena Misionero* 3, no. 8, pp. 10–11 (December 1982).

"Esto pasa porque no tenemos tierra." *Última Hora* (1 December 1978).

"Existiría premura para el estudio del proyecto de ley." *ABC Color* (12 May 1981).

"Exprópian tierras de Sommerfeld." *ABC Color* (10 November 1989).

"Exprópian tierras para indígenas mbyá apyteré." *Última Hora* (4 June 1988).

"Un extranjero en su tierra: El indígena." *Sendero* (April 1981).

"Finalizó un curso informativo para líderes indígenas auspiciado por Proyecto Marandú." *ABC Color* (14 March 1975).

"Finiquitado juicio contra el INDI." *Hoy* (31 July 1988).

Flores, Severo. "Las comunidades indígenas frente a la sociedad nacional." *Suplemento Antropológico* 19, no. 1 (June 1984): 97–99.

Fogel, Ramón. *El proceso de modernización y el deterioro de las comunidades indígenas.* Asunción: Centro Paraguayo de Estudios Sociológicos, 1989.

Fretz, Joseph Winfield. *Pilgrims in Paraguay: The Story of Mennonite Colonization in South America.* Scottdale, Penn.: Herald Press, 1953.

Frutos, Julio César. "El Estatuto del Indígena: Sus antecedentes cercanos." *Suplemento Antropológico* 17, no. 2 (December 1981): 73–85.

Galeano, Luis A. "Las transformaciones agrarias, las luchas y los movimientos campesinos en el Paraguay." *Revista Paraguaya de Sociología* 28, no. 80 (January–April 1990): 51.

Ganson, Barbara. "The Evuevi of Paraguay: Adoptive Strategies and Responses to Colonialism, 1528–1811." *The Americas* 45, no. 4 (April 1989): 461–488.

———. *The Guaraní under Spanish Rule in the Río de la Plata.* Stanford: Stanford University Press, 2003.

Garfield, Seth. Indigenous Struggle at the Heart of Brazil, *State Policy, Frontier Expansion, and the Xarainte Indians, 1937–1988.* Duke University Press, Durham and London, 2001.

"La Gauloise informa a la opinión pública." *ABC Color* (16 November 1980).

"El genocidio en el Chaco paraguayo." *El Pueblo* (4 February 1987).

"El gobierno se hará cargo del asentamiento de los toba-maskoy." *ABC Color* (15 January 1981).

González, Natalicio J. *Proceso y formación de la cultura paraguaya,* vol. 1. Asunción, Buenos Aires, Editorial Guarania, 1948.

González Casanova, Pablo; Marcos Roitman; and Xavier Albó. *Democracia y estado multiétnico en América Latina.* Mexico City: Jornada Ediciones, 1996.

Graber, C. L. *The Coming of the Moros.* Scottdale, Penn.: Herald Press, 1964.

Grubb, Barbrooke. *An Unknown People in an Unknown Land: An Account of the Life and Customs of the Lengua Indians of the Paraguayan Chaco, with Adventures and Experiences during Twenty Years' Pioneering and Exploration amongst Them.* London: London Seeley Service, 1918.

Grünberg, Friedl. "Estudio sobre el proceso de los Paï-Tavyterã de 1972 a 1988: Evaluación de las consecuencias a largo plazo del 'Proyectos Paï-Tavyterã.'" Unpublished manuscript. Asunción: Servicios Profesionales Antropológicos y Jurídicos, 1988.

"Grupos de indios guayaquíes aparecieron en zona de Abaí." *La Tribuna* (15 October 1959).

"Guías de turismo dan falsa imagen de maká." *Última Hora* (14 January 1980).

Guidieri, Remo, and Francesco Pellizzi. "Smoking Mirrors—Modern Polity and Ethnicity." In *Ethnicities and Nations: Processes of Inter-ethnic Relations in Latin*

America, Southeast Asia and the Pacific, edited by Remo Guidieri, Francesco Pellizzi, and Tambiah Stanley, 7–38. Austin: University of Texas Press, 1988.

————, and Stanley Tambiah, eds. *Ethnicities and Nations: Processes of Inter-ethnic Relations in Latin America, Southeast Asia and the Pacific.* Austin: University of Texas Press, 1988.

Gutiérrez, Natividad. *Nationalist Myths and Ethnic Identities: Indigenous Intellectuals and the Mexican State.* Lincoln: University of Nebraska Press, 1999.

Haas, Lisbeth. *Conquests and Historical Identities in California, 1769–1936.* Berkeley and Los Angeles: University of California Press, 1995.

"Habrá reunión de indigenistas latinoamericanos in Asunción." *ABC Color* (22 February 1972).

Hack, Henck. "Indios y mennonitas en el Chaco paraguayo I." *Suplemento Antropológico* 13, nos. 1 and 2 (Spring and Winter, 1978): 207–259.

————. "Indios y mennonitas en el Chaco paraguayo II." *Suplemento Antropológico* 14, no. 1 (December 1979): 201–248.

————. "Indios y mennonitas en el Chaco paraguayo III." *Suplemento Antropológico* 15, no. 1 (Spring, 1980): 45–137.

Hale, Charles. "Rethinking Indigenous Politics in the Era of the 'Indio Permitido.'" *NACLA Report on the Americas,* 38, no. 2 (September–October 2004): 16–21.

Hanratty, Dennis M., and Sandra W. Meditz, eds. *Paraguay: A Country Study.* Washington, D.C.: Government Printing Office, 1990.

"Hemos labrado mejores condiciones." *Última Hora* (31 December 1987).

Hicks, Frederick. "Interpersonal Relationships and Caudillismo in Paraguay." *Journal of Inter-American Studies and World Affairs* 13, no. 1 (January 1971): 89–111.

Hill, Kim. "Los aché del Paraguay oriental: Condiciones actuales." *Suplemento Antropológico* 18, no. 1 (June 1983): 149–177.

————, and Magdalena Hurtado. *Aché Life History: The Ecology and Demography of a Foraging People.* New York: Aldine De Gruyter, 1996.

Horst, René Harder. "Breaking Down Religious Barriers: Indigenous People and Christian Churches in Paraguay." In *Resurgent Voices in Latin America,* edited by Edward Cleary and Timothy Steigenga, 65–92. New Brunswick, N.J.: Rutgers University Press, 2004.

————. "The Catholic Church, Human Rights Advocacy, and Indigenous Resistance in Paraguay, 1969–1989." *Catholic Historical Review* 88, no. 4 (October 2002): 723–744.

————. "Consciousness and Contradiction: Indigenous Peoples and Paraguay's Transition to Democracy." In *Contemporary Indigenous Movements in Latin America,* edited by Erick D. Langer and Elena Muñoz, 103–132. Wilmington, Del.: SR Books, 2003.

"IBR solicitará 1,200 has. para indígenas mbyá apyteré." *Patria* (18 April 1988).

"Implementarán capítulo para derechos indígenas." *Noticias* (7 February 1992).

"El indígena como persona." *Última Hora* (8 August 1981).

"El indígena es una persona adulta, madura y educada." *Hoy* (7 August 1981).

"Indígenas agradecen apoyo del Presidente Stroessner." *Patria* (2 September 1986).

"Los indígenas del Chaco central trabajarán sus propias chacras." *ABC Color* (2 August 1976).

"Indígenas denunciaron acoso en el parlamento." *ABC Color* (14 October 1989).

"Indígenas denunciaron la invasión de sus tierras." *Hoy* (8 June 1988).

"Indígenas desean ser protagonistas." *Noticias* (16 September 1991).

"Los indígenas maskoy rechazan el ofrecimiento de Casado S.A." *Hoy* (21 May 1984).

"Indígenas pedirán indemnización en tierras a Itaipú binacional." *ABC Color* (26 February 1982).

"Indígenas quieren que se respeten sus comunidades." *Hoy* (7 June 1992).

"Indígenas quieren un lugar en el parlamento." *Última Hora* (17 April 1989).

"Los indígenas saben lo que quieren." *ABC Color* (2 August 1989).

"Los indígenas siguen siendo despojados de sus tierras." *La Tribuna* (3 September 1981).

"Los indígenas y la reforma constitucional." *ABC* (17 April 1991).

"INDI impidió ocupación de las tierras de Casanillo, en el kilómetro 220, la tierra es inhóspita." *ABC Color* (6 January 1981).

"INDI no organiza reunión de indígenas con el papa." *La Tarde* (27 January 1988).

"INDI y la futura constitución." *ABC Color* (12 February 1991).

Infanzon, Tristán. "Política indigenista, II: Conclusión." *Patria* (20 July 1968).

"Informe del Ministerio de Defensa Nacional." *ABC Color* (23 February 1973).

"Inícua explotación de ayoreos." *Hoy* (10 January 1987).

"Inquietudes indígenas." *Semanario El Pueblo* (21 February 1989).

"Itaipú ensanchó ruta que corta en dos un asentamiento indígena." *ABC Color* (17 September 1982).

"Itaipú ubicará a los avá chiripá en nuevas tierras." *Hoy* (19 April 1982).

Kidd, Stephen. "Religious Change: A Case-Study amongst the Enxet of the Paraguayan Chaco." Master's thesis, University of Durham, 1992.

Klassen, Meter P. *The Mennonites in Paraguay.* Vol. 2: *Encounter with Indians and Paraguayans.* Kitchener, Ont.: Pandora Press, 2002

Knight, Alan. "Racism, Revolution, and Indigenismo: Mexico, 1910–1940." In *The Idea of Race in Latin America, 1870–1940,* edited by Richard Graham, 71–113. Austin: University of Texas Press, 1990.

Kokueguara, Rembiasa. *Experiencias campesinas, ligas agrarias cristianas, 1960–1980.* Vol. 4. Asunción: Centro de Estudios Paraguayos Antonio Guasch, 1993.

Kowalski, Alejandro. "Aceptar al otro como constituyente de uno mismo." In *Después de la piel: 500 años de confusión entre desigualdad y diferencia,* edited by Alejandro Kowalski, 34–40. Posadas, Arg.: Departamento de Antropología Social, Universidad Nacional de Misiones, Fotograbados Iguazú, 1993.

Laíno, Rafaela Guanas de. *Familias sin tierra en Paraguay.* Asunción: Editora Litocolor, 1993.

Langer, Erick D., with Elena Muñoz. *Contemporary Indigenous Movements in Latin America*. Wilmington, Del.: Scholarly Resources, 2003.

"Le hicieron leer el mensaje al cacique." *El Diario* (21 May 1988).

Lewis, Norman. *The Missionaries: God against the Indians*. London: Penguin Books, 1988.

Lewis, Paul. *Paraguay under Stroessner*. Chapel Hill: University of North Carolina Press, 1980.

"El líder mbyá solicita que las autoridades intervengan." *Hoy* (24 October 1985).

Lima, Antonio Carlos de Souza. "On Indigenism and Nationality in Brazil." In *Nation-States and Indians in Latin America*, edited by Greg Urban and Joel Sherzer, 236–258. Tucson, Ariz.: Hats Off Books, 1991.

Llorente, Ángel, and Antonio Carmona. "Parte crónica del Proyecto Marandú, proyecto de la Interamericana Fundation [*sic*]." Unpublished manuscript. Asunción: Archives of Miguel Chase Sardi (ACHS), 1973–1976.

Loewen, Jacob A. "From Nomadism to Sedentary Agriculture." *América Indígena* 26, no. 1 (January 1966): 27–42.

Mainwaring, Scott, and Alexander Wilde, eds. *The Progressive Church in Latin America*. Notre Dame, Ind.: University of Notre Dame Press, 1989.

"Maká: Los artesanos del Paraguay." *Última Hora* (21 April 1980).

Mallon, Florencia E. "Indian Communities, Political Cultures, and the State in Latin America, 1780–1990." *Journal of Latin American Studies* 24, Supplement (1992): 35–53.

"Mantenerlos en hábitat tradicional es imposible." *ABC Color* (17 September 1989).

"Marandú: Prosigue curso en Caaguazú." *ABC Color* (21 June 1975).

"Más acusaciones contra Nuevas Tribus." *Hoy* (13 January 1987).

"Más firmas incurrieron en fraude." *El Diario* (28 November 1985).

"Maskoy: No ejecutaron hasta ahora la mensura." *Noticias* (27 April 1985).

"Los maskoy cultivan su tierra." *Diálogo Indígena Misionero* 9 no. 29, p. 5 (July 1988).

"Los maskoy solicitan expropiar tierras." *La Tarde* (4 June 1987).

Maybury-Lewis, David. "Becoming Indian in Lowland South America." In *Nation-States and Indians in Latin America*, edited by Greg Urban and Joel Sherzer, 207–235. Tucson, Ariz.: Hats Off Books, 1991.

———, and James Howe. *The Indian Peoples of Paraguay, Their Plight and Their Prospects*. Special Report no. 2. Cambridge, Eng.: Cultural Survival, 1980.

"Los mbyá denuncian la destrucción de su hábitat." *Última Hora* (26 August 1988).

"Mbyá denuncia quema de sus sementeras y Rancho-Tapyí." *Hoy* (9 August 1988).

McCreery, D. J. *The Sweat of Their Brow: A History of Work in Latin America*. Armonk, N.H.: M. E. Sharpe, 2000.

Melià, Bartomeu. *El guaraní conquistado y reducido*. Asunción: Universidad Católica, 1988.

———. *Una nación, dos culturas*. Asunción: RP Ediciones, 1993.

———. "La obra etnológica de León Cadogan." *Revista Trimestral*, INDI 2, no. 2 (1992): 19–24.

———, and Christine Münzel. "Ratones y jaguares: Reconstrucción de un genocidio a la manera del de los Axé-Guayakí del Paraguay oriental." *Suplemento Antropológico* 6 (1971): 101–147.

"Mennonitas: De perseguidos a perseguidores." *Nuestro Tiempo*, no. 14, pp. 39-41 (October 1986).

"Mennonitas ingresaron con topadoras a un asentamiento, nuevamente hostigan a indígenas mbyá." *Hoy* (10 July 1984).

Mennonite Central Committee. *1962 Workbook*. Akron, Ohio, 1963.

"Menonitas endurecen su postura." *ABC Color* (1 November 1989).

"Menonitas hostigan a los indígenas en Sommerfeld." *Sendero* (1 August 1986).

Métraux, Alfred. "The Guaraní." In *Handbook of South American Indians*, vol. 3, edited by Julian Steward, 69–94. Washington, D.C.: Government Printing Office, 1948.

"Miles de laicos hicieron marcha pública de denuncia." *Última Hora* (31 October 1987).

Miller, Elmer. *Los tobas argentinos: Armonía y disonancia en una sociedad*. Buenos Aires: Siglo Veintiuno Argentina Editores, 1979.

Miranda, Carlos R. *The Stroessner Era: Authoritarian Rule in Paraguay*. Boulder, Colo.: Westview Press, 1990.

Mörner, Magnus. *The Political and Economic Activities of the Jesuits in the La Plata Region: The Hapsburg Era*. Stockholm: Victor Pettersons Bokindustri Aktiebolag, 1953.

Muntzel, Martha, and Bruna Radelli, eds. *Homenaje a Leonardo Manrique C.* Mexico City: Instituto Nacional de Antropología e Historia, 1993.

Münzel, Mark. *The Aché: Genocide Continues in Paraguay*, doc. 17. Copenhagen: International Work Group for Indigenous Affairs, 1974.

———. *The Aché Indians: Genocide in Paraguay*, doc. 11. Copenhagen: International Work Group for Indigenous Affairs, 1973.

———. "Manhunt." In *Genocide in Paraguay*, edited by Richard Arens, 19–45. Philadelphia: Temple University Press, 1976.

Muratorio, Blanca. *The Life and Times of Grandfather Alonso*. New Brunswick, N.J.: Rutgers University Press, 1991.

———. "Protestantism, People, and Class in Chimborazo." In *Cultural Transformations and Ethnicity in Modern Ecuador*, edited by Norman E. Whitten Jr., 506–534. Urbana: University of Illinois Press, 1981.

"Nadie quiere al indio, dicen tobas-maskoy." *Hoy* (20 January 1981).

"Nativos analizaron constituyente." *Noticias* (3 June 1991).

"Nativos presentan propuestas para la nueva constitución." *Última Hora* (18 June 1991).

Nickson, Andrew. "Brazilian Colonization in the Eastern Border Region of Paraguay." *Journal of Latin American Studies* 13, no. 1 (May 1981): 111–131.

————. "Tyranny and Longevity: Stroessner's Paraguay." *Third World Quarterly* 10, no. 1 (January 1988): 237–259.

"No hay genocidio en el Paraguay porque no hay intención de destruir grupos indígenas." *ABC Color* (9 March 1974).

"Nos preocupa cambio en INDI." *Última Hora* (24 December 1980).

"Nos preocupa la situación de indígenas." *Hoy* (14 February 1989).

"Nos quieren dar tierras feas y con muchos esteros." *Última Hora* (1 July 1988).

"Nuestro hábitat está siendo destruido." *Hoy* (30 August 1988).

"Nuestro pueblo no puede seguir así." *Última Hora* (5 January 1984).

"Nuevas muestras de solidaridad para con maskoy." *Hoy* (22 July 1987).

"Nuevo rechazo a propuesta hecha por Carlos Casado." *Hoy* (31 January 1985).

"Nuevos y más títulos de propiedad a comunidades indígenas." *El Diario* (2 May 1988).

Oliveira, Roberto Cardosa. "Indian Movements and Indianism in Brazil." *Cultural Survival Newsletter* 5, no. 1 (1985): 12.

"Otras 3,000 firmas dan su apoyo a los maskoy [*sic*]." *Última Hora* (21 August 1987).

"El papa estará con los indios." *El Diario* (31 August 1987).

"El papa trajo esperanza." *Diálogo Indígena Misionero* Vol. 9, Issue 29, p. 11, (29 July 1988).

Paraguay: Latin America's Oldest Dictatorship under Pressure. Washington, D.C.: America's Watch Committee, August 1986.

"Paraguay Coup: Battle for Succession." *New York Times* (4 February 1989).

"Paraguay General Leads a Rebellion." *New York Times* (3 February 1989).

"Para los indígenas continúa el régimen de Stroessner." *Última Hora* (12 September 1989).

"Parlamento indio pidió se devuelva tierras a tribus con títulos de propiedad de las mismas." *ABC Color* (15 October 1974).

Perasso, José A. *Crónicas de cacerías humanas: La tragedia ayoreo.* Asunción: El Lector, 1987.

"Persigue hoy conferencias." *ABC Color* (31 May 1972).

Peterson, Robert W. *The Boy Scouts: An American Adventure.* New York: American Heritage, 1984.

"Piden expropiación de Sommerfeld." *Diálogo Indígena Misionero* 10, no. 33, pp. 4-5 (September 1989).

"Piden investigación de la emboscada." *Hoy* (9 January 1987).

"Población indígena no está en un proceso de extinción." *Hoy* (17 June 1989).

Polanco, Héctor Díaz. *Indigenous Peoples in Latin America: The Quest for Self-Determination.* Boulder, Colo.: Westview Press, 1997.

"Posición del INDI no satisface a los mbyá [*sic*]: No quieren tierras reducidas y ocupadas." *Hoy* (27 August 1989).

"Posiciones encontradas, del IBR y del INDI, ante el caso." *Última Hora* (30 June 1988).

"Posición final del INDI ante el caso Sommerfeld." *Última Hora* (28 August 1989).

Prieto, Esther. *Entre la resignación y la esperanza: Los grandes proyectos de desarrollo y las comunidades indígenas.* Asunción: Centro de Estudios Humanitarios, Intercontinental Editora, 1989.

———, and Guillermo Rolón. *Estudio legislación indígena: Legislación ambiental.* Asunción: Centro de Estudios Humanitarios, 1991.

"Primer Encuentro Interétnico se realizó en Coronel Oviedo." *Hoy* (3 June 1991).

"Privilegios de menonitas van en detrimento de indígenas." *Última Hora* (8 November 1988).

"Prosigue conflicto mbya [sic] en Sommerfeld." *Diálogo Indígena Misionero* 7, no. 23, pp. 4-5 (August 1986).

"Proyecto Caazapá: Urge solución para indígenas." *Diálogo Indígena Misionero* 8, no. 25 (May 1987).

"Proyecto de desarrollo de Caazapá." *Diálogo Indígena Misionero* 5, no. 13, p. 13 (June 1984).

"El proyecto de ley indígena podría ocasionar perjuicios." *ABC Color* (15 October 1981).

"Proyecto Marandú: Se busca informar a líderes indígenas de todo el país." *ABC Color* (23 April 1974).

Proyecto Paï-Tavyterã. "Recuento histórico-analítico de los trabajos con los Paï Tavyterã." Unpublished manuscript. Asunción: AENM, 1988.

"El pueblo maskoy frente a Carlos Casado S.A." *El Pueblo* (28 January 1987).

Ramírez, René. "Discurso de bienvenida dirigida a su santidad Juan Pablo Segundo." Unpublished manuscript. Mariscal Estigarribia: AENM, 1988.

Ramos, Alcida Rita. *Indigenism: Ethnic Politics in Brazil.* Madison: University of Wisconsin Press, 1998.

Rappaport, Joanne. "Las misiones protestantes y la resistencia indígena en el sur de Colombia." *América Indígena* 44, no. 1 (January–March 1984): 111–126.

"Reasentamiento debe ser una prioridad." *Hoy* (11 March 1982).

"Reclaman cese de presiones a comunidades mbyá-apyteré." *Última Hora* (9 April 1988).

Redekop, Calvin. *Strangers Become Neighbors: Mennonite and Indigenous Relations in the Paraguayan Chaco.* Scottdale, Penn.: Herald Press, 1980.

Reed, Richard. *Forest Dwellers, Forest Protectors: Indigenous Models for International Development.* Boston: Allyn and Bacon, 1997.

———. "New Rules for the Game." In *The Politics of Ethnicity: Indigenous People in Latin American States,* edited by David Maybury-Lewis, 310–328. Cambridge and London: Harvard University Press, 2003.

———. *Prophets of Agroforestry.* Austin: University of Texas Press, 1995.

Regeher, Walter. "Mennonite Economic Life and the Paraguayan Experience." Unpublished manuscript. Waterloo, Can.: AWR, 1990.

———. "Teorías de desarrollo y autogestión indígena." Unpublished manuscript. Asunción: AWR, 1983.

———. "Tierra y población en los departamentos de Alto Paraguay y Chaco." Unpublished manuscript. Neu Halbstadt, Para.: AWR, 1980.

Renshaw, John. *Los indígenas del Chaco paraguayo: Economía y sociedad.* Asunción: Intercontinental Editora, 1996.

———. "Paraguay, the Marandú Project." *Survival International Review* 1, no. 15 (Spring, 1976): 14–20.

"Retornaron indígenas que participaron." *ABC Color* (8 November 1975).

"Los ricos ganan 144 veces más que los pobres en nuestro país." *Última Hora* (2 December 1980).

Robins, Wayne. *Etnicidad, tierra y poder.* Asunción: Editora Litocolor, 1999.

———. "Importancia de la cultura indígena en el panorama socio-cultural del Paraguay." *Acción* 13 (August 1981): 8–25.

"Rodríguez inauguró una escuela para indígenas." *Última Hora* (1 October 1990).

"Un saldo a favor del indigenismo." *Última Hora* (27 December 1988).

"Samaniego: 'El aborigen suma su esfuerzo al desarrollo.'" *Hoy* (25 October 1980).

"Samaniego con indígenas." *ABC Color* (23 April 1989).

"Sanción del senado, exprópian Sommerfeld." *Última Hora* (1 November 1989).

Sanneh, Lamin. *Translating the Message: The Missionary Impact on Culture.* Maryknoll, N.Y.: Orbis Books, 1989.

"Satisfacción por capítulo indígena." *Noticias* (7 June 1992).

Scott, James C. *Domination and the Arts of Resistance: Hidden Transcripts.* New Haven, Conn.: Yale University Press, 1990.

"Se agudiza un problema de tierra con indígenas." *Hoy* (15 October 1987).

Seelwische, José. "Una interpretación del indígena desde las categorías de la iglesia." *Acción* 13, no. 51 (August 1981): 23–25.

———. "Los misioneros y la autogestión de los pueblos indígenas, la evolución de su comprensión y práctica en el equipo nacional de misiones." Unpublished manuscript. AENM.

"Se hizo cambio de guardia en la dirección del INDI." *ABC Color* (24 December 1980).

"Se inició ayer en San Bernardino reunión de líderes indígenas de la selva tropical." *ABC Color* (9 October 1974).

"Senado aprobó expropiación." *El Diario* (31 July 1987).

"Se prepara un proyecto de desarrollo rural de Caazapá." *ABC Color* (7 August 1980).

"Se saben más detalles del incidente con los nativos paï." *Última Hora* (14 October 1988).

Smith, Gavin. *Livelihood and Resistance.* Berkeley and Los Angeles: University of California Press, 1989.

Smith, Peter. "The Search for Legitimacy." In *Caudillos, Dictators in Spanish America*, edited by Hugh M. Hamill, 87–96. Norman: University of Oklahoma Press, 1992.

Smith, Robert, and Ramón Fogel. "The Invisible Guaraní: The Effects of Development Projects on the Chiripá and Mbyá of Paraguay." Unpublished manuscript. Lawrence, Kan., 1982.

Solidaridad de líderes paï con grupo de takuaritiy." *Última Hora* (12 October 1988).

Stahl, Wilmar. "Chaco Native Economies and Mennonite Development Cooperation." Unpublished manuscript. Filadelfia, Para.: Asociación de Servicios de Cooperación Indígena-Mennonita, 1994.

———. *Escenario indígena chaqueño, pasado y presente.* Filadelfia, Para.: Asociación de Servicios de Cooperación Indígena-Mennonita, 1982.

Stavenhagen, Rodolfo. "Challenging the Nation-State in Latin America." *Journal of International Affairs* 45, no. 2 (Winter, 1992): 422–440.

Stern, Steve J. *Peru's Indian Peoples and the Challenge of Spanish Conquest, Huamanga to 1640.* Madison: University of Wisconsin Press, 1993.

Stunnenberg, P. W. *Entitled to Land: The Incorporation of the Paraguayan and Argentinean Gran Chaco and the Spatial Marginalization of the Indian People.* Saarbrücken, Ger.: Verlag Breitenback, 1993.

Stutzman, Ronald. "El Mestizaje: An All-Inclusive Ideology of Exclusion." In *Cultural Transformations and Ethnicity in Modern Ecuador,* edited by Norman Whitten, 45–94. Urbana: University of Illinois Press, 1981.

"Los sufrimientos aumentan y no tenemos tierras donde vivir." *Última Hora* (6 June 1987).

Susnik, Branislava. *Los aborígenes del Paraguay.* Vol. 3, no. 1: *Etnohistoria de los chaqueños, 1650–1910.* Asunción: Museo Etnográfico Andrés Barbero, 1981.

Swepston, Lee. "Latin American Approaches to the Indian Problem." *International Labor Review* 117, no. 2 (March–April 1985): 179–196.

Taussig, Michael. "Culture of Terror—Space of Death: Roger Casement's Putumayo Report and the Explanation of Torture." *Comparative Studies* 26, no. 3 (1984): 467–497.

———. *The Devil and Commodity Fetishism in South America.* Chapel Hill: University of North Carolina Press, 1980.

———. *Shamanism, Colonialism, and the Wild Man: A Study in Terror and Healing.* Chicago: University of Chicago Press, 1987.

Teltsch, Kathleen. "U.N. Body Accuses U.S. on Paraguay." *New York Times* (6 April 1976).

"Los tobas-lenguas viven el sueño de la tierra propia." *Última Hora* (14 February 1977).

"Tobas-maskoy esperan ocupar los terrenos de Casanillo." *ABC Color* (24 November 1980).

"Tobas-maskoy podrán ocupar tierras." *Última Hora* (27 December 1980).

"Los tobas piden devolución de su tierra." *Última Hora* (2 December 1980).

"Tobas reclaman devolución de tierras que constituyeran su habitat original." *Última Hora* (15 March 1980).

"Transculturación del indígena es larga y difícil: La sociedad debe tomar conciencia de su realidad." *ABC Color* (8 July 1989).

Turner, Christina Bolke, and Brian Turner. "The Role of Mestizaje of Surnames in Paraguay in the Creation of a Distinct New World Ethnicity." *Ethnohistory* 41, no. 1 (Winter, 1994): 139–165.

Van Cott, Donna Lee, ed. *Indigenous People and Democracy in Latin America*. New York: St. Martin's Press, 1994.

Varese, Stefano. "Multiethnicity and Hegemonic Construction: Indian Plans and the Future." In *Ethnicities and Nations: Processes of Inter-ethnic Relations in Latin America*, edited by Remo Guidieri, Francesco Pellizzi, and Tambiah Stanley, 57–77. Austin: University of Texas Press, 1988.

———, ed. *Pueblos indios, soberanía y globalismo*. Quito: Ediciones Abya Yala, 1996.

Vázquez, Mirna. "Historia de la legislación indigenista paraguaya." *Suplemento Antropológico* 16, no. 2 (December 1981): 93–103.

Verdecchia, José Miguel. *Algunas consideraciones sobre las condiciones de éxito y fracaso en las asociaciones cooperativas campesinas en el Paraguay*. Asunción, Centro Paraguayo de Estudios Sociológicos, 1989.

von Bremen, Volker. "Los Ayoreode cazados." Unpublished manuscript. Asunción: Servicios Profesionales Antropológicos y Jurídicos, 1987.

———."Fuentes de caza y recolección modernas: Proyectos de ayuda al desarrollo destinados a los indígenas del Gran Chaco (Argentina, Paraguay, Bolivia)." Unpublished manuscript. Asunción: Servicios Profesionales Antropológicos y Jurídicos, 1987.

"Voz y voto en la convención reclaman otra vez representantes de indígenas." *ABC Color* (10 January 1992).

Wallis, Cristóbal. "Cuatro proyectos indígenas del Chaco." Unpublished manuscript. Salta, Arg.: Comisión Intereclesiástica de Coordinación para Proyectos de Desarrollo, AIAP, 1986.

———. "Las expectativas de los guaraní-ñandeva en torno a Laguna Negra. Carpeta Informes Originales." AIP. Asunción: Servicios Profesionales Antropológicos y Jurídicos, 1981.

———, and Victoria Lincoln. "Propuesta para un estudio sobre los Tapieté." Unpublished manuscript. Asunción: Servicios Profesionales Antropológicos y Jurídicos (formerly stored at AIP), 1979.

Warren, Harris Gaylord. *Rebirth of the Paraguayan Republic: The First Colorado Era, 1878–1904*. Pittsburgh: University of Pittsburgh Press, 1985.

Warren, Kay B. "Transforming Memories and Histories: The Meanings of Ethnic Resurgence for Mayan Indians." In *Americas: New Interpretive Essays*, edited by Alfred Stepan, 189–219. New York: Oxford University Press, 1992.

Whigham, Thomas. "Paraguay's Pueblos de Indios: Echoes of a Missionary Past." In *The New Latin American Mission History*, edited by Erick Langer and Robert H. Jackson, 157–188. Lincoln: University of Nebraska Press, 1995.

———. *The Politics of River Trade: Tradition and Development in the Upper Plata, 1780–1870*. Albuquerque: University of New Mexico Press, 1991.

Williams, John Hoyt. "Paraguay's Stroessner: Losing Control?" *Current History* 86, no. 516 (January 1987): 25–35.

———. *The Rise and Fall of the Paraguayan Republic, 1800–1870*. Austin: University of Texas Press, 1979.

"Y se mueren los indios, sin tierra y sin cultura." *Última Hora* (1 August 1981).

Zogbaum, Heidi. *B. Traven: A Vision of Mexico*. Wilmington, Del.: Scholarly Resources, 1992.

Zook, David H., Jr. *The Conduct of the Chaco War*. New Haven, Conn.: Bookman Associates, 1960.

Index